SERVING G

"Chaplains share the hardships, dangers, and loneliness, as well as the wonderful camaraderie known only to those who face grave danger and serve together for each other and for their country. Dr. Dorsett has skillfully written the stories of the chaplains who made their contribution during World War II. This is a tremendous work of interest to military historians, spiritual leaders from all faith groups, and patriotic Americans."

—Carlton W. Fulford, Jr., General (Ret.) U.S. Marine Corps

"Through intensive study of published and unpublished records—as well as from many interviews with World War II veterans—Lyle Dorsett has written a compelling history of the military chaplaincy during that great conflict. The book is chock-full of inspiring stories of faithful service rendered by Catholic, Protestant, and Jewish chaplains—often literally under fire. But also in purely secular terms, *Serving God and Country* shows how important the chaplains were for maintaining morale among troops, and also on the home front. This is one of those rare books that delivers excellent history and realistic inspiration in equal measure."

—Mark A. Noll, Francis A. McAnaney Professor of History,
University of Notre Dame

"Lyle Dorsett does a superb job at capturing the spirit, culture, and challenges chaplains of all denominations faced during World War II. Lyle not only tells the chaplain's story, but also the commander's and the GI's story of what their chaplain did for them. In particular, how chaplains were instrumental in facilitating the free exercise of religion with the result of helping soldiers overcome the harsh realities of war. This is unique in chaplain historiography."

—Chaplain (LTC) Robert Nay, 5X Skill ID,
Military Historian, U.S. Army

SERVING GOD AND COUNTRY

U.S. Military Chaplains in World War II

LYLE W. DORSETT

CALIBER

DUTTON CALIBER

An imprint of Penguin Random House LLC
penguinrandomhouse.com

Previously published as a Berkley Caliber hardcover in 2012 and
a Berkley Caliber trade paperback in 2013

First Dutton Caliber trade paperback edition: June 2022

The Library of Congress has catalogued the Berkley Caliber
hardcover edition as follows:

Dorsett, Lyle W.
Serving God and country : U.S. military chaplains in World War II / Lyle W. Dorsett.
p. cm.
ISBN 978-0-425-24786-0
1. World War, 1939–1945—Chaplains—United States. 2. Military chaplains—United
States. I. Title.
D810. C36U635 2012
940. 54'780973—dc23   2011038762

Dutton Caliber ISBN: 9780593187463

Printed in the United States of America
1st Printing

BOOK DESIGN BY TIFFANY ESTREICHER

For Bill, Dan, Elizabeth, Henry, and your children.
May the dedication and selflessness of those who have gone before
inspire you to spend your lives Serving God and Country.

Put down somewhere, too, everything you see and hear which will help later on to recapture the spirit of this tragic, marvelous, and eye-opening time: so that, having recaptured it, we can use it for better ends.

Jan Struther, in *Mrs. Miniver* (1940)

PART ONE

CHAPTER ONE

THE WAR AND SPIRITUAL POWER

Battles are won by military power, but wars are won by spiritual power.

CHAPLAIN (MAJOR GENERAL) WILLIAM ARNOLD[1]

THROUGH fog, smoke, and screams Sergeant Bob Slaughter charged into a storm of bullets and shrapnel and, as he phrased it, "somehow survived" the bloody first wave of the Normandy invasion on June 6, 1944. A month later, after he and fellow soldiers of the Twenty-Ninth Infantry Division had battled their way about twenty miles southward, they were pinned down near the heavily fortified French city Saint-Lô. Well-dug-in Germans rained a barrage of mortar and artillery shells down on what remained of Slaughter's battle-decimated company. In the confusion of blinding smoke, flying debris, cursing, and yelling, frantic soldiers dug foxholes and listened for orders from battle-weary platoon leaders. Bob Slaughter and another member of his squad hastily dug a hole for cover until American artillery support could weaken the German fortifications. He and his comrade had no sooner scooped out their shallow shelter than a third man plunged in with them. Slaughter looked up and saw a white cross painted on the uninvited guest's helmet. The intruder immediately asked if they by any chance knew where he might find Sergeant Bob Slaughter. Astonished by the coincidence, Slaughter confessed he was the man. Without wasting time on introductions, the chaplain apologized for not finding him sooner but explained that locating anyone in the confusion of invasion preparation had been almost impossible. The chaplain quickly informed Slaughter that his father had died a few weeks earlier at home in Roanoke, Virginia. Slaughter's mother had sought the assistance of her Presbyterian pastor to get the news overseas to her son. The pastor had managed to get the message moving through channels until it reached the chaplain assigned to Slaughter's battalion and, finally, its destination near Saint-Lô.

In 2009 Bob Slaughter was still in awe of that battlefield chaplain. Although he neither learned the clergyman's name nor saw him again, sixty-five years later the combat veteran remained deeply grateful to the clergyman who had risked his life to carry the message in the midst of harrowing enemy fire. Furthermore, the courageous news carrier took time to express condolences and to apologize because, under the circumstances, he could not ask the sergeant's commanding officer to grant him an emergency leave to comfort his grieving mother.[2]

SIX MONTHS LATER a young combat infantry officer along the Belgian-German border, engulfed in another deafening episode of war, crawled out of the Ardennes forest holding a compress on his wounded leg. Falling off the front line to get stitched up, Lieutenant Henry Cobb looked up to see a chaplain rushing into the woods, where the Germans were raining down a storm of artillery shells on the battered Americans who had been caught by surprise in the Battle of the Bulge. Cobb recalled that he recognized the chaplain as the priest who had given him and some other soldiers Holy Communion several hours earlier. The Catholic priest was charging full speed toward the woods, into an inferno of fire, smoke, deafening explosions, and splintering trees. The wounded officer yelled: "Where in the devil do you think you are going, Father? All hell is breaking loose up there." The chaplain ran past Cobb, muttering "That is why I need to be there."

Henry Cobb never learned the chaplain's name and he never saw him again. But more than sixty years later, the aging World War II veteran still marveled at the priest's disregard for his own safety in a quest to comfort and encourage beleaguered and dying men.[3]

A YEAR EARLIER, on the Pacific island of Saipan, Jewish chaplain Milton Rosenbaum hunkered down in a slit trench with twelve marines. Japanese mortar shells exploded all around and enemy fighter bombers strafed the entrenched Americans. One of the men bellowed: "Chaplain, what about a prayer?" Rosenbaum cried out over the battle noise, "The Lord is my Shepherd, I shall not want. . . ." A dozen voices joined the chaplain in reciting the ancient Psalm. The young man who remembered the incident said the chaplain was the only Jewish man in the trench. In combat, discrimination because of creed simply did not exist.[4]

Such encounters were common throughout the war. Similar stories involving Jewish, Catholic, and Protestant chaplains—across North Africa, Europe, Asia, on every island in the Pacific, and aboard numerous ships in combat on the high seas—testify to the heroism of ministers, priests, and rabbis who served God and the

United States of America. These unsung heroes continually ignored their own safety to minister to the spiritual needs of the men and women who were serving their country during World War II, regardless of race or creed.

THIS VOLUME IS the story of the brave men who voluntarily left the relative comfort of their civilian ministry callings to care for the spiritual needs of more than 12 million men and women who served in America's armed forces during the war. Their story is important because as Chaplain (Major General) William Arnold, U.S. Army chief of chaplains in World War II, phrased it: "Battles are won by military power but wars are won by spiritual power."[5]

A major thesis of this book is that military chaplains were absolutely essential to America's victory. Indeed, without the role played by clergy in keeping the soldiers', sailors', and marines' courage up and morale high, the enormous sacrifices required to sustain and win a war simultaneously fought on three continents and numerous Pacific islands would not have been possible. Likewise these members of the armed forces, all too often ignored by historians of the great conflict, were indispensable to keep morale and production up on the home front, among people who continually feared for the physical and spiritual well-being of loved ones so far from home.

In brief, the history of the United States in World War II is incomplete without the story of the chaplains, and I have written this book in hope of giving these men their proper place in the panorama of America at war between 1941 and 1945. Although scores of chaplain autobiographies have been published over the years, most of these books are relatively unknown. Indeed, many of these volumes were self-published and therefore difficult to find. In any case, much of the story is hidden in archives, periodicals, and the memories of men and women who interacted with men of the cloth. We are fortunate, however, that the late Donald F. Crosby, S.J., wrote a first-rate history of Catholic priests who served in the Second World War. In *Battlefield Chaplains: Catholic Priests in World War II*, Crosby bemoaned the fact that there was no similarly thorough study like his of Protestant and Jewish chaplains, or an overview of all three faith communities ministering in the side-by-side conflict.[6]

This book is a modest attempt to fill that void, and it is my desire that it will give long-overdue recognition to twelve thousand men who sought neither glory nor fame for themselves.[7] It is likewise hoped that this book will encourage other Christian and Jewish historians to fill the gaps I have left. Finally I confess one other purpose: to challenge a new generation of young Americans to consider offering their lives "For God and Country" as chaplains in the armed forces. The thoughtful reader of these pages will discern that the need for chaplains among our military personnel is as great now as it ever was, and perhaps from the World War II experience some lessons can be gleaned that will enhance the military's efforts to sustain morale and courage in the face of extremely difficult times.

TO FIND CLUES as to what inspired these quietly courageous chaplains in the 1940s, it is instructive to ponder the words of one of America's most famous preachers and pastors during World War II. Peter Marshall, a native of Scotland who had come to America as an impoverished young man in his twenties, eventually made his way to seminary, gained a well-deserved reputation as a powerful preacher, and was called before his thirty-fourth birthday to the pastorate of New York Avenue Presbyterian Church, one of Washington, D.C.'s most prestigious churches. Soon after assuming his pastorate in Washington, Peter Marshall was invited to speak at a Christmas service attended by President Franklin D. Roosevelt and his family; he also became close to senators and congressmen of both parties, and during President Harry Truman's administration he became the chaplain of the United States Senate. In a sermon titled "The Tap on the Shoulder," delivered during the anxious days of World War II, Reverend Marshall said:

> *By what right does a man stand before his fellows, Bible in hand, and claim their attention?*
>
>   *Not because he is better than they are,*
>
>   *Not because he has attended a theological seminary and studied Hebrew, Greek, and theology.*
>
>   *But primarily because he is obeying a "tap on the shoulder."*
>
>   *Because God has whispered to him in the ear*
>
>   *and conscripted him for the glorious company of those voices crying in the wilderness of life.*
>
>   *The preacher is conscious of being called, as we say, and that means that he is responding to an inward urge that could not be resisted . . .*
>
>   *an urge that grew out of a providential arrangement of his life and his circumstances to the great end that he should become an ambassador of the Chief—an urge that grew into a conviction that only by obeying could he ever find that joy and satisfaction of a life lived according to the plan of God.*
>
>   *God brought Moses from minding the sheep,*
>
>   *He took Amos from the herds of Tekoa,*
>
>   *He beckoned Peter, James, and John from the fishing boats and their nets.*
>
>   *. . . The true minister is in his pulpit not because he has chosen that profession as an easy means of livelihood, but because he could*

*not help it, because he has obeyed an imperious summons that will
not be denied.*[8]

Reading hundreds of letters by rabbis, ministers, and priests who
described how they originally came to their vocations and how they
subsequently felt constrained to serve men and women in the armed
forces during the war, it became abundantly clear to me that most
of them sensed that they had received a supernatural "tap on the
shoulder" and that they would know no peace until they answered
their divine call.

CHAPTER TWO

THE PATH TO PEARL HARBOR

THE COSTLY END OF AMERICAN INNOCENCE

Any peace is not better than any war.

ANDY ROONEY, *MY WAR*[1]

AT the first light of dawn on July 3, 1943, navy chaplain Carol Lemons began the grim task of searching for men who'd died the previous night during a Japanese bombing raid on Rendova (Solomon Islands). Lemons remembered that although he had buried several men over the previous two days, this "was our first experience with mass death. The gruesome sights burned deeply into our inexperienced minds."[2] A husband and the father of three little children, Lemons was still a few months shy of his thirty-second birthday. He vividly recalled that "with each body, resentment increased within me, not so much toward Japanese pilots, who were just doing their job, but toward the minority of irresponsible Americans who caused us to unilaterally disarm following World War I and leave us totally unprepared for World

War II."[3] Chaplain Lemons laid much of the blame for the "59 Americans killed, 97 wounded—in addition to [destruction of] boats, tents, big guns, food, fuel, ammunition, and much other equipment" on the people he labeled naïve American isolationists in the 1920s, and especially on the idealistic American politicians and journalists in the late 1930s and early 1940s who simply refused to prepare us for war. These leaders, said Lemons, argued that America had no duty to defend helpless nations overrun by Germany and Japan, and that America's security would be best enhanced if the nation remained neutral and gave the world a peaceable example by not building up its military arsenal. To the mind of Lemons and plenty of his contemporaries, such "unrealistic dreamers" ultimately cost the United States a prolonged war and countless lives and casualties.[4]

BY THE EARLY 1930s it grew evident to any clearheaded observer of the world scene that Germany, Italy, and Japan were determined to fulfill their expansionist designs on weaker nations despite the condemnation of people in the free world. In 1931 Japan occupied Manchuria and in 1933 withdrew from the League of Nations, with Germany following the same course several months later. In 1934 Japan repudiated the Washington and London naval treaties and rapidly launched construction of a modern fleet of naval vessels. And in 1935 Hitler began stripping German Jews of their rights as citizens, while Italy's Benito Mussolini, without any provocation, invaded Ethiopia.

During 1936 and 1937 the political and military status quo changed dramatically. Germany occupied the Rhineland that had been demilitarized since the Treaty of Versailles. Hitler and Mussolini formed the Rome-Berlin Axis; Italy withdrew from the League of Nations; and Japan began to invade and occupy China. During 1937 Peking and Shanghai fell to the Imperial Japanese forces, and in December that year the Japanese inflicted the infamous Rape of Nanking that startled the world with its mass murder and brutality.

In 1938 Neville Chamberlain, who had become prime minister of Great Britain in 1937, made it clear that he would rather surrender to Germany's demands than risk war. In early 1938 British foreign secretary Anthony Eden resigned over Chamberlain's policy of appeasement, but his gesture brought no change at Number 10 Downing Street. Indeed, in the immediate wake of Eden's resignation, Germany annexed Austria and invaded the Sudetenland of Czechoslovakia. Then, at the Munich Conference in September 1938, France and Britain caved in to Hitler and forced Czechoslovakia to cede the Sudetenland to Germany. During November, Japan proclaimed a "New Order" in Asia—belligerently announcing their domination of the Western Pacific and Southeast Asia.

Despite these blatant acts of aggression, the mood of appeasement was as strong in the United States as it was in Britain and France. The U.S. Congress passed a series of Neutrality Acts in the 1930s designed to keep America isolated from the spread of militarism in Europe and Asia. To be sure, President Franklin Roosevelt disagreed with the isolationist posture in Congress. He realized that his nation's freedom was inextricably linked to Western Europe's and Britain's. Nevertheless, American public opinion stood with Congress in marked opposition to any actions that might drag America into war.

When the Nazis invaded Poland in September 1939, causing Great Britain and France to declare war on Germany, the American people voiced sympathies with their old allies, but a majority remained unyielding in their determination to remain neutral. Even in 1940, when Germany invaded Norway, Denmark, Belgium, France, and the Balkans and then attempted to bomb Britain into submission, most Americans still believed they could stay out of the war.

The rapid collapse of the free world in Europe, plus Japan's reception into the Axis Alliance with Germany and Italy, caused the United States to break with neutrality enough to begin providing economic and military aid to Axis enemies, all the while voicing determination to stay out of war. During autumn 1940 Roosevelt convinced Congress to induct the National Guard into federal service. He also persuaded the Senate and the House to legislate the first peacetime draft in U.S. history.

ON DECEMBER 7, 1941, Imperial Japan destroyed America's illusion that national security lay in isolationism. Japanese naval and air forces launched a surprise attack on the U.S. Navy fleet at Pearl Harbor in Hawaii that revealed the U.S. military to be as unprepared for war as the nation as a whole. In just one hour and fifty minutes the Japanese sank or disabled 19 ships, destroyed more than 150 airplanes, and killed 2,335 soldiers, sailors, and marines. Civilian casualties included 68 killed and nearly 1200 wounded.

The devastating assault began at 7:55 A.M. local time. While Americans on the mainland were reading their newspapers, drinking coffee, and making their way to and from Sunday worship services across the continent, the dreadful news began to break. Regular radio programs were interrupted to announce that the Empire of Japan had bombed our military installations—planes, airfields, mess halls, and barracks at Pearl Harbor. Americans learned that the number of casualties were unknown but enormous.

The news came to Washington, D.C., in early afternoon, and soon citizens congregated around the White House—standing in solidarity with their beleaguered president and waiting for his response. During these afternoon hours President Roosevelt called together his cabinet and congressional leaders, while military leaders hastily made their way to Washington. The crowd of onlookers, already five deep, pressed against the tall, iron fence around 1600 Pennsylvania Avenue—waiting patiently but anxiously for word from their leader.[5]

People gradually gathered along narrow streets near the White House and on the steps in front of the old State Department Building and around the nearby Revolutionary War cannon and anchor. As darkness engulfed the Capitol, voices could be heard singing "God Bless America."[6]

Throughout the afternoon and evening, while Americans tried to process the savage attack on a place that seemed at once far away yet right in their midst, the President made plans to address Congress and the American people the next day amid a flurry of phone calls, telegrams, and face-to-face meetings.[7]

It quickly became evident that the horrid news about Pearl Harbor was only one piece of a widening conflict. The Japanese were launching assaults on the Philippines, Wake Island, Midway and Guam, as well as Britain's installations in Hong Kong and on the Malay Peninsula.

On December 8, after trying to assess all of the bad news, pinpoint placement of all of America's meager armed forces, and calculate current military strength, President Roosevelt made his way to the rostrum of the House of Representatives while the crowd stood and applauded. The President's words reverberated throughout the House of Representatives and over the radio waves into almost every home, school, and workplace in America:

Yesterday, December 7, 1941—a date which will live in infamy—
the United States of America was suddenly and deliberately
attacked by naval and air forces of the Empire of Japan.

Roosevelt set forth a list of devastating attacks on the United
States.

The facts of yesterday and today speak for themselves. The people of
the United States have already formed their opinions and will
understand the implications to the very life and safety of our Nation.
As Commander in Chief of the Army and Navy I have directed
that all measures be taken for our defense. . . . Hostilities exist.
There is no blinking at the fact that our people, our territory, and
our interests are in great danger.

With confidence in our armed forces—with the unbounding
determination of our people—we will gain the inevitable triumph—
so help us God.[8]

In the wake of the President's address, Congress declared war on
Japan, with only one dissenting vote. On December 11 Germany
and Italy declared war on America, and eight days later Congress
extended the military draft from men between the ages of twenty-
one and thirty-five to men between the ages of twenty and forty-
four. Isolationism was gone and with it all hope that the belligerence
of the Axis powers would not touch the Unites States of America.

THE U.S. ARMY, Navy, Coast Guard, and Marine Corps scrambled
to meet the national emergency. When Japan attacked, America's
military strength—including federalized National Guard units—
stood at only 1,800,000. By the end of 1942 military personnel

numbered almost 3,860,000, with an additional 5,000,000 added in 1943, and it reached a total of nearly 11,500,000 in 1944. At war's end more than 12,000,000 men and women served on active duty.

All of the nation's major industries—construction, transportation, manufacturing, and food processing—converted to wartime demands. The professions, too, were pressured to provide quotas. With millions of military personnel in need of training, demands for doctors, nurses, dentists, dieticians, and lawyers grew proportionately.

The U.S. military, by any reasonable standards, performed astonishingly well. Their task of taking ordinary young men and quickly training them into powerful and versatile fighting forces that would eventually defeat well-trained and combat-experienced enemies in Europe, North Africa, and Asia defied all odds, including the careful calculations of Axis leaders.

Recruiting undisciplined and peaceable men to fight and kill was no easy task. But the military trainers—from boot camps and basic training stations to the most advanced and specialized programs—overall performed their tasks well. Medical and dental professionals came alongside to keep bodies fit and repair the physical damage caused by rigorous physical training and the ravages of combat.

Career military men, especially those who had survived the stress and devastation of combat in World War I, understood that the need to prepare and sustain men for the physical and mental strain of military engagement was only part of the task. The challenge of helping keep morale strong and courage high required that the religious and spiritual needs of military personnel also be met. It must be stressed that during the era of World War II, a Jewish and Christian worldview—and with that a rather keen sense of morality based on the Ten Commandments—exercised a dominant influence over American thought and behavior. If few people actually obeyed the entirety of the Law believed to have been given by God to Moses and passed on to the Jewish and Christian faithful, most people in the United States did believe such a lifestyle to be good for both the individual and society. Most Jewish and Christian members of the armed forces would have affirmed the importance of the commandments set forth in the Hebrew Scriptures and succinctly summarized in the Christian New Testament in Jesus Christ's response to the question "What is the greatest command of the law?" "Thou shalt love the Lord thy God with all thy heart, and with thy soul, and with all thy mind. This is the first and great commandment. And a second is like unto it: You shall love thy neighbor as thyself. On these two commandments hang all the law and the prophets."[9] To the point, military leaders recognized that training men to kill the enemy and sustaining them in this dreadful task required chaplains who could help combatants maintain their humanity and religious convictions in the worst of times.

The political and military leaders also needed chaplains to help bolster morale on the home front. Catholic priests, Jewish rabbis, and Protestant ministers who maintained regular contact with the men and women in uniform could also assure families and friends at home that their sons and daughters were attending worship services and finding spiritual guidance and counsel in training camps, aboard ships, and even in combat areas around the world.

If these home front concerns seem overly protective to twenty-first-century Americans, we must be mindful that standards of morality and spirituality were markedly different in the late 1930s and early 1940s. Andy Rooney, a World War II veteran who became a well-known syndicated columnist and television commentator, recalled that he had "led a sheltered high-school life." He and his friends didn't smoke, didn't curse, and didn't sleep with their girlfriends. William Manchester, a celebrated journalist and historian of the postwar years, stressed in his memoir of combat experience in the U.S. Marine Corps during World War II that by the standards of the late 1970s, when he wrote *Goodbye, Darkness*, the values and behavior of that wartime stood worlds apart. Manchester had to inform his post–Vietnam War era readers that in the 1940s we really loved our country and families and we saw it as our responsibility to care for one another—even to the point of putting a senile aunt in a back bedroom rather than banish her to a state hospital. Furthermore, "debt was ignoble. Courage was a virtue. Mothers were beloved, fathers obeyed. Marriage was a sacrament. Divorce was disgraceful. Pregnancy meant expulsion from school or dismissal from a job." Manchester recalled that "boys responsible for the crisis of impregnation had to marry the girls," and "couples did not keep house before they were married." Women were called "ladies" and did not resent it. And "gentlemen always stood and removed their hats when a woman entered the room." There was a "precise relationship between the sexes, so that no one questioned the duty of boys to cross the seas and fight while girls wrote them cheerful letters from home; girls you knew were still pure because they had let you touch them here but not there, explaining they were saving themselves for marriage." This marine veteran who received two Purple Hearts said these folks were imbued with the sentiments of "God Bless America." They were those who celebrated Christmas and Hanukkah, and were convinced that these values would be preserved and would help bring victory.[10]

We can part the curtain and peer back into the spirit of that time by glancing at popular reading tastes. To be sure, the best-selling nonfiction books, according to *Publisher's Weekly*, were focused on the war: William Shirer, *Berlin Diary* (1941); Marion Hargrove, *See Here, Private Hargrove* (1942); Wendell Wilkie, *One*

World (1943); Bob Hope, *I Never Left Home* (1944); and Ernie Pyle, *Brave Men* (1945). Fiction best sellers, on the other hand, brought issues of faith and human dignity into homes and hearts of an ever-growing reading public: A. J. Cronin, *The Keys of the Kingdom* (1941); Franz Werfel, *The Song of Bernadette* (1942); Lloyd C. Douglas, *The Robe* (1943); Lillian Smith, *Strange Fruit* (1944); and Kathleen Winsor, *Forever Amber* (1945).[11]

With such religious and human values deeply ingrained in the culture, it logically followed that the military establishment saw the recruitment of chaplains as one of the highest priorities for disciplining and sustaining the morale of military personnel.

WHILE PREVAILING CULTURE, common sense, and the history of American warfare united army and navy leaders about the need for chaplains, major obstacles stood in the way of quick and easy recruitment. First of all, even if interventionism had gradually grown in the late 1930s and early 1940s, isolationism persevered as the nation's dominant mood. Indeed, just prior to December 7, 1941, 80 percent of Americans did not want to fight either Japan or Germany. To the point, a spirit of pacifism permeated American religion and culture. The utter failure of America's World War I aim to "Save the World for democracy," proclaimed by outspoken and triumphal Christians—among them President Woodrow Wilson—was dashed by the carnage of war and the deterioration of any semblance of peace within a few years after the cessation of hostilities.

Countless American clergy in World War I enthusiastically supported the war effort and celebrated it as a holy crusade—a war fought for the glory of God. But the reality seen in pictures of muddy rat-infested trenches, barbed wire, bayonets, poison gas, and men maimed by artillery shells, machine gun and rifle bullets, culminating in several million deaths and millions more in casualties—revealed the glorious cause to be a revelation of hell on earth.

"No More War" became the cry of guilt-ridden religious leaders. In 1935 New York City's Riverside Church hosted a gathering of 251 rabbis and ministers who, according to historian Gerald L. Sittser, made a pledge before God and the assembled witnesses that "in loyalty to God" and in "the spirit of true patriotism" they "renounce war and never will . . . support another." In the same vein polls taken among clergy in the 1930s declared that more than 60 percent believed churches should take a stand against war, and many clergy expressed unwillingness to serve as chaplains if war did come.[12]

Journalist Andy Rooney remembered that while he was a student at Colgate University during the tumultuous years between 1939 and 1941, it became quite fashionable among college students, academics, and intellectuals to oppose war. Rooney recalled that he and many of his classmates were encouraged in their antiwar leanings by a popular economics professor, Kenneth Boulding. The Quaker teacher impressed Rooney and other undergraduates with his unqualified statement that "Any peace is better than any war." Rooney remembered, "I liked that a lot." And it was a position he maintained until he was drafted, served with the U.S. Army in Europe, and then came upon the German death camp at Buchenwald in spring 1945, where "for the first time, I knew for certain" that Professor Boulding was wrong and "that any peace is not better than any war."[13]

During the time Andy Rooney studied at Colgate in New York, John Morrett pursued graduate work for ordination to the priesthood at the Episcopal Theological School in Cambridge, Massachusetts. Morrett, a 1939 graduate of Ohio State University, served in the college Army ROTC program and was commissioned in the U.S. Army Reserves upon graduation. He remembered that he and another seminarian felt quite isolated in seminary because their dean, the presiding bishop, and most of their fellow students vociferously expressed their opposition to war. In fact during June 1941 Morrett was urged by faculty and students to resign his commission and finish his theological education. Despite peer pressure, John Morrett volunteered for active duty and deferred studies for ordination until after World War II.[14]

The strong antimilitary and antiwar sentiment that Morrett met among Episcopalians, and that Rooney found among academics and Quakers, was common. The Presbyterian Church's General Assembly had declared that "war is a violation of human personality and is repugnant to the Christian conscience, and we repudiate it as a means of settling international disputes." And this sentiment was typical among mainline denominations on the eve of the Pearl Harbor firestorm. One of the main reasons church leaders manifested even more of an antimilitary and antiwar posture than the people in the pews was that the clergy had been trained in seminaries that increasingly embraced a humanistic worldview that assumed human nature was basically good.[15]

Although President Roosevelt had done all he could, within the limits placed upon him by Congress, to prepare the nation for war, only Japan's attack on Pearl Harbor exposed the dangerous state of America's unpreparedness. Even counting the inadequately trained federalized National Guard units, there were only slightly more than 1.75 million military personnel. And despite the quotas each branch of the armed forces had placed upon themselves to recruit chaplains, they were far short of their goals. On December 7, 1941, the army had only 137 chaplains on active duty and 770 reserves eligible for call up, and the navy identified 105 chaplains on active duty and 87 more men eligible to be called.[16]

In the immediate wake of Japan's attack, many of America's young men stood in long lines to volunteer for military service. Their numbers manifested an impressive display of patriotism, but they were not even close to meeting the needs of such a national emergency. The new draft law, on the other hand, quickly pulled tens of thousands of men into the armed forces, providing the army and the navy with enough personnel to meet the urgent crisis.

Recruiting chaplains, however, was another matter. Clergy could not be drafted. Furthermore, the military establishment, by law, had to rely on the various religious denominations and their ordination and licensing councils to do the recruiting. Prior to December 1941 most of Protestant and Catholic opinion—especially at administrative and leadership levels—opposed the concept of "just war." And America's Jews, even in the face of growing evidence of Nazi German atrocities inflicted on Europe's Jews, by no means led a charge for military intervention.[17]

Understandably, U.S. military leaders were seriously concerned. Even if the nation's Jews responded to the call, their numbers comprised less than 10 percent of the armed forces. Much more problematic was the Christian posture. Would Protestants and Roman Catholics be willing or able to meet their quotas? To the mind of many observers it would have required an act of God to transform the antiwar sentiments—especially within the denominational seminaries and power structures. For instance, when John Harold Craven, a young Baptist who was a college student and a marine reservist, informed his denominational leader of his desire to be a marine chaplain, the man responded by tersely expressing his doubt if a truly Christian man could even consider being a marine. Not easily discouraged, Craven prayed to God to transform men of power within the Missouri Baptist Association.[18]

John Craven learned what aspiring military chaplains discovered across denominations and traditions. Religious institutional leaders quickly, albeit cautiously, joined the American public in changing their attitude toward war. Whereas 80 percent of Americans before December 7, 1941, believed we could and should stay out of war, public opinion had shifted nearly 180 degrees by early 1942.[19] Although a small core of pacifists faithfully clung to their convictions despite Japan's attack and Germany's and Italy's declarations of war against the United States, Jewish and Christian institutions answered the call from the armed forces for spiritual and moral leadership. In fact, John Craven and many others like him found that the pathway to the chaplaincy was slowed down most by an unpredictable but consistently stubborn obstacle known as governmental and military bureaucracy. The armed forces at once made desperate appeals for chaplains yet seemed to stand in the way and say "you shall not enter."

CHAPTER THREE

MILITARY TRAINING AND THE CARE OF SOULS

THE SPIRITUAL DIMENSION OF STATESIDE COMBAT PREPAREDNESS

[The] duties of the chaplain require many qualities and abilities which are completely foreign to the daily activities of the average priest, minister, or rabbi in civil life. It is part of the job of the Chaplain School to help in the difficult adjustment and transition of men of all faith, Negro and white, from all areas of the country, to the most honorable status of chaplain in the United States Army.

CHAPLAIN (COLONEL) WILLIAM D. CLEARY
FAITH OF OUR FIGHTERS[1]

AT first glance the story of John Craven's struggle to become a military chaplain is almost beyond belief, especially considering that he was seeking neither special treatment nor a variance of military regulations. Actually, the navy was desperate for chaplains, and John Craven, a highly qualified, ordained minister who was also a U.S. Marine Corps reservist with experiential knowledge of the Navy Department, was readily available and his denomination had endorsed his application with enthusiasm. Yet all of these assets notwithstanding, it took the navy three-quarters of a year to process and act on the application.[2]

If this story were unique, it would be of little significance. Applications sometimes do get misfiled. But alas, Craven's experience was quite common in 1942. Seeing the context, however, makes the snafus more understandable.

THE CHAPLAIN CORPS of both the navy and the army relied on the ordination and governing structures within the Christian and Jewish religious communities to recruit and endorse chaplains. The armed forces established age and physical guidelines, and they required—with some denominational exceptions—a four-year college degree and three years of seminary education. The military also maintained that one year of pastoral ministry was desirable but not mandatory.

The navy, like all federal agencies, including the armed forces, was caught off guard with a peacetime bureaucracy. The Navy Chaplain Corps worked overtime in 1942, streamlined procedures, and operated efficiently by 1943. Even so, as late as 1944 and 1945 the navy could not procure more than 77 percent of their quota of one chaplain for every 1,250 personnel. Although the causes of the shortfall were numerous, the navy did speed up the process by compromising regulations. For instance, the age limit of thirty-eight years became flexible if the other qualifications were in place. Men in their forties and fifties, especially if they had previous military chaplaincy experience, were brought on board to help with procurement and stateside duties. One former chaplain, B. R. Patrick, who had retired in 1932, requested to be returned to active duty as soon as he learned of the attack on Pearl Harbor. The Navy Chaplain Corps, desperate for spiritual leadership, accepted this seventy-two-year-old veteran and assigned him to the naval hospital at Norco (Corona), California. He served admirably until March 1945, when he retired a second time.[3] Such flexibility notwithstanding, the system creaked along.

THE DEPARTMENT OF the Navy had no monopoly on what became derisively called the "hurry up and wait policy," (i.e., hurry up and meet our urgent need but be patient and put your life on hold while we sort out our priorities and get to your application). The army's needs far exceeded the navy's because they had determined that a chaplain was required for every one thousand active duty personnel. Furthermore, three-quarters of the armed forces served in the army. A random sample of the official files of the approximately nine thousand men who served as army chaplains reveal that in 1942 and early 1943 many men who answered the call and already had denominational endorsements waited months to receive their orders for chaplain school. Men with families and churches waited in limbo, demonstrated remarkable patience, but they sent letters and telegrams to remind the army about the considerable inconvenience these delays caused.[4]

One of the more comical delays involved an ordained minister in Aurora, Illinois. Gilbert Johnstone was born in Scotland in 1906. He was thirty-six years old when he volunteered to be an army chaplain. Johnstone met all the qualifications. He had begun his formal schooling with two years at the University of Edinburgh, and then he emigrated to the United States to get a degree from Chicago's Moody Bible Institute because of that institution's strong emphasis on biblical studies, missions, and evangelism. After finishing at Moody, he spent four years at Northern Baptist Seminary in the Windy City, where he earned a bachelor of Theology degree in 1936. Ordained a Baptist, the sturdy Scotsman, who stood five-foot-six and weighed in at about 170 pounds, worked among homeless men at an Aurora, Illinois, rescue mission while serving full-time as the pastor of a local church. Reverend Johnstone's application met delays that lasted eight months. Despite his persistent requests imploring the army to let him serve his adopted nation, it seems someone in the chain of command did not approve his application because he was not certain the reverend was a U.S. citizen. Finally, a superior officer intervened and demanded that Johnstone be accepted, acidly pointing out that his citizenship was with our closest ally, who had been fighting the Axis two years before we entered the war.[5]

In fairness to the armed forces, bureaucratic delays were not always the consequence of incompetence or lack of support staff. Because of the magnitude of the national emergency, all pre-1942 procedures were inadequate. Indeed, by 1945 the number of U.S. military personnel (men and women) reached more than 12,500,000. Approximately 8,300,000 men served in the army and 145,000 women served as WACs and nurses. In the navy there were more than 3,300,000 men, 82,000 women WAVES, and 11,000 nurses. The coast guard included 161,500 men and 10,000 women SPARS. And the marines had approximately 458,000 men and 18,400 women. That drafting, recruiting, processing, equipping, and training this many people in less than five years was sometimes done awkwardly and inefficiently is not nearly as remarkable as the fact that it was done well enough overall to defeat well-trained and combat-experienced Axis forces.

ARMED FORCES BUREAUCRATS did not stand alone in inefficiency. Their ineptitude could always be rivaled by the Catholic, Protestant, and Jewish organizations that had to approve every candidate and faithfully help procure more as the need increased each year. Chaplain Issac Klein, for example, who eventually spent four years as a combat chaplain in Europe, remembered his entrance into the chaplaincy this way: "I discovered soon that volunteering your services was not as simple as I expected. There were several hurdles to overcome." The Jewish Welfare Board, comprised of representatives from Orthodox, Conservative, and Reform rabbinic bodies, was plagued by internal disagreements, and the board had to jointly approve each Jewish candidate before the army or the navy could make a final decision. Writing his memoir in 1974, Rabbi Klein's perspective thirty years later caused him to "smile" at the "irrelevance" of the board's questions. Their queries revealed "that committee had a very faint idea of what the chaplaincy entailed." Klein remembered that "some of the rabbis were particularly anxious to find out whether my observance of Jewish dietary laws and the Sabbath restrictions would interfere with my chaplaincy work, and at what point I would relax their observance." He recalled that he answered his questioners "with a spirit of humor, spiced with quotations from the Talmud."[6]

Among the approximately three thousand Roman Catholic priests who became military chaplains, the story of John P. Foley, S.J., provides a glimpse of the ladders of ecclesiastical authority some priests needed to climb over before securing approval from the Church. Foley, who had taught Greek and English at Boston College, was appointed academic dean in 1940. After December 7, 1941, the Jesuit academician expressed his desire to go into the navy, but "the situation was delicate." He had important responsibilities at Boston College and he knew permission "would not come easily." First he needed permission from the New England Jesuit provincial. The nod from the provincial did not come without some clever maneuvers on Foley's part. And after securing his provincial's approval, he still needed green lights all the way through the college chain of command. From there Foley needed the blessing of the military ordinariate in New York. All of these levels of authority proved to be favorable to Father Foley's application, but the process took many months and caused him to wonder if the war would end before he could be activated.[7]

To Father Foley's utter dismay, weeks of red tape delayed his physical examination, and then the order's military ordinariate slowed the process by trying to convince Foley he would be better off in the army. But the persistent priest held his ground, and after four more months of waiting, he boarded the train for the U.S. Navy Chaplain School at Norfolk, Virginia.[8]

Hurdles that slowed the commissions of Protestant ministers were as varied as the more than one hundred denominations that responded to the call for chaplains. Some of the most fundamentalist and conservative denominations refused to work through national denominational organizations such as the Methodists or National Lutherans, even if they were in the same tradition. Likewise, they would not affiliate with the larger Protestant umbrella group titled the General Commission on Army and Navy Chaplains, sponsored by the ecumenical Federal Council of Churches in America. Therefore, in September 1942 the independent groups calling themselves Evangelicals or Fundamentalists organized the American Council of Christian Churches. In the same separatist vein, some sacramental and liturgical churches as well as Baptists maintained their exclusive denominational practice. Among these were Missouri Synod Lutherans and Southern Baptists, just to mention two.[9]

Consequently there was a proliferation of Protestant certifying agencies, and this caused more work for the military. Protestant disunity, for instance, dictated a procurement process that was less streamlined than what came from the Catholic and Jewish boards. On the other hand, decentralization among Protestants allowed for more grassroots or congregational-level influence in the selection process.

Among the most marginalized and underrepresented Christian traditions were the small independent fundamentalist churches and the African-American denominations. Most pastors of black and rural white congregations represented the economically disadvantaged in those areas, especially in the South, the Ozarks of Missouri and Arkansas, and among the mountain people in Appalachia. Few of these pastors had college degrees or seminary training. Consequently the predominantly African-American denominations could supply only a small percentage of the quota of chaplains they were allotted. The Colored Methodist Episcopal Church could only fill a fourth of their quota, the Colored Baptists 13 percent, and the Primitive Baptists less than 10 percent. The African Methodist Episcopal Denomination, on the other hand, had high clergy credentialing requirements, and they filled their quotas with college- and seminary-trained clergy. Ultimately, white clergy from the middle and upper classes served people of color and whites who entered the armed forces from the most disadvantaged social and economic classes.[10]

CRITICS APLENTY FOUND imperfections on both government and civilian sides of the recruitment system. But the process gradually worked fairly well. The army ultimately commissioned more than 9,000 chaplains, and the navy put 2,742 into service between December 7, 1941, and August 31, 1945. In the final analysis, most of these volunteers served ably—even exceptionally well.[11]

Once their appointments came through, the candidates were hurried off to chaplain schools. The army's first facility, at Fort Benjamin Harrison, Indiana, opened in early February 1942. Each recruit class lasted twenty-eight days, consisting of two hundred hours of instruction, including military organization, law, graves registration, first aid, customs and courtesies, map reading, use of equipment for field services, and physical training. The schools were extended to five weeks in 1944, and eventually most classes required six weeks for completion.

Only four classes went through Fort Benjamin Harrison, because the facilities were too small to accommodate the rapidly growing mission. The last classes there ended in August 1942. The U.S. government sought assistance from some of the nation's larger colleges and universities to make dormitories, classrooms, chapels, and athletic fields available at $10.50 per student per day. Although many institutions of higher learning offered their campuses, the army contract went to Harvard.[12] The Ivy League school won the bidding war because it was near a major city and its housing, academic buildings, and athletic facilities were excellent. The trump card, however, was the name. Even these "sky pilots" and "chappies," as World War II chaplains were dubbed, were not free from the temptation to snob appeal that came with boasting they had "studied at Harvard."

Naval chaplain candidates initially trained at the Norfolk Naval Station, remaining there until March 1943. But as with the army, the navy's needs outstripped the original facility and an academic institution was needed for the mission. The navy school remained on the Virginia coast, leaving Norfolk and occupying several buildings at William and Mary College in Williamsburg. Like Harvard, William and Mary had name appeal, but by far the greatest considerations were superb mess facilities, good dormitories, and an environment, including the beautiful Sir Christopher Wren Chapel, that appealed to the navy's deep sense of history. Furthermore, William and Mary provided excellent separate facilities for enlisted men and women who were candidates for the special rating (W) in order to serve as chaplain assistants for helping with clerical tasks and music.[13]

The navy school lasted eight weeks, making it two to three weeks

longer than the army class. There were many reasons for this differ-
ence. First of all, the navy required more academic courses, particularly Applied Psychology and History. Second, naval candidates had to
master customs, procedures, and regulations for the navy and the
marines.[14] The military worlds of the marines and the navy, despite
both being in the same department, were in many ways different. Typically the navy relocated chaplains each year, often moving them from
naval bases to ships and sometimes to marine camps. Consequently, a
navy chaplain needed to be at home in any Navy Department environment. Lieutenant Leland Carol Lemons, for instance, spent his first
year with the marines and Seabees in combat in the Solomon Islands.
Because of naval reassignment policies, after one year with the marines,
Lemons returned to the States and served as base chaplain of a naval
air station in Indiana. Then after twelve months he was assigned as the
Protestant chaplain to an aircraft carrier, USS *Manila Bay*.[15] To say the
least, it required additional training to be this versatile.

AS A GROUP, most chaplain candidates did well in their academic
courses in chaplain schools. Most arrived with at least seven years
of higher education, and men in some traditions, like Jewish rabbis
and the Catholic Jesuits, had chosen their calling, in part at least,
because of their love for learning. Most all of these chaplain candidates, regardless of their denomination, possessed above average
minds well disciplined in Greek, Hebrew, and Latin. Furthermore,
records at the National Archives reveal that many of these clergy
had studied French or German as well as biblical languages.[16]

Jesuit priest William J. Leonard twice offered himself as a chaplain, but his provincial said no. The third time his superior said yes.
Leonard remembered that he found the academic classes at Harvard to be "thin. But the experience was worthwhile in that we

learned something of close-order drill, marched in formation over half of Cambridge, picked up the more common army jargon, and in general became less self-conscious in our khaki, so that when we joined units we were posted to we were not as ignorant or clumsy as we might have been." What proved to be one of the most valuable parts of his chaplain school education was getting to know men of other faith traditions. "I had never in all my life talked to a Protestant minister. Now one was my roommate, several counted cadence with me in the same section, I sat with thirty or more in class."[17]

Father Leonard's interfaith experience was commonplace by design. The armed forces knew that in many wartime circumstances all chaplains were going to have to minister to men and women outside their traditions. Consequently, they housed chaplain candidates so as to deliberately cause interaction. Rabbi Isaac Klein wrote that "whether design or by sheer chance, each of the six men in my room was of another denomination. My roommates were Episcopal, Presbyterian, Christian Disciple, Baptist, and, probably by oversight, the only other rabbi in that class of a hundred and seventy." Klein maintained that "the arrangement proved to be a great source of liberal education and it started the first morning." As each man began his own time of devotions, Rabbi Klein urged the men to stop eyeing one another with curiosity and instead take turns explaining what they were doing. "This suggestion was readily accepted by all in the room, and our dormitory room became a classroom." Prior to chaplain school the Massachusetts rabbi had no idea that there were six Presbyterian denominations and each proudly stood on their distinctiveness. He discovered that Episcopalians were similar to Catholics and that neither the Baptists nor the Disciples were sacramentalists. His greatest surprise came when he learned that some of these groups eschewed any use of alcoholic beverages.[18]

True friendships were forged among disparate faith groups at

Harvard, Norfolk, and Williamsburg as men roomed, ate, marched, and shared weekend passes together. Most chaplains not only gained comrades and an education, they were prepared to minster to men of all faiths and to look forward to a postwar era of more unity. Indeed, Chaplain Klein celebrated the fact that "the Chaplains' Corps wrote an inspiring chapter in the history of understanding, cooperation and appreciation between the clergy of all faiths."[19]

No one in the military command structure expected these men to conduct formal worship services that included all faith traditions. To be sure, chaplains were representatives of their own traditions. Nevertheless, they learned in chaplain school to minister to all men and women. This meant they must listen to problems, offer counsel, give encouragement, pray comfort for the wounded and dying, and bury each one in a dignified way. As the *Army Chaplain Technical Manual* phrased it: "The chaplain is the servant of God for all, and no narrow sectarian spirit should color his utterances, nor should his personal work assist only a special group."[20]

UPON GRADUATION FROM chaplain school, the navy and army commissioned the chaplains (first lieutenant in the army and lieutenant junior grade in the navy), granted them a brief leave, and gave them orders to report to their duty posts. In some cases, of course, this meant still more training. An army chaplain assigned to an infantry unit would be assigned to train for infantry duty alongside men who had just finished basic training. For an infantry chaplain this required several weeks of advanced physical training, including demanding obstacle courses, miles of marching, and living outdoors in all kinds of weather.

A man like Edward K. Rogers, a Lutheran chaplain who had attended Thiel College in Pennsylvania, where he lettered in football and wrestling and then listed boxing, swimming, and skiing as hobbies, delighted in the rigors of his training with the First Infantry Division. Although Rogers was thirty-six years old, married with three daughters, a dozen years out of seminary, and a decade and a half out of college when he entered the chaplain program, he was tough as horse hide and kept up with all the officers and enlisted men.[21]

Not every chaplain adapted so well. One African-American was fifty-six years old when he entered the Harvard school. His age caused one fellow student to question why the army allowed a man over fifty into the program unless it was because he was so big and strong. The aged warrior was probably given a waver in part because of the acute shortage of black chaplains. Why the man was brought into the program aside, a Jewish candidate befriended the black brother, bound up his blistered feet, and both of them continued to encourage each other, finished the program admirably, received their commissions, and no doubt brought racial reconciliation to a heightened level.[22]

Some chaplains in training had neither the physical fitness of Edward Rogers nor the heart of the African-American man in his fifties. Alvin O. Carlson, a Presbyterian pastor, was forty-two years old when he entered chaplain school. He was initially passed over because of age, but his correspondence reveals an unusual persistence. He wrote several letters to the army chief of chaplains saying he was willing and able to help fill the dire need for pastors in the army. Bespectacled, slightly balding, and less than trim, Carlson stood five-eleven and weighed about two hundred pounds. Pastor Carlson, a well-educated man with degrees from the University of Minnesota and McCormick Theological Seminary, was married and the father of three minor children. Evidently motivated by a rush of patriotism, he made it through chaplain school with no problems. Upon graduation in January 1944 his comfort zone changed. Carlson was assigned to the Thirty-Fifth Infantry Division, and preparations were being made to whip these men into fighting shape to be shipped overseas.[23]

Totally unprepared for the rigors of infantry, Carlson now showered a volley of letters on the same chief of chaplains he had implored to let him into the army. Carlson's letters are full of self-pity. He notes that he is forty-two years old and not physically strong enough to be in the infantry. He entreats Chaplain William Arnold to see if some mistake has been made in placing him in "a very active marching unit" and one that is rumored "soon to go overseas." Chaplain Arnold informed Lieutenant Carlson, "You are within the age limit for overseas duty. Chaplains are being sent who are three years beyond your age." But Carlson was not impressed. He wrote again complaining, "I am now with this regiment and am on a special mountain training period in West Virginia." He noted he was having to write from the corner of a tent kitchen and that "we are sleeping in sleeping bags out in the open, and we have had drenching rain for two days, and today it is very cold with low temperatures on their 3500[-foot] mountain elevation."

Carlson's several requests for a reassignment to a non-infantry unit that was not slated for combat were promptly and sharply denied. In late February 1944 a chaplain personnel officer informed Carlson that chaplains were in short supply. Furthermore, "We believe that you will become acclimated to your present unit prior to departure. . . . We suggest . . . that you orient yourself to your present assignment and that before long you will be enjoying it just the same as your other fellow chaplains."[24]

Carlson finally abandoned all hope of reassignment. In fact, he acclimated and shipped out with the Thirty-Fifth Infantry Division. He was promoted to captain, assigned to the front lines of combat with his unit in France, and was wounded in the heavy fighting for Saint-Lô in July 1944. Carlson returned to fierce fighting as soon as he recovered, and he went on to distinguish himself and serve with much valor. He was awarded the Bronze Star, the Purple Heart, and the highest commendations from his battalion: "This officer is aggressive in his work. He has a keen interest in his men. Is a man with an appeal to soldiers. His combat service has brought him perspective and stature to command respect and he is particularly successful in bringing service to small units often neglected."[25]

The case of Chaplain Carlson was not unique. In 1943 a Dominican, Jean P. Cossette, finished Harvard Chaplain School and was assigned to the Eighty-Third Infantry Division. In a fashion similar to Carlson, the priest performed well until he began his ministry and training with the infantry. Cossette implored the chief of chaplains to reassign him. The thirty-five-year-old clergyman claimed to be too weak and too sickly to keep up with the rigorous training routine of the Eighty-Third. Chaplain Arnold evidently played no favorites. A Catholic himself, he in essence told the Dominican to stop whining and get moving. Like Carlson, Cossette also survived training and went on to be an outstanding combat chaplain in Europe. Genuinely loved by the men, he stayed in the thick of combat to be with them and was awarded the Bronze Star with an Oak Leaf Cluster, having served in heroic fashion in two major battles.[26]

ENDORSING AGENCIES REPRESENTING Catholic, Jewish, and Protestant faiths had little understanding of what kind of men the armed forces needed as chaplains. Military leaders, on the other hand, had active duty experience, and many of the senior officers had combat experience from World War I. Therefore they possessed a keener sense of the attributes men needed to become effective chaplains. They understood that the spiritual leaders must do more than preach, teach, and care for the souls of people of their own traditions. Of course they would lead worship, preach, teach, and offer spiritual nurture. But their calling was to help civilians become combatants, adjust spiritually and psychologically to a radically different way of life, and at the same time assure families and communities back home that military life would not destroy the moral values and souls of their loved ones in uniform.

Faculty in chaplain schools did their best to teach candidates how to conduct worship services in chapels and out in the field, or aboard ship, and how to counsel men and women about the commonest issues people would face. The schools likewise taught chaplains to become bridges between officers and enlisted personnel, as well as how to function as conduits of communication between the military base and the local communities where most troops would go for weekend liberty.

Once the chaplains finished school and reached their first stateside assignment, commanders of the various camps and bases usually made their own requirements clear regarding the role of the chaplains. To be sure, some commanders disliked "preachers" and "Holy Joes," but most unit commanders let it be known that worship was a right and that therefore, whenever possible, opportunities for it should be extended to all personnel. Chaplains were to be welcomed and encouraged, as long as they did not attempt to interfere with orders.

Brigadier General F. B. Prickett, commander of the Seventy-Fifth Infantry Division at Fort Leonard Wood, Missouri, made his position perfectly clear in a memorandum he had distributed to all unit commanders on October 6, 1943. He prefaced his directive by stating that among "the four freedoms of the Atlantic Charter for which we contend is freedom of religion. Religion is basic in American life and fundamental to our survival as a strong people." He went on to assert that "a religious life will be considered the normal life for all personnel." The general noted, "I commend regular habits of church attendance." He said his ambition was for "everyone" to attend "at least one church service each week. This is not simply to achieve a

record, but to maintain a life." He argued that commanders needed
to realize that a successful religious program has a positive effect on
"the attitude and practice of officers and non-commissioned officers." Although "there will be no compulsory church attendance,"
he did stress that "to attend religious services is part of an *officer's
leadership*." General Prickett commended "the practice of all personnel carrying a Prayer Book or a Testament," and ones that would fit
in the pocket would be supplied by the chaplains. He explained the
desirability of each soldier having a personal prayer book by saying
that if a person was in peril or was in need of spiritual help—yet isolated from a chaplain—the valuable aid would be in his pocket.[27]

General Prickett's nine-point memorandum did not stop there.
He emphasized that "in view of our positive religious emphasis,
ridicule or disrespect of a man's religious habits, devotions or church
attendance will not be tolerated. Personal epithets or disparaging
comments will not be permitted." He made it "the duty of officers
and non-commissioned officers to prevent ridicule or disrespect in
barracks or elsewhere."[28]

Chaplains assigned to the Seventy-Fifth Infantry Division were
no doubt encouraged by this directive, but they were given some
strong words of exhortation as well. It is hard to imagine that any
chaplain received clearer words of responsibility from a home front
bishop or overseer than those from this divisional commander: "I
am holding the chaplains of this division to a very high standard.
They have a very grave responsibility with such a high percentage
of teen-age men and an average of only 21.9 years [of age]." The general got specific about his requirements:

*The chaplains are more than morale builders; morale building is
every officer's duty. The primary function of chaplains is to be ministers of religion to the officers and men of this command.*

In order to do this work most effectively, the chaplains are train-
ing with the men—going into the field—living with the troops—
getting close to them—understanding their psychology.

The commander allowed no quarter for laziness. Chaplains
would be in the field, but they needed to be careful to find "adequate
time for professional preparation." Beyond this, chaplains are devot-
ing "and will continue to devote long and intense hours in counseling
men who come to the Chapel offices, particularly in the evenings."

The general concluded his memorandum with these words: "The
religious life of this command is fundamental. I invite the cooperation
and loyalty of every officer and enlisted man in maintaining it."[29]

DURING 1942 THE army constructed over six hundred chapels.
Made of wood and usually painted white, these worship facilities,
designed to seat 350 people, were furnished with oaken pews, two
tables, and pine podiums or pulpits. The front area could be converted for Catholic, Protestant, or Jewish services within minutes—
complete with standards, banners, and other items necessary for
each tradition's worship. These mass-produced chapels had office
space in back for a chaplain and his assistant, outfitted with wooden
desks and a few bookcases and storage shelves.

Similar structures were built for the expanding naval bases and
marine camps. Throughout the camps and bases, facilities were spartan, but so were most of the hastily constructed buildings thrown up
between 1942 and 1944 to meet massive and ever-growing demands
of various kinds. Indeed, most camps and bases were always under
construction. Sounds of hammers and saws, the smell of fresh lum-
ber, and the waving of brushes spreading gray, white, or olive-drab
paint were part of the monotonous but functional landscape.

There is no evidence that anyone complained about the austerity of chapel facilities, but if any person had such a mind, that person could be pointed to places where the chapels were even more austere. In many stateside locations during 1942 and early 1943, a large tent sufficed for a chapel until the standard frame building could be erected. Chaplain J. H. Cosby spent most Sundays holding services on the beach. In cold weather he could be found on Sundays commandeering trucks to ferry troops from Camp Davis, a North Carolina coast artillery camp, to several local churches in surrounding communities. It is doubtful that he had a course on networking churches at chaplain school, but the forty-two-year-old Baptist from Virginia stood in the gap and made certain that every soldier who was willing to worship on Sunday could be provided with roundtrip transportation both morning and evening.[30]

Once the chaplains received their unit assignments, they carried out the general guidelines of what they had been taught to do. Depending on the chaplain's tradition, he distributed little volumes of Scriptures in Hebrew and English, or various Catholic missals or prayer books, often with his name stamped inside as a way of introduction. The chaplains organized regular worship services and recruited volunteers to serve as vocalists for small choirs, readers for the Scripture lessons, and in some denominations Communion assistants. Typically a chaplain would post a sign near his chapel office, complete with his name and the hours when he would be available. While most signage was little more than a name and WELCOME, the more creative attracted attention with military humor. One board read: CRYING TOWELS AVAILABLE DAILY. Others proclaimed PARSONAGE, PADRE, INC., and YOU HEARD THAT IF YOU HAVE A COMPLAINT—"TELL IT TO THE CHAPLAIN" WELL, HERE HE IS. And yet another offered this hope: IF THE CHAPLAIN CAN'T HELP HE CAN POINT YOU TO THE ONE WHO CAN.[31]

The chaplains stamped their own personalities on nearly everything they did. The prescribed "Sex and Hygiene" lectures—something all chaplains in both the army and navy were required to give, varied as widely as the backgrounds and experiences of the rabbis and clergymen. One chaplain assumed the troops lived in a fog of innocent ignorance, and no doubt many of his listeners did. The chaplain explained that the Bible teaches that sex is good in marriage—the place God intended it to be. But "sex misused may bring a taste of hell on earth." The chaplain went on to inform the men of venereal diseases that infected prostitutes and loose women who were not part of the ancient profession. He warned, too, of the terrible pain that comes for a "nice girl" who is taken advantage of and then left alone when you ship out. She is marked for life as an unwed mother, or she might cause trouble for you after you are long gone, as she demands you step up and shoulder fatherly responsibilities. The chaplain further cautioned that at best the soldier or sailor who seeks sexual satisfaction outside of biblical boundaries will carry a guilty conscience home to his wife or tawdry memories into the honeymoon bedroom. One priest struck a different chord when he said, "The greatest motive to chastity: you're a temple of God."[32]

Other chaplains employed more graphic approaches. Marine Corps camps, naval bases, and army camps commonly showed stark black-and-white films of male and female private parts infected with sexually transmitted diseases. These reel-to-reel displays left nothing to the imagination and served as unforgettable complements to sexual morality and hygiene lectures. In short, some chaplains used the Bible, others appealed to loyalty toward loved ones at home, and despite the fact that the military required chaplains to give these talks, some enterprising clergy brought in military medical doctors to offer their warnings to the cynical men who were prone to ignore anything a clergyman had to say on any subject—especially sex.

Chaplains were not fools, and all of them were at least ten to fifteen years older than the majority of their enlisted personnel. Therefore they knew that many men would succumb to peer pressure and temptation. They would drink too much and find themselves in situations they'd never planned to be in. For that reason most sky pilots did not condemn the military for making condoms and prophylactic kits available to men as they went on leave, and the most pastoral chaplains assured the troops that if they did stray and found themselves despondent or in any kind of trouble—"tell it to the chaplain." He would help.

Successful chaplains endeared themselves to the soldiers and sailors by being good to their word. The best chaplains followed up formal lectures by mingling in the mess halls, talking with men on bivouac, dropping into the barracks, and inviting the troops to simply come by the office for a chat.

The chaplains who became the most effective at helping the men stay morally straight and emotionally strong recognized that the young soldiers, sailors, and marines were often homesick, especially during the first months away from home. While in boot camp and basic training they were on the go most hours of the day and often into the night, so there was little spare time to think of anything but running the next mile or completing the endless chores and catching some sleep. But once these recruits were placed into their post basic training schools or combat training units, occasional weekend liberty brought leisure and the evenings were often free. Consequently, chaplains did their best to create a small space that became a home away from home, offering themselves as listening and caring father figures to the throngs of men and women who sorely missed the warmth of hearth and home.

Several veterans confessed that their military experience was their first time away from home. Lads in their late teens especially longed for their mother's cooking, evening puzzles and games on the kitchen table, noises of siblings playing, or someone reading aloud during the hours between supper and bedtime in that era before television and personal computers commanded the family's center of attention. To be able to drop in on Chappie for a cup of coffee and a brief chat could lift the spirits and brighten the week. Wilmar Bernthal, an army enlisted man, recalled his homesickness being away from his family and future wife in Frankenmuth, Michigan. To Bernthal, his chaplain at Fort McClellan, Alabama, brought joy to his spirit by simply being present and offering a few activities that provided some semblance of home away from home to a Northern lad in the rural South. In similar fashion an Alabama Catholic who found himself "pretty homesick" up north, despite the crowds of people in New York, found solace through fellowship by simply attending a Catholic mass.[33]

Savvy army and navy chaplains knew that the most effective way to steer men away from trouble and help lead them out of dark nights of the soul was to offer plenty of activities and entertainment rather than sermonize on the "Thou Shalt Nots." They organized a variety of athletic events, including boxing and wrestling matches, and baseball or football games. If they lacked equipment for sports, and that was often the case, enterprising chappies took a jeep to the nearest town, where they bought items in the sporting goods stores or begged them from members of local churches.

Besides athletic activities, inventive chaplains started little libraries, complete with selections of fiction, poetry, history, and biography, as well as books on religion. Once again the chaplains learned to glean from local communities. They bought discarded books from second-hand shops but also employed civilian rabbis and pastors in towns near the bases to ask their congregations to donate books for a chapel library.

Always urging the men and women to get their eyes off themselves, chaplains organized them on liberty to go into nearby cities and towns to serve local civilians. The idea for the Marine Corps "Toys for Tots" program, where the marines acquire secondhand toys

and then distribute them to needy children at Christmas, began in
World War II with chaplains taking troops to San Diego or Los Angeles to bless disadvantaged children. In the same vein, all branches of
the armed forces took up collections among themselves so that they
could go to town and buy food, clothing, or toys for people in need.
One fascinating example of this can be found in records of the 142nd
Mobile Gun Battalion. Out in the Texas desert, at Camp Maxey, an
isolated artillery training camp within sprawling Fort Bliss, a tender-
hearted chaplain discovered a little Indian church across the border
in Oklahoma. Precisely what that Choctaw community needed is not
in the records, but we do know that the chaplain and his men pooled
$55.25—a tidy sum in 1944 from men in a remote desert camp—
and delivered it to meet the needs of some marginalized people.[34]

Chaplains did more than teach men and women to help the
needy, they taught them to save. Many members of the armed forces
took advantage of their chaplain's offer to be their banker. Chappies
offered to keep money in a safe place, and in the same fashion they
volunteered their services as postmasters, lending librarians, athletic directors, father confessors, counselors, and distributors of
sundry items begged from local churches.

Not surprisingly, almost all chaplains understood that their primary responsibility was to feed and nurture souls. They personally
led or found committed laymen to teach Bible classes and also
organized small discussion groups. For those who desired it, they
put together one-to-one or small group accountability meetings
with the purpose of holding men to task for feeding their souls in
daily devotions and keeping short accounts with God about their
personal habits and behavior.

Some evangelical chaplains brought civilians to camps and bases
to provide Friday or Saturday night programs and in some cases to
remain several days for evening services. Many evangelical chaplains

at army camps in Southern states spread the word that an unusually magnetic speaker named Eddie Martin would like to hold meetings. A Baptist evangelist, Martin represented the Pocket New Testament League out of New York. Letters in the wake of his meetings, which were held in dozens of camps in Texas, Alabama, Georgia, and the Carolinas, enthusiastically endorsed him and his team. The secrets of Martin's success were many. First, "outsiders" were always a breath of fresh air to soldiers. They grew weary of men and women in uniform. Martin, however, brought more than a fresh voice from civilian life. His wife frequently traveled as part of his team, and she often worked with local women and helped offer socials for the troops. Serving with the Martins was a "singing trio" of three female vocalists. Chaplain (Major) James A. Bryant wrote in early 1943 that Martin and his group "rendered an invaluable aid . . . among the men of our unit." He went on to celebrate the "girls" in the trio. They not only rendered the "grand old hymns and Gospel songs" in a way that presented "the Word of God in a most attractive manner, but, I honestly feel, did more to bring the virtues of womanhood to the minds of the men who are deprived of the restraining influence of wives, mothers, sisters, and sweethearts than any other single influence since their induction in the armed service."[35]

A regimental chaplain at Camp Butner, North Carolina, agreed with Bryant and thanked the Pocket New Testament League for sending the preacher. He also wrote: "I believe the idea of a ladies unit is a good one. We have had so much trash brought us through other organizations that it is a blessing to see real Christian womanhood stand before our men and present the Gospel as they did."[36]

Outside speakers resulted in a welcome change from military routine at all military bases and camps. Also, local women living near these bases encouraged the troops by organizing service clubs. Women's groups always provided homemade refreshments, and they frequently arranged for films, slides, and lectures. Such activities invariably elevated the spirits of military personnel of all religious traditions. Whatever the content of the entertainment or talks, morale was lifted by these women because they brought the flavor of home into the predominantly male military environment.[37]

Eddie Martin and the women who accompanied him were unusual in that they were intentional about encouraging the black troops. Unlike some groups of outsiders, they made a concerted effort to include the frequently segregated African-Americans in their swings through a camp. For example, they ministered at the Colored Service Club at Camp Bowie, Texas, and their records show that they "appeared before the Negro Personnel" at Hunter Field, an Army Air Corps base in Georgia.[38]

PERHAPS THE MOST isolated and neglected members of the military were those who were incarcerated in the guardhouses, stockades, and brigs. Chaplains brought light to these men and helped them get straightened out to rejoin their units. These ministers visited the ill and wounded in sick bays and hospitals, and they wrote letters home for men who were disabled, and for those who could not write well enough to communicate with loved ones.

Chaplains not only tended to their units and ministered to the incarcerated, infirm, and semiliterate, they became advocates for wives and mothers of servicemen who needed doctors, rent money, or letters of assurance that their men were receiving soul care as well as training to fight. Many chaplains in the navy and army took names and addresses of those enlisted personnel who attended chapel services. Then they put their chaplain assistants to work helping send printed postcards to families at home assuring them that their loved one had been to chapel.

For example, Mrs. Jack Dorsett received a postcard from army chaplain Raymond Draffin informing her that her husband, Private First Class Jack J. Dorsett, "has been true to his Christian profession by participating in our Communion service. Our prayers mingle with yours for his continued devotion and faithfulness to Christian obligations." But the blade could cut the other way as well. A Catholic priest, Chaplain Philip A. Holland, sent a four-paragraph letter to an army man's wife, informing her that her husband was not "attending to his religious duties. There is absolutely no excuse other than laziness or indifference" to account for his failure to go to Mass. The priest's hope was that his wife could encourage his attendance.[39]

ALTHOUGH CHAPLAINS WERE not readily available everywhere in 1942, or present in all combat areas of Europe and Asia, and every ship on the high seas, by 1943 almost no woman or man in uniform in the United States was without benefit of clergy care if he or she wanted it. Not every Jewish person in the armed forces could always find a rabbi, but Protestant and Catholic chaplains did their utmost to scour the base and find one or, if necessary, contact the nearest town or city for a civilian rabbi to come and help.

That the armed forces intended military personnel to know that the care of souls was of paramount concern is manifested in this notice printed on the back of the Protestant Order of Worship at the Reception Center Chapel in Fort Leavenworth, Kansas, for the morning service on Sunday August 15, 1943:

> The Chaplains are in their offices in
> the Chapel each morning and at any
> other time by appointment. If you wish
> to see either of them, feel free to

do so. They are here to help you with
any problem you may have.

————————————

In each barracks in camp there is a
Schedule of the religious services for
the coming week. Be sure to attend any
of the services listed there. You will
be more than welcome.

————————————

READ YOUR BIBLE DAILY.

Similar invitations met men in other branches of service. The "Order of Morning Worship" at the U.S. Naval Training Center in Great Lakes, Illinois, in 1942 advertised that "the chaplains will welcome personal interviews with men who desire baptisms," and a post-chapel bulletin at Moore Airfield, California, carried these words on September 12, 1943:

> *The literature on the table in the vestibule is for you. Take at least one pamphlet with you today. If you are interested in the other literature or wish to discuss some problem with the Chaplains, why not make arrangements today?*[40]

NOTICES OF CATHOLIC masses as well as Jewish and Protestant services were widely circulated and posted at all stateside military installations. Locations of chaplains' offices were as easy to find as those of the mess halls and post exchanges. Soul care and worship were clearly high priorities.

PART TWO

CHAPTER FOUR

Entering Harm's Way

THE EARLY STAGES OF WAR IN THE PACIFIC

Chaplains must be permitted to minister in harm's way if they are to carry out their combat role effectively. This role, to be truly effective, must be executed in forward combat areas.

GENERAL A. M. GRAY, U.S. MARINE CORPS[1]

A RE you ready to be killed?" With these words the navy's district chaplain in New York greeted Father George W. Wickersham just prior to his departure for the naval training school for chaplains at Williamsburg, Virginia. The district leader's cryptic question startled the thirty-year-old graduate of Harvard College and the Virginia Theological Seminary. Nevertheless, the aspiring chaplain recalled he answered his elder's gallows humor with the comment "to the effect that I could hardly wait."[2]

The district chaplain aimed to lighten the official tone of the interview. But he also intended to puncture the lofty idealism that led many men into war. Years later, Wickersham confessed that despite daily news reports of battle casualties on Pacific islands and continuous sinkings of merchant ships in the Atlantic, the thrill of adventure and the constant flow of patriotic music and speeches meant that Americans saw all ships as "galleons of freedom, and to the men on deck always gave the 'thumbs up' sign which was almost inevitably returned." Having no idea of the pain and devastation that lay ahead, Wickersham admitted, "I wanted to be aboard, and aboard I was going. Was I ready to be killed? I guess that I was just about ready for anything. Indeed, I could hardly wait."[3]

Chaplain candidates like Wickersham by no means stood alone in the patriotic parade. Early in the war, Chester Root joined the navy as an enlisted man. He finished boot camp in San Diego and was trained to be a medic assigned to the Marine Corps as a corpsman. Root remembered being caught up in a high tide of patriotic enthusiasm. He enjoyed wearing his uniform, listening to the rousing military band music, and being applauded by California civilians while he excitedly awaited orders "overseas" with the marines. It was not until his troop ship reached New Caledonia that the reality began to sink in that this war was not a festive adventure. Sobering reality dawned in the minds of sailors and marines when, for the first time, they saw body bags and listened to horrific stories about a place called Guadalcanal. Chet Root would soon care for wounded, maimed, and dying Second Division marines on Tarawa and Saipan, and then he would be nearly killed by a Japanese hand granade on Tinian in late July 1944.[4]

CHAPLAINS RECEIVED THEIR baptisms by fire the same way as medics and combatants.

It was a Marine Corps general who insisted that "chaplains must be permitted to minister in harm's way if they are to carry out their combat role effectively." And this role, "to be truly effective, must be executed in forward combat areas" because men's concerns for their souls, God, and life hereafter grow with each step closer to the front lines of combat.[5]

Chaplains from all branches of the armed forces unflinchingly took their places alongside the men in the areas of fiercest fighting. Indeed, by war's end 24 of the navy's 2,742 chaplains had been killed in action and 46 Purple Hearts were awarded to chaplains serving with the navy and the marines. Army chaplains had it even worse. Except for the Army Air Corps, the Chaplain Corps sustained the highest per capita casualty rate in the army, with 77 killed and 275 wounded out of the approximately 9,000 active duty men of the cloth.[6]

That America's military chaplains would always be found with the most vulnerable combatants in harm's way during World War II was clearly manifested during the Japanese attack on Pearl Harbor. Among the 2,335 soldiers, sailors, and marines killed that morning of December 7, 1941, were two chaplains. Father Aloysius Schmitt, a Catholic, died when the USS *Oklahoma* capsized after three torpedoes ripped her underside. And almost simultaneously, Protestant chaplain Thomas Kirkpatrick, a Presbyterian serving on the USS *Arizona* perished when the battleship he served was sunk. Survivors of the battleship *Oklahoma* reported that Chaplain Schmitt assisted several sailors to get through a porthole before he drowned. No one lived to disclose Kirkpatrick's last minutes.[7]

Men rescued from the *Oklahoma* and the *Arizona* could not recall seeing their chaplains before the attack, but it is likely that the ministers on those ships were preparing for Sunday morning worship services in the hold of their vessels. Indeed, chaplains on other ships were setting up for worship, as were chaplains on shore. Army chaplain Terrence G. Finnegan, the senior chaplain of the chapel on Oahu, recalled looking outside the little chapel while his assistant set up for Mass. He was thinking: "What a bright, peaceful morning and how beautiful are the formations of planes coming in from the sea." No more than five minutes later those planes began raining down a firestorm of bombs, torpedoes, and machine gun bullets on unsuspecting and unprepared American civilians and military personnel.[8]

Chaplain Finnegan furiously drove his rickety 1931 Buick around Oahu Barracks, saying last rites over scores of dead and dying men around the airfield and artillery area. Quickly other chaplains appeared among the wounded and dying, doing all they could to assist nurses, doctors, army medics, and navy corpsmen who began to descend on the most war-torn areas. Confessions were heard, civilian men, women, and children were comforted and prayed for, and then after nearly two hours of bombing and strafing, the yellowish planes with the blood-red balls painted on the wings and fuselage, turned away. And then began the torturous task of identifying the dead.[9] Chaplain Albin L. Fortney remembered the morbid work this way:

> It was not an easy task. We had to use every means possible to determine the identity of bodies: clothes, letters, contents of pockets, billfolds, laundry marks, organization insignia, fingerprints, personal identification. In many cases there was so little remaining of a body that only our own resourcefulness would make an identification possible.[10]

Identifying the dead did not end the heartaches experienced by military chaplains at Pearl Harbor. Next came the painful task of writing personal letters of condolence to families of those killed, as well as letters of assurance and hope dictated to chaplains by wounded soldiers and sailors who were too disabled to write.

Experiences of chaplains at Pearl Harbor proved to be a prelude to four years of similar activities. Until the cessation of hostilities in August 1945, chaplains scattered throughout the Pacific would attempt to conduct their so-called "normal" duties, such as worship services, administering sacraments and ordinances, offering religious instruction, counseling troubled souls, providing athletic and entertainment activities, visiting the sick, and performing endless administrative chores. At the same time—all over the great Pacific—

whether aboard ships or in the jungles or sands of the land, these ordinary tasks were frequently interrupted by the chaos of combat.

IN THE AFTERMATH of America's declaration of war on the Axis powers, tens of thousands of newly trained marines and navy and army personnel were mobilized and strategically placed among our allies in the Pacific. Australia, New Zealand, and New Guinea became essential entry points for American fighting forces, as well as storage bases for materials necessary to sustain an ever-expanding Pacific military enterprise. Consequently, army and marine divisions peacefully invaded the Pacific nations of our allies. From these strategic locations American troops continued to be trained and supplied while the upper echelons of the military machine planned their course to halt Japan's offensive onslaught. The Japanese had already overrun American bases with their march through the South Pacific. Consequently the immediate objective in the Pacific became keeping open the lifeline connecting the west coast of the United States with Hawaii, New Zealand, and Australia.

During the first months of 1942 it grew clear that the only successful defense of Australia, New Zealand, and New Guinea would be a good offense. Therefore General Douglas MacArthur pushed U.S. forces from southeastern New Guinea north and westward to drive out the enemy, while U.S. Marines, followed by the U.S. Army, launched a major offensive at Guadalcanal that would require six months of deadly combat with unprecedented casualties to the navy, the army, and the marines.

Support for these military operations caused hundreds of U.S. naval vessels to line up, drop anchor, and then take turns entering ports to unload military personnel and millions of tons of supplies from the United States. For more than three years cargo and troops flowed in and out of these Pacific areas, enabling the United States and her allies to send out the men and materials to halt and eventually roll back the powerful Japanese aggressors.

Continuous physical training and simulated combat exercises toughened the troops to meet the Japanese, but another enemy— boredom—threatened to devastate morale in every port and camp base in New Zealand, Australia, and New Guinea. To combat this insidious opponent, military leaders granted frequent weekend liberty, and the troops were allowed more free time in the evenings than they had typically enjoyed during stateside training. Nevertheless, these privileges notwithstanding, homesickness flooded the ranks and men grew impatient with playing war games.

Except for the better educated and intellectually reflective military people, more discretionary time coupled with monthly pay that went farther in the staging countries than it did at home did not translate into reading books, visiting cultural sites, and taking sightseeing trips. On the contrary, many of America's young military men coped with boredom and psychological depression by drinking, gambling, and pursuing recreation with the opposite sex.

Military chaplains valiantly battled the problems emanating from idleness. They organized sports events, as well as concerts and plays. They also held Bible classes and provided worship services twice on Sundays and on weeknights. But neither the army nor the navy found enough chaplains to meet these recreational needs. Indeed, official army reports on chaplain activities in the Pacific revealed frequent times when troops arrived and there were simply no chaplains to cover basic weekly worship services. During one season at the Milne Bay, New Guinea, staging area, twelve thousand army personnel had no chaplain.[11] There were times in 1943 and 1944 when the army reported "it was not uncommon to have 150 or 250 ships in the harbor at one time." To make matters worse, many of these ships had no chaplains, and the troops were kept on board because "debarkation had to be delayed." Possible navy and army chaplains would be brought aboard to conduct worship services, and in some cases clergymen in the port cities would be ferried out to the ships, where they conducted services.[12] One Second Marine Division enlisted man was so intrigued by the sight of a civilian pastor in a suit, white shirt, and tie, vested in a Geneva gown, that he took pictures to send home to his family.[13]

Military officers and enlisted men without formal theological training frequently organized and conducted worship services among their fellow sailors and soldiers aboard ships and in land-based staging areas. Some of these meetings were ably done and extremely well received. African-American troops were exceptionally well qualified to do this for two reasons. First of all, black men who had been pastors of churches at home but were disqualified from being military chaplains, because they lacked the required college degree plus three additional years of theological training, served their people better than many of the regular chaplains who took them under wing but did not know their culture. And second, because of racial segregation, African-American troops had fended for themselves so often that they were quite proficient at making do with what was available.

Of all military personnel, the Jewish troops were the most deprived of chaplain care from men of their own tradition. To be sure, Catholic and Protestant chaplains did their utmost to stand in the gap. But only up to a point did that satisfy the troops. Like the African-Americans, Jewish personnel organized laymen-led services. And whenever possible local rabbis were impressed for duty. The American Jewish Welfare Board even set up trust funds to compensate an Australian national, Rabbi Max Schenk, to minister to Jewish soldiers and sailors in Sydney and environs. Although the efforts of a devoted man like Schenk met some needs, Catholic chaplain James J. O'Donnell discovered in late 1942 and early 1943 that in his remote area of Australia the nearest rabbi was seven hundred miles away. Consequently O'Donnell secured a local Methodist church, and as the chaplain phrased it, "a Jewish boy led his buddies in the service."[14]

WAGING WAR ON boredom took place in more places than public worship services. Some of the most effective battles were won in the one-to-one counseling sessions chaplains held with those under their charge. Plenty of homesick men needed little more than a cup of coffee and some encouraging fatherly conversation from a sky pilot who cared enough to listen. For some men, though, the burdens were greater, and a different level of soul care was required. Chaplains helped many men find healing and peace in the wake of socially destructive activities. While marines had no monopoly on drunkenness and fighting, enough of the leathernecks dubiously distinguished themselves by excessive drinking and brawling that some New Zealanders popularized a ditty designed to humorously deride the Corps:

Here come the raggedy-ass marines,
They're on parade today;
We love to see them come and go,
But we hate to see them stay.

A navy corpsman serving with the marines, and allowed to wear either the marine or the navy uniform, admitted that he decided which uniform to wear on liberty in New Zealand depending on whether the sailors or the marines had done the most damage to Wellington the night before.[15]

Because of antics that were far from amusing to New Zealand and Australian civilians, chaplains diligently worked with local ministers and community leaders to mend torn military-community

relations. And on the military side, chappies listened to lots of confessions by men with wounded consciences that caused more pain
than the black eyes and broken teeth after street and barroom
brawls. To be sure, plenty of revelers and brawlers felt no remorse
for their antics. Yet testimonies are legion that many men were
spiritually, psychologically, and emotionally distraught when chaplains listened and prayed with those who had engaged in activities
they had been raised in homes and churches to avoid.

Chaplains of all branches of the armed forces made pastoral calls
to men thrown into detention by MPs for disorderly conduct. Some
of these men paid a big price in loss of rank and pay for escaping
boredom through fighting, disrespectful behavior toward an officer,
or failing to return to camp or ship on time to avoid AWOL.

Some of the most delicate soul care problems confronting chaplains involved counseling married men who had one-night stands
with local women or engaged in extramarital relationships where
a New Zealand or Australian woman became pregnant. While un-
married men sometimes received permission to marry the woman
they'd impregnated, and claimed they loved, for married men—or
men who left a local married woman pregnant while her husband
was away from home fighting the Japanese—this was a much more
complicated situation, with widespread effects.

Given the gravity of so many problems, it becomes clear why
senior officers—even those who were not personally attracted to any
religious persuasion—saw the need for chaplains. Personnel being
sharpened for combat needed wholesome alternatives to problematic
entertainments that left men stricken with venereal diseases, pulled
out of service doing brig time, causing divisive problems with civilians in the host community, and nearly immobilized by depression
and guilt. Chaplains were needed to simultaneously provide creative
preventive activities and effective restorative soul care.

And chaplains did not have to do this work alone. In Australia and New Zealand Christian churches, organizations, and servant-hearted individuals did much to provide wholesome activities for military men on leave. The civilians in these allied countries worked tirelessly and generously alongside chaplains to keep men out of temptation's way.[16] Given the low percentage of Jewish population, the Jewish troops often did not have this resource available to them. Certainly Jewish troops were welcome at Christian religious or social gatherings, but understandably, not all were comfortable in those environments.

GENERAL A. M. Gray had insisted that chaplains would have to be permitted to "minister in harm's way" if they were to be effective. To the man they would meet the challenge courageously and well, in the same way chaplains faced it at Pearl Harbor in 1941. But for most of these Pacific-based chaplains, the kind of harm the troops faced was not delivered by the Japanese. Chaplains of all traditions confronted the enemy of boredom and its effects with the same purpose and effectiveness with which they would later face bullets and bombs. They compassionately cared for the souls of military personnel who discovered that they were often their own fiercest enemies. The sky pilots performed ably, handling difficult situations that neither their theological and seminary training nor their military chaplain schools had fully equipped them to expect.

By mid 1942 and early 1943 most of the Pacific-based chaplains had entered fully into combat alongside the combatants under their spiritual care. This time they would all be part of a mass offensive movement designed to take the horrors of war to the ones who had attacked them on December 7, 1941. Like the crews and troops God called them to pastor, these chaplains prayed they would have the courage and skills to sail and walk into a dreadful level of harm's way.

CHAPTER FIVE

TAKING THE OFFENSIVE IN THE PACIFIC

The closer you got to the front lines of combat the more inter-
ested men became in worshipping God and making a commit-
ment to Him.

RICHARD T. SPOONER (MAJOR, USMC, RET.)[1]

JAPANESE forces made rapid and significant advances throughout the Pacific in early 1942. In January, General Douglas MacArthur secretly fled to Australia in order to take command of Allied forces in the Southwest Pacific, and by early May the Philippines had fallen into Japanese hands when General Jonathan M. Wainwright surrendered himself and a garrison of 11,500 men who had valiantly fought the aggressors for four months. During the time Americans were fighting a losing battle on Bataan and Corregidor, the British not only suffered losses in the Philippines, they were overwhelmed by superior Japanese forces in Malaya, Singapore, and much of Burma.

Japanese naval and land forces also quickly crushed Dutch opposition and occupied the Netherlands East Indies. They established control of much of Indonesia and then attacked New Guinea. Their strategy was to occupy New Guinea and from there launch an invasion of Australia. With a massive display of their supposed invincibility, the haughty Japanese bombed two locations in Alaska and then invaded Attu and Kiska, two of the westernmost islands of the Aleutians.

But Imperial Japan fatally misjudged America's will to fight and her ability to quickly mobilize a massive army and navy. The would-be rulers of Asia also miscalculated America's engineering and industrial genius and strength, which would eventually support more than 12 million men and women in uniform. Japanese leaders likewise failed to understand the resilience of the American character and will to win, which grew out of a deep-rooted faith in God, stemming from the nation's strong Jewish and Christian heritage.

The spiritual fiber of the United Sates had been cut from the same cloth that defined Australians and New Zealanders. Consequently, the ANZAC forces for the most part welcomed the Yanks, worked alongside them rather well, and jointly these allies began to slow down and then reverse Japan's imperialistic thrust.

EARLIEST EVIDENCES OF America's latent prowess came at sea. On May 7 and 8, 1942, an air battle raged in the Coral Sea. This was the first naval engagement in history where ships did not engage ships; it was a contest where carrier-based airplanes fought for two days. Although the United States lost the carrier *Lexington*, American planes sank one Japanese carrier and severely damaged two others, and also crippled several more ships.

American naval air superiority stopped Japan's attempt to seize Port Moresby in Southern New Guinea and thereby thwarted the Japanese plan to sever Australia's supply line to her troops in New Guinea.

If the Battle of the Coral Sea retarded Japan's advance, the massive naval and air Battle of Midway the following month (June 3–6, 1942) put the Japanese navy completely on the defensive for the first time in World War II. This Central Pacific engagement saved Midway Island from falling to the Japanese, while simultaneously destroying 275 Japanese planes and sinking 4 of her aircraft carriers. The U.S. victory at Midway eliminated Japan's threat to Hawaii and effectively halted the Japanese offensive.

These pivotal sea engagements at once restored a balance of naval power in the Pacific and enabled the United States to successfully execute three critical offensives against the Japanese forces. In less than five months, joint U.S. and Canadian forces humiliated the Japanese in the Aleutians; the warriors from the land of the Rising Sun evacuated Kiska before the Yanks and Canadians arrived, and in little more than eight weeks all Japanese resistance had been eliminated on Attu.

With impressive swiftness North American military forces eliminated Japanese aggression in the Aleutians. But the liberation of New Guinea and concomitant securing of Australia's and New Zealand's perimeters would prove to be much more costly.

THROUGHOUT 1942 AND most of 1943 Japan occupied much of Northern New Guinea. Nevertheless, stubborn Australian, New Zealand, and American forces under the leadership of General Douglas MacArthur repulsed every Japanese attempt to seize Port Moresby in Southern New Guinea, and gradually quelled Japan's aggression on other parts of the massive island.

New Guinea proved to be one of the most challenging concentrations of combat in the Pacific. Besides engaging well-equipped and -trained Japanese troops, Allied units had to secure vast areas of coastal and mountainous terrain. Sustenance of the physical and psychological health of these fighting men in the densest of jungles proved to be a gigantic task. New Guinea's jungles manifested an appetite to destroy our fighting men that was equal if not superior to the Japanese. Indeed, heavy and continuous rain, mosquito swarms as dense as dark clouds, malaria, dysentery, and body sores formed an alliance that ravaged the bodies and morale of American and ANZAC forces.

Survival under such wretched conditions required troop movements, supply logistics, and medical maintenance unfamiliar to Americans. To be sure, ANZAC troops instructed Yanks and helped them acclimate, but soul care became increasingly essential to bolster dreadfully low morale, and neither the Australians, the New Zealanders, nor the Americans had enough chaplains to meet the demand.

No one questioned the need for chaplains in the dense jungles of New Guinea. Supplying that need, on the other hand, became a high-priority challenge. Under the most ideal conditions during World War II a battalion of one thousand to fifteen hundred men would have two Protestant, one Catholic, and one Jewish chaplain. But placing even one chaplain among scattered and constantly moving companies became almost impossible, especially in such difficult terrain.

When a tough chaplain did get with the men, he became a channel of spiritual grace that strengthened morale and the will to continue the fight. Chaplain Delbert P. Jorgensen from Comfrey, Minnesota, provided a glimpse of a sky pilot's work in New Guinea. Jorgensen had worked diligently in the staging camps to build relationships with the men, but with only moderate success. Once they entered combat in the jungles, on the other hand, attitudes changed. "The campaign brought us together as never before. We

were one, regardless of rank, and I learned to know the men inti-
mately where I had only a casual acquaintance with them previously."[2] Chaplain Jorgensen, an energetic and sturdy man of
Scandinavian ancestry, said the change came because "I was with
[the men] constantly. I hiked with them in the dense damp New
Guinea jungle. I slept with them under a shelter half on the wet
ground. I have stumbled along with them in blinding rain on a slip-
pery track." Jorgensen went on to say that he "dug graves for the
dead, served as pall bearer, and buried them." He also "worked as a
litter bearer to evacuate the wounded," and he scrounged extra
rations and cigarettes for his exhausted men.

Chaplain Jorgensen revealed that as important as all of these
things were, he found the spiritual dimension of his service "of
much greater worth." Nevertheless, he sensed divine protection as
he "had to dodge the fire of snipers and machine gun bullets" in
order "to visit the men in the front lines and there [chat] with them
individually, trying to instill in them greater faith in God." He
remembered one particularly sad yet encouraging encounter. A sergeant who suffered from a dreadful wound and knew he was dying
said, "Chaplain, I have not always lived as I should, but I tried to be
a good Christian." The Protestant chaplain knew he had no time for
small talk, so he asked the sergeant: "Do you trust Christ?" The
weak voice answered, "Yes." Jorgensen said that a few hours later "I
buried his body, but his soul had gone to be with the Lord."[3]

The shortage of chaplains in 1942 and 1943 meant that only a
small percentage of combatants received the personal spiritual care
offered by Delbert P. Jorgensen. Because the army knew the importance of soul care during such trying times, it responded in the same
fashion it did in similar situations—it improvised. One of the most
impressive and courageous chaplains who actively interacted with
men had been trained as a paratrooper before being deployed to the

Pacific. In September 1943, for instance, Chaplain Robert Herb, a Protestant and Luzerne, Pennsylvania, native, and Chaplain John J. Powers, a Catholic from Oneonta, New York, gathered their packs and Communion sets, harnessed themselves in their chutes, and were dropped in among U. S. Army fighting men far into the jungle.[4]

IMPROVISATION TOOK MANY other forms. A common approach involved enlisted men—most of whom were nonprofessionals yet deeply devout laymen—who went to their commanding officers seeking permission to hold preaching and Bible teaching meetings. Unless such requests interfered with pursuing military objectives, they were usually granted. These gatherings proved to boost morale. Because priests, rabbis, and ministers serving as chaplains at every home front military installation sought to place either Catholic missals, New Testaments, or Jewish Scripture and prayer books, in Hebrew and English, in the hands of every person who professed faith in their tradition, many combatants carried their own spiritual reading, which could be used in public worship as well as private devotions.

African-American soldiers surpassed everyone else when it came to organizing and conducting their own services. Frequently without benefit of chaplains, even in the rear echelon areas, these men made do extremely well with lay preachers. Although there was one highly respected black Catholic chaplain, Father John W. Bowman, in the Ninety-Third Infantry Division, almost 100 percent of the troops in the mostly African-American division were Protestant and low churchmen to the core. "Every colored unit, with one exception," according to a battalion commander, "has one or more preachers. They conduct Sunday and Weekday services, an undertaking rarely found in white units. The services are dignified, devotional, and moving."[5]

In one African-American battalion, Corporal D. C. Morton was singled out for praise by his commanding officer. Because there was no regular chaplain for the unit, Morton stepped up on his own and took responsibility to provide as much pastoral care, preaching, and worship leadership as his other duties allowed. Although he had taken some evening classes in Bible and Theology at Morehouse Theological School in Atlanta, Georgia, before entering the army, this gifted and respected leader had never been ordained or served as a church pastor.[6]

Despite the overall effectiveness of laymen in bolstering combatants' morale, astute observers realized that more needed to be done for troops in remote areas. President Franklin D. Roosevelt became aware of the lack of chaplains in many areas of the Pacific, so he, being a great improviser himself, did what he could to supplement the efforts of lay religious leadership. Working in concert with national Jewish, Catholic, and Protestant agencies, he recruited some high-profile religious leaders in America and put the Army Air Corps to work flying them as close as possible to the troops who seldom saw a chaplain.

Among the civilian leaders the President tapped was an African Methodist Episcopal Church leader, Bishop John Andrew Gregg. The Chicago-based bishop had a commanding demeanor. He stood more than six feet tall—unusual for men in the early 1940s. Standing among men who averaged five-foot-four to five-foot-nine, this broad-framed, wide-shouldered clergyman was as gigantic in reputation as he was in physique. Gregg served as a representative of the Fraternal Council of Negro Churches, comprised of eleven denominations with more than forty thousand churches and six million members.

Bishop Gregg was not only a highly respected and recognized leader among black Christians, he was a stellar preacher who exuded charm and wit and simply electrified military personnel with his contagious smile, gray beard, and bespectacled eyes—all accentuated by the black Homburg hat he wore despite high heat and humidity. The sixty-six-year-old AME bishop cheered African-American and white soldiers all over the Southwest Pacific.[7]

The visitation of Bishop Gregg certainly encouraged men, and it also proved to be effective for public relations back in the United States. The press and radio networks delighted in assuring home front folks that their loved ones were having religious needs cared for by the best and the brightest—right up near the front lines. This public relations concern is evident in photographs that were taken and published in U.S. newspapers. In August 1943, for example, the *Chicago Times* published a photo that no doubt comforted folks on the home front who worried about their loved ones. The caption read: "Near God in New Guinea." The photograph captured a small jungle clearing, complete with a makeshift altar, logs for seating soldiers clothed in damp and dirty combat fatigues, and Father Joseph B. Boggins, S.J., facing the altar and saying Mass for approximately forty kneeling army men. Chaplain Boggins had been a math teacher at Chicago's St. Ignatius High School before entering military service. And for Catholics, this picture spoke volumes of comfort.[8]

BESIDES TRYING TO reach scattered combatants with "para-trooper padres," courageous civilians, and hastily constructed altars, other types of improvisation were attempted with mixed results. The U.S. Army assigned pilots and planes of the Thirteenth Air Force to airlift Australian and American military chaplains into areas quite near the front lines. Of course, it was most effective if a battalion chaplain could be moved to the locations of his own troops, but even jeeps and other land vehicles could not traverse much of the jungle to reach men scattered over many miles. When airplanes were given the task, it became at best difficult and at worst dangerous.

Army chaplain Albert Hart, for example, was determined to do all he could to reach men in his unit who were separated from him by dense jungle and water. A Los Angeles native, Chaplain Hart tried every way he could to reach his isolated men—by jeep, on foot, and by boat. Heroically he persuaded an Army Air Corps pilot with a small plane to get him in as close as possible to vegetation-covered terrain. The California family man made several flights to serve his men. But on one particularly difficult run, the plane went down, and Arthur Hart gained the unfortunate distinction of being the first chaplain to die in New Guinea.[9]

Chaplain Hart's fate did not deter other chaplains from improvising in similar fashion. Probably no World War II chappie in any branch of the armed forces matched James Edwin Orr's flight record, accumulated in his relentless push to serve men and women without regular on-site soul care. James Edwin Orr distinguished himself as a chaplain-at-large for the Thirteenth Air Force, where he served in the Southwest Pacific from 1943 to 1946, moving from location to location in a modern rendition of an eighteenth- or nineteenth-century itinerating Methodist evangelist. Born in 1912 in Northern Ireland to an American father, Orr had U.S. citizenship from birth. From his childhood, Edwin Orr proved to be unusually intelligent and eager to learn. Moving to the United States in the 1930s, he also traveled to the British Isles, Scandinavia, South Africa, Europe, and much of China before his thirty-first birthday. His military records reveal that besides his native English he was proficient in French, Norwegian, Swedish, German, Spanish, and Chinese. He also had managed to earn a technical degree from Belfast Community College, an M.A. from Northwestern University

(Illinois), and three degrees (Th.B., B.D., and Th. D.) from Northern Baptist Theological Seminary (Chicago) by 1943.[10]

Most officers and enlisted personnel saw Orr as a high-octane
genius with burning ambition to communicate the Christian Gospel to every isolated enclave in the Southwest Pacific. One of his
Efficiency Reports in early 1945 identified the Interdenominational
Protestant this way: "This officer has a pleasant manner, rather
eccentric, but good natured."[11]

Chaplain Orr reached many remote spots as he hopped from the
Dutch East Indies to New Guinea, to scores of islands in between.
No record survives of the flight hours he logged but one thing is certain. He pushed himself so hard that by summer 1945 he wrote, "At
present I am under medical care due to fatigue."[12] Orr had served
virtually thousands of Yanks from 1943 to 1945. But he nearly
wrecked his health to do so.

Chaplain Orr was respected for his devotion to duty, but he
bothered some officers and a few chaplains because of his overt
evangelism. Standing five-foot-six and weighing less than 130
pounds, Dr. Orr was nevertheless strong of body and will. He saw
himself as an evangelist in the spirit of the apostle Paul. He confessed he had no respect for Christian chaplains of the more liberal
persuasion—especially those who believed all men and women
would go to Heaven because Almighty God was too loving to condemn anyone to Hell. "I have little more than pity and contempt for
a minister of a denomination who flouts the teachings of his Church
but makes a mock of its doctrine [of final judgment]. I respected the
faithful Roman Catholic and Hebrew chaplains," he continued, "but
not the false prophets in my own camp."[13]

If Orr was a stormy petrel who offended chaplains who saw
evangelism as unloving, crude, and in poor taste, he earned the
respect of African-American troops who found him quite attractive

for several reasons. First of all, he went out of his way to serve black troops with a fervor equaled by few white chaplains. Second, his determination to evangelize the men and women in uniform by telling them they needed to confess their sins, repent, and give their souls over to the care of Jesus Christ did not seem to offend African-American soldiers, because most of them came from traditions that were evangelical and strongly committed to missions. But finally, Orr was welcomed and respected among the African-Americans because he listened sympathetically as they raised the question of why they should risk their lives to fight for the preservation of America's freedom when they were sorely discriminated against in the United Sates and even segregated in the army. Orr urged these fighting men to speak honestly; he listened to their questions and agreed that the black men's criticisms were valid. He also suggested that as bad as things were for them, their fate would be worse if America lost the war. If the enemy won the war, Orr feared that the African-Americans would be re-enslaved by the Germans and Japanese who practiced horridly brutal racism.[14]

WHILE SCORES OF chaplains served fighting men in New Guinea, others sailed with a task force directed to drive the Japanese off an island a thousand miles from the northeastern coast of Australia. In July 1942 America and her Pacific allies were shocked to learn that Imperial Japan had invaded a narrow island about ninety miles long, at the southern end of the Solomon Island chain. Named Guadalcanal, this small place in the Solomon Sea did not exist in the geographic knowledge and vocabulary of most Americans. But during the six months from August 7, 1942, to early February 1943 Guadalcanal would become a name that would live for decades in the annals of marine, navy, and army history. This speck of real estate in the South Pacific looms large in World War II history because of Japan's decision to build an airstrip on Guadalcanal, in order to bomb Australia and New Zealand while simultaneously disrupting American shipping to those countries.

Marine Corps General A. A. Vandegrift, commander of the newly organized First Marine Division, sailed from Norfolk, Virginia, for New Zealand with a division that, in his words, had "not yet attained a satisfactory state of readiness for combat." To the general's mind the First Marine Division needed at least six months in New Zealand so he could prepare his men for combat. But to his utter astonishment, he had no sooner landed in Wellington, on New Zealand's north island, than Admiral Robert Ghormley requested an immediate meeting. Ghormley served as commander of the South Pacific, and he informed Vandegrift of the bad news about Japan's occupation of Guadalcanal and the airfield being constructed. To the point, Vandegrift learned that General Douglas MacArthur, in concert with Admiral Chester Nimitz, had ordered the invasion of Guadalcanal on August 1. This gave the First Marines less than five weeks to prepare for combat and sail for the Solomons. Although Vandegrift was able to persuade his superiors that his division was not nearly combat ready, they only extended his orders by six days.[15]

The inexperienced and hastily trained First Marine Division embarked on July 22. Richard Tregaskis, a courageous and skilled newspaperman who accompanied the marines, noted that only a few senior officers knew the precise place of invasion. On Sunday, July 26, Tregaskis observed, "there were services on the deck, facing a canvas backdrop on which a Red Cross flag was pinned." Because the newspaperman had no previous experience on a U.S. naval vessel during a worship service, he made no mention that the Christian chaplains usually ran up a white flag with a dark blue cross for worship. Evidently Father Francis W. Kelly from Pennsylvania had not been given a flag for this troop transport, and therefore he made do with a Red Cross flag, which was the best substitute he could find before the division's hasty departure. Tregaskis described Chaplain Kelly as "a genial smiling fellow with a faculty for plain talk." His sermon, the second of the day, was delivered at a first service for Catholics, and "this one was for Protestants." The brief sermon "dealt with duty, and was obviously pointed toward our coming landing somewhere in the Japanese-held territory." Tregaskis explained Father Kelly, "who had been a preacher in a Pennsylvania mining town and had a direct, simple way of speaking which was about right for the crowd of variously uniformed sailors and marines standing before him."[16]

Noticeably absent was mention of any service held the evening before for Jewish men. Typically, if there were only one or two chaplains available to care for everyone, the law of averages said they would be Christian, because they comprised 95 to 96 percent of the chaplain force, as well as the troops. It is probable that Kelly appointed a Jewish marine to lead Jewish men in prayer, or he would have read Scripture and prayed with them himself.

The following Sunday, August 2, Richard Tregaskis noticed that as more ships were congregating in the vicinity, and a sense of invasion being imminent, "church services were crowded this morning, for the day of our landing is drawing close and more and more of the men aboard, 'the Padre,' Father Reardon told me, want to settle themselves in some sort of spiritual self-understanding and be prepared for at least the possibility of death." The chaplain informed the tall, slender, and bespectacled newspaperman that many of the men sensed that "this is the last Sunday for Communion and the straightening of souls." Tregaskis's diary reveals that some of the Catholic men lingered after the service. They knelt by the bare wall and made the sign of the cross as they rose to leave.[17]

A while later, Protestant sailors and marines gathered in the ship's hold for a solemn worship service. The mess hall temporarily serving as a church was crowded to capacity. "There was a sermon . . . there were hymns, and, after the services, communion," and many men lingered longer than usual for meditation and prayer.[18]

THE U.S. MARINES waited five more days before they took part in the first major American offensive in the Pacific Theater. On Friday, August 7, nineteen troop transport ships began unloading their human cargo, of fighting men laden with heavy packs, weapons, ammunition, canteens, and steel helmets, into noisy and clanking landing crafts for the initial invasion of Guadalcanal. To everyone's surprise only tiny pockets of resistance met these youthful and hastily trained Americans. Troops swiftly overran the air base and renamed it Henderson Field, while cargo ships began unloading tons of water, food, fuel, ammunition, and other supplies required to sustain the siege of an island that from a distance looked like an emerald-green paradise rimmed by pristine beaches.

The relative quiet of the first few hours proved to be nothing more than a deceptive tactic of the Japanese. Before even half of the supplies necessary to support the troops could be unloaded, Japanese bombs and mortars began to pound the supply dumps and troops being amassed on the airfield and nearby beaches. Then a massive fleet of Japanese ships surprised the Allied task force, destroying one Australian and three American heavy cruisers. Consequently, the U.S. Navy retreated before they lost more men and ships, leaving the marines with no more than half of their supplies and no naval artillery support.

In the wake of this naval disaster, the Japanese launched heavy counterattacks on the marines—day after day and night after night. As the marines sought to hold on to the airfield, they were besieged by deafening artillery and mortar attacks all day and then deprived of sleep at night by flares illuminating the darkness and continuous banzai attacks on their foxholes and trenches. Added to these assaults were the continuous strafing and bombing by Japanese airplanes.

The casualties mounted with each passing day. Rows of dead had to be buried before the stench overwhelmed the living. Chaplains removed muddied dog tags and prayed over the dead, and they made notes of temporary grave locations in hopes that the men could be exhumed and reburied in proper graves—complete with wooden markers—once the island had been secured.

Twenty-four-hour-a-day combat took a psychological as well as a physical toll. Without sleep for days on end, some men broke under pressure and had to be taken back behind the front lines. Others fought on with the shakes, while still other men grew so numbed to conditions that they made dreadful and often fatal mistakes.

Many veterans of Guadalcanal testified that even more devastating to morale than constant harassment from the Japanese, and from mosquitoes, reptiles, leeches, and jungle vegetation, was the knowledge that they had been abandoned by the navy. And they were running dangerously low on food—they survived only by drastically cutting rations and foraging rice and canned fish from Japanese outposts and camps they could overrun.

Although no one can quantify the impact of military chaplains in such hellish conditions, the evidence reveals that the Holy Joes jumped into the most dangerous places, by day and night, bringing what seemed to many combatants the very presence of God, to soothe men's souls with words of assurance, hope, and encouragement.

IT REQUIRED SIX months, from August 7, 1942, to February 9, 1943, for Guadalcanal to be wrested from stubborn Japanese forces.

After several weeks the navy returned to support the marines, and on January 10, 1943, the army's Twenty-Fifth Infantry Division arrived to relieve marines on several front lines where they had advanced against Japanese marines and soldiers for more than five months, and held a perimeter around the airfield.

During the half year of fighting on Guadalcanal numerous chaplains distinguished themselves as they sought to bolster the faith and morale of men living in constant danger. One of the Catholic chaplains, Father Thomas M. Reardon, a thirty-year-old native of New Jersey, whom Richard Tregaskis observed on one of the troop transports, celebrating Mass and praying with men before the August 7 invasion, for 125 days never got off the beach where he landed with the First Marine Division, Fifth Regiment. It was not that Reardon shirked his duty to move inland, it was simply the matter of so many wounded and dying being on the beach, and waves of hundreds more being continually brought to the field hospital in hopes that they could be evacuated to ships, that kept him there, to serve the dead and dying.[19]

During his four months on the beach, Reardon recalled that "we had almost no medicine, almost no food except Japanese food. At times we had no pills for malaria. We were all alone."[20] During the first month or more, the priest assumed they would never get off "the Canal." He referred to the beach as his "parish," and some marines helped him build an altar out of empty ammunition boxes, and they designed a cross from empty shell casings. For eighty-five days Chaplain Reardon never changed clothes; he lost fifty pounds, seldom had even a few minutes for private prayer, and like many of the marines he served, suffered from streptococcal infections and malaria. Despite the fact that he eventually collapsed into unconsciousness, had to be evacuated, and came perilously close to death, the faithful chaplain could look back on the experiences at Guadalcanal and say, "I really felt close to God."[21] While he celebrated Mass for men who had pulled back for a brief respite, he remembered, "it was as if the war didn't exist. Only the Mass existed."[22]

A brief glimpse of Chaplain Thomas M. Reardon's ability to bring light to the darkness of Guadalcanal came from a non-Catholic marine who came upon the priest's little makeshift chapel: "Speaking in a tone of most sincere compliment, [the young man said] 'The Catholic Church is like the Standard Oil Company. It has stations wherever you go.' "[23]

EARLY IN 1943 another Catholic priest demonstrated remarkable courage and determination to serve men in combat regardless of their religion or unit. Born in Philadelphia in 1911, Father Matthew Francis Keogh had served as a prison chaplain in Pennsylvania until the war.[24] Historian Donald Crosby wrote that "Keogh always managed to show up where the fighting was at its worst. He seemed to have an instinct for where the Japanese would strike next—and where he would therefore be needed the most."[25]

One night in January 1943, Keogh ministered in an unusually brave manner. He was wounded and subsequently awarded the Purple Heart for an injury he sustained during a Japanese bombing raid. Nonetheless, the seemingly omnipresent chaplain volunteered that same night to lead a reserve battalion to a battlefield location because he knew the battlefield terrain of that area better than anyone else at that location. For this deed, which violated Geneva Convention regulations that chaplains could not employ aggressive action, Chaplain Keogh received the Bronze Star.[26]

This violation of the Geneva Convention was not Father Keogh's only time to ignore regulations. A valiant chaplain who visited the wounded in tent hospitals at night and combed the battle lines during daylight in search of the wounded and dying, Matthew Keogh caused the men of the Seventh Regiment to wonder if he lived without sleep. In any case the marines loved him because, as the late Father Donald F. Crosby phrased it, he "offered Mass for the marines every weekday and said three or more Masses on Sunday." Besides this, the marines delighted in the fact that "despite regulations explicitly forbidding chaplains to carry firearms, he habitually stalked around the island with a loaded pistol and a cartridge of extra bullets." One veteran of Guadalcanal, according to Crosby, possessed "several photographs of him, each showing him brandishing his weapon and loaded cartridge belt. He also carried his gun into combat, though no evidence has emerged that he actually fired his weapon in battle."[27]

A Protestant chaplain who served "the Canal" in a different regiment, but nevertheless knew Keogh well, insisted—perhaps with a grin and a gleam in his eye—that "Navy Chaplains assigned to the Marines in the South Pacific area were permitted to carry a weapon to protect themselves against wild animals." Wyeth Willard, a highly decorated chaplain and one who was greatly admired by the troops, said, "I carried a Colt .45-caliber revolver, which was my constant companion." He quoted his fellow chaplain Father Keogh, who purportedly exclaimed, "You've got to help the Lord once in a while."[28] Evidently Chaplain Carol Lemons, another Protestant chaplain who ministered to Seabees and Marines during these months, decided to "help the lord once in a while" too. His unpublished autobiography reveals that in the face of threats of Japanese infiltration at night, he kept two .45-caliber pistols—one under each side of his blanket.[29]

PISTOL-PACKING CHAPLAINS WERE not the only clergy who won admiration from the fighting men. Glyn Jones, a Baptist who braved heavy combat with the First Marine Division on Guadalcanal and Cape Torokina, was awarded the Silver Star for his heroic actions on "the Cape." On Guadalcanal his work might have been less remarkable, but it certainly was no less significant. In an article written for the *Army and Navy Chaplain*, Jones recalled getting among the men just after foxholes were dug in preparation for the probability of a banzai (suicide) attack. Jones sat on the edge of a foxhole and read from St. John 14: "Let not your heart be troubled . . ." He said "a marine with a Testament in his hand interrupted me to ask which passage I was reading. As I answered him, I looked at the other men. Grimy, sweating, unshaven, they were relaxing on the edges of their foxholes and in the hands of many of them were Testaments, rosaries, and prayer books." Jones took care to mention that no one did this for show. There was no self-consciousness, "it simply seemed at that moment to be the most natural thing to do."[30]

Chaplain Jones admitted that there is a danger of glamorizing "the chaplain's role in combat." Indeed, once men are in battle, the chaplain can give them little that they do not already possess. "They are upheld by religion who have learned and practiced the 'Presence of God,' just as those who have thorough training in proper tactics." A Baptist in his late twenties who had spent most of his life in northern New England, Jones did concede that men without a religious background could still be helped during a lull in the fighting in the midst of a battle zone, where it was not uncommon for men to ask: "What happens when you die?" Jones saw it as a God-given privilege to help men learn the answer to this question.[31]

The U.S. Army, as well as Navy, had combat chaplains on Guadalcanal. Among them was a Presbyterian, Jacob Stephen MacKorell, Jr., who was awarded the Bronze Star. Born and raised in South Carolina, MacKorell held degrees from Davidson College in North Carolina and Union Theological Seminary in Richmond,

Virginia. When he was assigned to First Battalion, Thirty-Fifth Infantry Regiment, Twenty-Fifth Infantry Division, he accompanied his men on Guadalcanal when they relieved some battle-weary marines in January 1943. During subsequent combat engagements Chaplain MacKorell distinguished himself for heroic action in some of the areas of fiercest fighting in the Pacific Theater. During one Japanese bombing raid on Guadalcanal his field Communion set was completely destroyed, except for fragments of two glass cups. Although MacKorell grieved the loss of his altar set, he knew he was fortunate to be alive.[32]

MacKorell made an especially positive impression on Jewish soldiers in the Twenty-fifth Infantry Division. He went to great lengths to meet their spiritual needs, often finding Jewish officers to assist in worship services by serving as readers. In one month alone, he organized three Jewish services and buried with dignity three Jewish enlisted men who were without benefit of a rabbi.[33]

The carnage in 1942 and early 1943 in places like New Guinea and Guadalcanal caused officers and enlisted men to ask such questions as "Why does a Sovereign God allow war?" "How can Christians who have been taught to love their enemies kill men without destroying their own souls?" Even chaplains, who had supposedly wrestled with such questions during their theological training, now faced the challenge of applying their academic answers to real life. If men questioned the goodness of God by early 1943, their cries for answers would only increase, because the war in the Pacific had only begun to reveal the extent of man's inhumanity to man.

CHAPTER SIX

"CLIMBING UP THE LADDER TO TOKYO"

By their patient, sympathetic labors with the men, day in and day out and through many a night, every chaplain I know contributed immeasurably to the moral courage of our fighting men.

ADMIRAL CHESTER W. NIMITZ[1]

C LIMBING up the ladder to Tokyo" was the way Admiral Chester W. Nimitz described the Allied offensive in the Pacific. Throughout 1942 and early 1943 this warfare revealed at least three things. First of all, the Japanese were not invincible! The Aleutians, New Guinea, Guadalcanal, and smaller Solomon islands such as Florida and Tulagi proved that they could be defeated. Second, it became clear that even if Japan could be stopped, it was going to require an unusually costly war of attrition to liberate the islands and countries they had overrun and occupied. Indeed, victory on just Guadalcanal cost the Marine Corps enormous casualties: 1,152 dead and 2,799 wounded.[2] Added to these dreadful costs were thousands more navy and army causalities in both the New Guinea and Guadalcanal areas of the Pacific. As one chaplain described it, "Green-clad marines, blue-dressed sailors, and khaki-garbed men lay together in common dust—heroes all."[3] To sharpen the picture, the Japanese, who had launched banzai attacks with apparent disdain for their own losses—one night they lost 1700 men in a single attack on "the Canal"—apparently would rather die than surrender, because death was honorable and surrender a disgrace. To the point, 50,000 Japanese were killed on Guadalcanal. Third, it became abundantly evident that heroic efforts would have to be made to bolster and maintain the morale of young men called to continually put their lives on the line to liberate island after island with names they had never heard of—and that were held by an enemy manifesting a fanaticism unparalleled in modern history.

HONEST OBSERVERS AGREED that the old adage "there are no atheists in foxholes" was simply not true. To be sure, many men drew close to God when they sensed the imminence of death. And plenty of so-called "combat conversions" were forgotten as soon as the fighting stopped and troops were taken to safe places for rest and relaxation. Robert H. Rivers, a veteran marine airman, enjoyed recalling an incident that took place in the wake of a Pacific island being secured. Basking in the comfort of clean clothes, fresh water, and decent food, three young junior officers began strutting their university-born scorn for the Bible and the picture of God revealed therein. Several officers and NCOs listened in as the self-styled intelligentsia of the junior officer corps expressed their disdain for the chaplain who obviously trusted the veracity of the Holy Scriptures and the God to which the writ pointed. What impressed the onlookers—including Robert Rivers, who admittedly seldom entered a chapel—was the smiling demeanor of the chaplain, who impressively employed his superior logic and education to demolish their glib presuppositions and generalizations.[4]

If religious debates like the one observed by Rivers were not typical, it was true that as the veterans of Guadalcanal and Tulagi made their way back to New Zealand and Australia for a well-deserved season of rest, religious services were not as heavily attended aboard the troop ships. Many men's minds were on liberty leave and home more than anything else.

Chaplain Arthur Glasser, who had served the Seventh Marines, First Division, and crossed back and forth with the men on troop transports, admitted that attendance was equally poor at the camp chapel services back in Australia. But he did not blame it all on indifference toward God and religion. He acknowledged that some men grew so obsessed with Australian women and the inexpensive and free-flowing whiskey and beer that they set aside their moral compasses. On the other hand, he recognized that the camps, with their bare buildings and tent facilities, were unattractive to men who had grown weary of military and austerity. Therefore, when the Australian people showered the Yanks with gratitude for helping halt the Japanese offensive toward their land, the Americans gladly accepted their accolades, as well as invitations to dine in their homes and worship in their churches. Consequently Australian congregations were often overflowing with American men in uniform.

Glasser himself, a tall, strong, and handsome graduate of Cornell, Carnegie Institute of Technology, and two theological schools, frequently accepted invitations to preach in a variety of settings in Melbourne and smaller cities. The superior officers encouraged this evangelical Baptist with a magnetic personality to speak from pulpits and in as many home gatherings as possible because it promoted goodwill between the Americans and the Australians.[5]

The situation Chaplain Glasser found in Australia dovetailed with Second Marine Division Chaplain Wyeth Willard's experiences in New Zealand. The population on both the South and North islands totaled only 1,641,000. Most of the American military personnel congregated on the North Island, in the Wellington and Auckland areas. Despite the fact that tens of thousands of soldiers, sailors, and marines continually poured in and out of that land, the people were warm and generous, and quite a few good marriages came out of wartime relationships.

Chaplain Willard, born in 1905, was a graduate of Brown University who did graduate studies in a first-rate theological seminary and became a published author before World War II. Already in his late thirties when he became a military chaplain, this urbane Protestant made friends easily in New Zealand and became a highly sought after speaker among Wellington's Christian community. During the time he spent in New Zealand between his tours of duty with the Second Marines—first on Guadalcanal and then Tarawa— he secured his commanding officer's permission to speak at "three or four outside speaking engagements each week." In Wellington he did evening services in Methodist, Baptist, Episcopal, Presbyterian, and Brethren churches. He accepted speaking engagements at three colleges and several YMCAs and other para-church organizations.[6]

Chaplain Willard was a powerful preacher. Although his ordination was in the Baptist denomination, he communicated well with all traditions and won the acclaim of business and professional leaders on New Zealand's North Island. Despite his ecumenical posture, the passionate preacher was an evangelist at heart. He preached in the tradition of America's Billy Graham, who already in the early 1940s was making a name for himself as a revivalist preacher in the Southern and upper Midwestern parts of the United States. Willard's New England accent and his preaching that called men to repent of their sins did not offend the local folks. He spoke with a fresh voice and was loved in New Zealand.

Colonel Elmer E. Hall, the commander of the Eighth Regiment and Willard's superior officer, absolutely delighted in the positive impact of his preaching and speaking. Consequently Colonel Hall, a native of Baker, Oregon, called the celebrated chaplain to his office and asked if there was anything he could do to encourage him in his work. Willard replied: "Sir, do you mean exactly what you say?" "Yes, I do," snapped the colonel.

"In that case, the first thing you may do for me is to attend services [at the regiment's chapel] each Sunday." "I'll be there," said the colonel. And he was good to his word, never missing a Sunday until the regiment shipped out. His personal commitment to Sunday morning worship had a salutary effect on the attitudes of the men toward chapel.[7]

CHAPLAINS LIKE GLASSER and Willard did more than public relations work with the local population, they diligently sought to monitor relationships between their troops and New Zealand women. Sometimes there were difficult problems to solve, but most of their efforts in this direction involved making certain that marines and sailors who applied for permission to marry New Zealanders were responsible men who were seeking a lifelong relationship with reputable women. The navy insisted that backgrounds had to be checked on both persons, and a chaplain was required to do more than counsel the couple, he sought to meet the woman's family. For the good of both the man and the woman, any serviceman who intended to marry other than an American citizen had to produce $200 in cash to cover his wife's passage to the United States. Furthermore, the serviceman had to "submit evidence by letter that he would be gainfully employed after the war." Evidence of the American man's character was delivered to the woman's family, and an American "officer was dispatched to investigate the home of the girl to ascertain whether she was worthy of American citizenship." Chaplain Willard wrote that "of the many who applied for permission to marry, the greater number were able to make all the hurdles."[8]

Chaplains in Australia and New Zealand worked closely with the Military Police, helping to get American troublemakers off the streets and find ways to repair damage done to people and property. This required building good communications between American military and New Zealand local officials. Overall this enterprise went well, given the thousands of military personnel involved.

As part of their trouble-shooting ministry, chaplains visited men who spent time in the brig. They devoted time to the rehabilitation of these men in the same way they cared for troops sidelined in hospitals. This latter duty required much attention, inasmuch as some regiments of marines had as many as 70 or 80 percent of men infected with malaria and other jungle diseases.[9]

BY 1943 THE military usually had enough Protestant and Catholic chaplains to provide regular worship services and one-to-one counseling sessions in training and rest locations like Australia and New Zealand. Most of the chappies saw it as their duty to mix among the men and women in the R & R areas and let them know they were available to offer counsel in their Quonset hut or tent offices. In order to make the folks feel welcome and remove any stigma that might be attached to a visit with the chaplain, some sky pilots encouraged visits by adding a touch of humor to their invitations.

Chaplain John Anderson, for example, a Presbyterian serving with the Second Marine Division, handed out yellow cards:

SYMPATHY CHIT

Don't Like The Chow!
U.S.M.C. Got You Fouled Up?

———————————

If You Have Trouble With Your
Mother-In-Law, The "Top," Your
Second-Best Girl, Or The Sheriff
Tell It To The Chaplain
This Card Entitles You To
Ten (10) Free Visits To The
Wailing Wall (Pure Coral)
Chaplain John Anderson
2nd Marines 2nd Mar. Div. F.M.F.[10]

A problem that sorely challenged the Chaplain Corps of both the army and the navy was meeting the needs of Jewish service personnel. Even in the noncombat areas there were not enough Jewish chaplains to provide Jewish men and women with even the most basic religious rites, let alone offer the personal counsel available to nearly all Christians. With only 311 active duty Jewish chaplains in World War II and well over a half million Jews in uniform, Christian chaplains were expected to stand in the gap. All chaplains took this responsibility seriously and they did it as well as they could. One thing Chaplain Wyeth Willard did was secure the services of a Wellington spiritual leader, Rabbi Katz. As long as the troops were in the Wellington area, he provided religious services for American

Jews. But of course he could not handle the counseling and the sick bay visitation chores.[11]

DURING THE SECOND half of 1943, General Douglas Mac-Arthur's Allied forces of U.S. and Australian armies and navies continued to hammer the resistant Japanese and gradually drive them out of New Guinea. While the stubborn Japanese fighters made the warfare there as horrid as anywhere in the Pacific, both American and Australian chaplains discovered that the "Green Hell" of the jungles did as much to hamper Allied advances and morale as anything the skilled and experienced Japanese could inflict. Historian Donald F. Crosby wrote that in many ways, New Guinea "seemed less an island than a horror of nature: a cauldron of bugs, snakes, bats, leeches, ants and scorpions all thriving in the island's soupy humidity."[12]

The chaplains knew they needed to help keep the soldiers' morale up, yet they could not disguise their own loathing for the island. One Catholic chaplain from Ohio suggested "we ought to give it to the Japs and make them live there." Another chaplain urged Allied strategists to pull out all the Allied troops and then seal off the country, leaving the Japanese to suffer the hell of the jungles "to the fullest."[13] If these observations failed to engender positive thinking, the fighting men probably found more encouragement from such acerbic humor than they would have from any pep talk on keeping their eyes on Heaven.

WHILE SOME OF the Allies slogged it out with Imperial Japan in New Guinea during the last months of 1943, combined forces of Australians, New Zealanders, and Americans began the so-called "climb up the ladder" of the Pacific islands of the Solomons, the Gilberts, the Marshalls, the Marianas, and the Bonin Islands. The aggressive Admiral Chester W. Nimitz was willing to pay as heavy a price as necessary to put Allied airplanes on islands within effective bombing range of Japan.

In July 1943 one of the first steps "up the ladder" came in the New Georgia campaign. The story of one chaplain's undaunted determination gives a glimpse of how a man who saw himself as missionary to combatants helped keep morale high in the face of dreadful conditions. Born in New Haven, Connecticut, in 1901, Paul Redmond graduated from high school in 1918. A lover of the sea, he joined the U.S. Navy and served on the battleship USS *Wyoming* for more than a year during and after World War I. Soon thereafter he sensed a call to the priesthood. He studied at Providence College and St. Thomas Seminary in Connecticut. Later he was ordained into the Dominican Order. The priest continued his formal schooling after ordination and earned a Ph.D. at Catholic University. Immediately after Pearl Harbor, Father Redmond applied for a commission and volunteered to serve as a navy chaplain. He went through a whirlwind chaplain school at Norfolk in less than three weeks and then went to Quantico Marine Base for special training with the marines. By February 1943 he had been assigned to a raider battalion.[14]

Redmond became the first of only a few chaplains to serve with the Raiders, because this elite fighting outfit was considered too physically demanding for men with the background and age of a typical chaplain. On paper Redmond could never have made it with the Raiders. Twice the age of the boys in such units, this Dominican priest was already forty-one years old when the war began, making him at least ten years older than the average military chaplain. But Paul Redmond was no ordinary man. He stood six feet tall and weighed 190 pounds. Even more impressive than his size, this lean, tough, and resilient Ph.D. could keep up with any of the eighteen-year-olds in running and other forms of physical training.

Marine Corps divisions seldom reached and maintained their goal of sixteen chaplains. Therefore, the commanders who understood the crucial role played by these spiritual leaders in sustaining morale almost always insisted that chaplains be excluded from joining the first waves of invasions. It is true that some Marine chaplains persuaded commanders to let them go in with the initial assault, but Chaplain Redmond distinguished himself in a rather unique situation. Before the main assault on New Georgia, a team of two Raider battalions and two army battalions invaded the coast, and Chaplain Paul Redmond was in their midst. When asked if it was wise for him to join in on the assault, he replied: "These are my boys. They will need me most out there. I'm going with them."[15]

For his valorous conduct during two separate assaults, the "old man" from New England was promoted to lieutenant commander and awarded the Legion of Merit. The citation reads:

For exceptional meritorious conduct in performance of outstanding services on New Georgia, Solomon Islands, on July 1, and July 20, 1943 during heavy fighting at Viru Inlet and Bairoko Harbor. He repeatedly ignored intense machine gun, rifle, and mortar fire so that he might comfort the wounded and administer the last rites to the dying in the front lines. When the fighting had subsided, he helped in the hazardous work of recovering the dead, and preparing a proper place for their burial. Throughout both actions Chaplain Redmond's calm demeanor, and his willingness to proceed to any point, however dangerous, where his presence was needed were a constant inspiration to his men.[16]

In another area of New Georgia invaded by the army, Jewish chaplain Elliot David gathered a group of eight Jewish soldiers for a brief Yom Kippur service. These army men found this time with their chaplain and comrades especially meaningful in a Central Pacific combat zone. They were thousands of miles from home, and there were no nearby cities with Jewish rabbis and civilian Jewish communities. Gathering Jewish soldiers together was no longer primarily for socializing and fellowship. As professor of Religion Deborah Dash Moore phrased it, such intimate services out there "took on different dimensions."[17]

A FEW WEEKS later Allied Forces would climb still farther up the ladder to be within effective bombing range of Japan. And the farther up the Allies climbed, the more determined the Japanese were to halt their advance. The Japanese sacrifice of fifty thousand men on Guadalcanal proved to be a mere down payment on what their increasingly fanatical military leaders were willing to pay. Consequently, every American who had experienced combat in 1942 and during the first nine months of 1943, or had talked to those who had, could sense the Sword of Damocles hanging over their heads and those of their fellow warriors. A hush settled on the decks and in the quarters of troop ships heaving to and fro like the deep breathing of a wounded man gasping for air.

On one troop transport in a fleet churning its way toward Bougainville, the word spread throughout the ship on the evening of October 31, 1943: "D-day is November 1."

"H-hour will be at 0715—chow starts at 0300." The Third Marines were ready for their initiation to combat.[18]

A marine officer, John Monks, who published what he saw and heard in that ship, recalled that a seriousness—almost a quiet—settled throughout the small vessel. "Canteens were filled for the last time aboard the ship. The men . . . took a last look at their [fire] arms, their packs, and their helmets, and then climbed into their hot canvas bunks."[19]

Men exchanged "good luck" and "it's goin' to be a short night." And one officer, Captain Bert Simpson, stood before the ship's only chaplain, Father Foley:

> *"I control the lives of two hundred men tomorrow, Father. . . . That's a big responsibility. I'd like to feel there was someone more powerful than I helping me to make the right decisions. I'm a Protestant but there's no Protestant chaplain aboard. Would you give me your blessing?"*
>
> *"Kneel down, son."*

John Monks remembered that Chaplain Foley then administered a blessing. Finally the chaplain asked the number of Simpson's debarkation net. Simpson replied: number four. The chaplain instructed the captain to tell his men who want a blessing to look over to where Foley was standing before they climbed down the net. "The next morning Father Foley was there, and each man in G. Company of the Second Battalion, Third Marines, received his special blessing."[20]

Captain Monks did not forget Chaplain Foley's ministry to these men, and he also remembered the service given later to G Company by Chaplain George Michael Kempker. During some of the heaviest fighting in Bougainville, Monks noticed that Kempker had been on the front all day just like he had been since they landed. On this day the infantry officer observed that the thirty-year-old chaplain was "always where the men needed him" and "had always been there since the day we landed." Captain Monks wrote: "In the middle of the afternoon the Father, who walked unhesitatingly in amongst the snipers, who had been through the barrage, who was always in the heat of battle, was laying out eleven dead marines. He was busy writing down their names and special numbers from their dog-tags and covering them over with ponchos."[21]

Chaplain Kempker, who would be awarded the Silver Star before Japan surrendered, had a sense of humor that bolstered morale as much as his courage. On one occasion when through misidentification a young man's name had been placed on the KIA list, the mislabeled man's buddy noticed it and informed the young man of the mistake. When Herbert L. Desimore saw his name on the Killed in Action list compiled by Kempker, he rushed out to find him: "Father, my name is Desimore. Have you got me on the list?" asked the worried lad. The chaplain immediately analyzed the situation and played it to the hilt. Carefully checking his book, he turned to Desimore and said his records were correct. Desimore was dead. Indeed, he was "dead and buried." Desimore asked him to "knock it off," but everyone else got a good laugh that broke some of the tension in combat for a few moments at least.[22]

A Protestant chaplain exuded a similar sense of how humor encouraged men whose lives were frequently on the line. During a lull in fighting this Holy Joe, while "standing in the chow line, was drenched with hot soup." The warriors who witnessed the accident roared in laughter when the chaplain quipped: "Will some laymen please say a few appropriate words?"[23]

WHETHER IT WAS through humor, a listening ear, or prayers and blessings on the edge of battle, anything the chaplains could provide to bolster morale became increasingly vital as the Allies advanced each step closer to the Japanese homeland. To the point, as every battle in the Central Pacific became more costly, there was no way to shroud the costs with patriotic songs, flying flags, or jargon. Consequently, the Navy Department distributed one large home front poster with photographs of a wounded man being helped off the front line by two battle-weary navy corpsmen. The collage also included graphic pictures of a dead marine lying facedown in the sand, a destroyed landing craft on the edge of a beach, as well as sundry other twisted and smashed pieces of military equipment rendered useless by enemy artillery. The boldface title of the poster read IT'S A LONG ROAD TO TOKYO and underscoring the cost were these words of General A. A. Vandegrift's: "EACH THING LOST MUST BE REPLACED. . . ."

Even local newspapers began to eschew all vestiges of the glamour of war. Journalists certainly celebrated Allied victories, but increasingly they underscored the enormous toll required to remain on the offensive. The *Kansas City Star*, for example, in early July 1944 ran a large photograph showing a chaplain on the deck of a ship reading from a Bible or prayer book. In front of the minister were seven flag-draped bodies of fighting men who were poised for burial at sea. Serving as pallbearers were somber-faced fellow warriors in combat helmets and battle fatigues.[24]

The mood on troop transports grew more sober with each passing battle. There were still calisthenics and drills on deck during the day, and throwing footballs and baseballs and shooting dice and playing poker went on as before, but the evening and nighttime chatter were toned down. Men became increasingly pensive as they sensed that the invasion was imminent. They spent more of their idle time writing letters to loved ones, sharpening and resharpening combat knives and bayonets, and cleaning well-oiled pistols and rifles one more time.

No wonder the mood grew more somber with each battle. After each successive victory there were reports that American casualties were "the highest to date."

One of the bloodiest struggles in the Pacific Theater was on the little atoll named Tarawa. This stepping stone to Japan was smaller than the state of Connecticut, and the U.S. Marines took it in seventy-six hours. Nevertheless, there were over 8,000 casualties on both sides. Nearly 1100 Americans died on this coral island and more than 2200 were wounded. As one historian described it, "Tarawa stands as one of the most violent battles in the 200-year history of the U.S. Marine Corps. . . . It cost 194 [Japanese and American] lives per acre, of which 34 per acre were American Marines."[25]

The carnage on Tarawa ultimately exacted a 17 percent casualty rate from the Americans, and Japanese losses grew much higher. The closer the Allies came to Japan, the more fanatical the Japanese became. On Tarawa nearly 5,000 Japanese troops met the invaders. Only 17 surrendered. Most of the Japanese died fighting, but many took their own lives rather than face defeat and what they deemed the humiliation of surrender.

Chaplains, like surgeons and combatants, frequently worked days and nights on end without sleeping. Relying only on odd naps of a few minutes to an hour, they faced ever-growing needs to serve the troops. While some chaplains moved from one platoon to another, praying for men and passing along words of encouragement, they also frequently assisted medics and corpsmen by providing emergency care to the wounded. Chaplains commonly offered their hands in carrying fallen soldiers and marines to tent hospitals behind the front lines, and they devoted countless hours to listening to the last words of dying men who could no longer be helped by surgeons.

With the mounting casualties and the needs of the fighting men growing, chaplains seldom gave much thought to whether they were ministering to men of their own tradition. Photojournalists caught on camera the hastily prepared Holy Communion services. One picture from Cape Gloucester displays a lopsided altar that appears so precariously held up by four ammunition boxes that it is doubtful it survived the time required for the consecration. Combat chaplains sometimes placed a stole around their necks, but in the midst of battle on the sides of hills and foxholes, in places like Tinian and Iwo Jima, the candid cameras often revealed a bare-headed minister or priest bent over to serve the sacrament to combatants who held their rifles in one hand and their helmets in the other—with mouths open to receive the wafer.[26]

Depending on the chaplain's own religious tradition, he might take Communion from man to man, offering the sacrament to those who wanted it along the way. The chaplains from the liturgical and sacramental traditions not only had their field Communion sets that enabled them to serve a platoon or more of men at a time, they usually had small Communion sets that fit into one hand or a pouch, allowing them to accommodate three or four men whom they might encounter on the run.

Chaplains of non-liturgical traditions would often forgo the Communion kit and carry instead a New Testament and a few sheets of gospel music. If there was a lull in the fighting, the word might be spread among a platoon that the chaplain was on the side of yonder hill and he was going to have a brief worship service for anyone who could come. S. G. Silcox, an enlisted marine from Illinois, recorded his recollection of such a service on Tinian in 1944:

> A chaplain came down the line and invited us to come down the hill for services. I went down. He laid his cloth across a rock. [It was probably the standard navy-issue small white flag with a dark blue cross.] He stood behind the rock laying his pistol on one side and his small carbine on the other. He passed out sheet music of some old familiar hymns, "Rock of Ages," "Onward Christian Soldiers," and "Amazing Grace." As I sat there I thought: I have attended church

in everything from the hills to some of the most beautiful churches in the United States, but this was really different.[27]

A CURSORY READING of published war-time memoirs of military chaplains serving troops fighting in the Pacific reveals how torn these ministers were about where to spend their precious time, especially when they were needed in so many places. They could be spotted in front-line locations like foxholes praying with men or attending to the wounded as they assisted a medic. On the other hand, men were agonizing and dying on the beaches awaiting transport to hospital ships. Then there was the responsibility of helping identify and bury the dead before the tropical heat caused a stench that made everyone sick. Chaplains kept notes of hastily dug graves, and they tried to hang dog tags on crude stakes that served as crosses. Over each body—if possible—they said a solemn prayer—"We therefore commit this body to the ground; earth to earth, ashes to ashes, dust to dust." There was also the horrid duty of overseeing mass burials of scores of men whose bodies were torn apart and where rain and sun had hastened decay before any accounting could be made. Some combatants tried to assure the folks at home that all bodies were identified and carefully accounted for. Despite heroic lengths to maintain rosters of men who were KIA or MIA, some men were lost in the jungles and decimated by artillery blasts. Fragments and truncated remains giving off nauseous stench, sometimes had to be buried in ditches with the help of Seabees and their bulldozers.[28]

Identifying the dead, covering bodies with ponchos, interring remains in temporary graves, carefully marking all graves on maps as well as on top of the ground took much time. On some islands five or six chaplains could be seen ministering over the graves of two or three dozen men.[29] The emotional strain on chaplains, corps-men, and medics—all of whom were relentlessly attending the wounded, dying, and dead—caused mental and psychological pain of singular gravity.

Chaplain William F. O'Neill's time in the Central Pacific provides some insight into the widespread needs faced by ministers during the major island battles. Born in 1905 in Connecticut, Father O'Neill had earned three university degrees and was teaching at Duquesne University when the war began. After he became a navy chaplain, he eventually served the Sixth Marine Division.[30] On one island he could be found "crawling from foxhole to foxhole assisting the men who needed to see a priest or were suffering from severe wounds."[31] A giant of a man by the standards of the 1940s, O'Neill stood well over six feet tall, and he was dubbed "Big Joe" by the men who knew him. With the courage to complement his strength, he single-handedly evacuated many wounded from the fray—"carrying them in his arms or dragging them over his shoulders." An observer wrote that he was "worth as much to the boys of his regiment as a trainload of ammunition."[32]

But the duties of a chaplain like William Francis O'Neill did not end there. All chaplains were expected to write letters of condolence to a man's next of kin as soon as possible after they had buried his remains. O'Neill recalled that he wrote letters "until his hands ached."[33]

The hearts of chaplains ached as much as their hands. The majority of combat chaplains carefully wrote personal letters and told the family something encouraging about their deceased loved one. Sometimes the chappies also mailed an item that belonged to the loved one—giving the family something to cling to during their time of need. A soul physician whose name has long been forgotten removed the sterling silver ID bracelet from the body of Marine

Corporal Samuel P. Grimes, Jr. This young man had been wounded on Saipan and then patched up to fight another day. Grimes was severely wounded on Tinian and taken to a hospital ship off the island, where he died. The navy chaplain wrote Grimes's mother in Kansas City, Missouri, and sent her son's silver ID bracelet along with a letter of condolence.[34]

Chaplains on hospital ships were just as important in the overall war effort as those on the ground in the thick of battle. Their lives, like the lives of all the officers and sailors, were increasingly at risk as the Pacific War went on, because Japanese kamikaze planes targeted them as well as other vessels. Nevertheless they performed their duties, often for days on end without sleep, right alongside the surgeons and nurses. Robert Spivey, a West Virginia lad, joined the marines when he was sixteen. His mother was his accomplice in lying about his age because she'd grown weary of his obsession with signing on and knew that neither she nor he would find peace until he enlisted. Spivey served the marines well. He was wounded in the Marshall Islands but recovered well enough to continue fighting. Several weeks later, however, a large piece of shrapnel tore through his rib cage and pierced his left lung, and at the same time a bullet entered the other side of his thoracic cavity. He lost a lot of blood and was hurried off the island to a hospital ship. On the ship, where he was being iced down and prepared for surgery, a Catholic chaplain came and told him he wanted to give him last rites because the doctor had said he probably could not save him. Spivey told the chaplain, "No, don't do that. I can't leave my mother this way." He passed out and woke up later remembering the kind chaplain. Although Bob Spivey had been raised a Methodist, he so valued the attention of the priest—the only chaplain who attended him—that he later took instruction and converted to the Catholic faith.

That Robert Spivey never knew the name of the chaplain who

helped heal his soul while nurses and doctors worked to repair his body, was by no means unusual.[35] Typically, enlisted men did not remember chaplains' names. And the good chaplains, no doubt, preferred for the men to meet the Lord they represented rather than themselves. As Bishop Fulton Sheen phrased it—and he could have been speaking for other ministers, as well as priests—"The priest does not belong to himself; he belongs to Christ. He need never worry who he is. He is not his own. He is Christ's." He is merely an "ambassador."[36]

ROBERT SPIVEY'S CONVERSION to a different tradition was no more unusual than his ignorance of the chaplain's name. The fiery marine, looking back from the perspective of more than sixty years, somewhat bitingly commented that he converted to Catholicism because no Protestant chaplain ever bothered to visit him on the hospital ship, let alone pray with him and take him seriously as a person.[37]

It is quite likely that there were no other chaplains on Spivey's hospital ship. In fact, many such vessels had only one chaplain aboard. Consequently a caring chaplain with a magnetic personality could win men to his faith without even trying. Many men converted because of their longing for fellowship. The author of GI Jews discovered that Jewish soldiers were often out there on their own, without Jewish comrades. Many men converted to Christianity, or at least were tempted to do so, because they were lonely.[38]

Of course conversions went more than one way. Catholics became Protestants and Christians became converts to the Jewish faith. But by far the most common conversions came from the ranks of men who belonged to a religious tradition by no more than name. All military personnel were required to claim a religion for their official files and for their identification tags. Each branch of the armed forces put a P (Protestant), C (Catholic), or H (Hebrew) on every dog tag. This became a way of finding an appropriate chaplain in a time of need. It was also useful for determining symbols for a grave marker. Inasmuch as countless members of the military had no real commitment to a particular religion, it is understandable why many so-called conversions took place during the war. In truth, many essentially nonreligious people experienced genuine conversions. Protestant chaplains commonly baptized converts—most of whom were new believers despite what their dog tags read. Certainly some folks did thoughtfully, carefully, and prayerfully convert to a totally different tradition from the religion they had truly embraced when they entered military service. But more often than not, though, it was the tepid Christian who became a born-again Christian, or the fellow baptized as an infant whose Baptist friend or chaplain convinced him that he needed "believer's baptism" to be truly baptized.

Among the several thousand World War II chaplains there were plenty of Catholics and Protestants who were willing to minister to men of any faith. But deep in the depths of their own hearts and souls many believed their tradition to be superior. Therefore they were quite willing to proselytize and give instruction to any man or woman in uniform who expressed interest. It is only to be expected that when chaplains submitted regular reports to their commanding officers, they would proudly record growing numbers of baptisms and swelling attendance at religious instruction classes.[39]

ALMOST ALL ARMY and navy chaplains reported increased conversions and baptisms in the wake of the bloody slaughter at Tarawa. To the mind of most combatants the odds of surviving the climb up the ladder rungs to Japan without a serious wound or death seemed improbable. From the perspective of those men who had already survived combat, they knew they had a decided edge over greenhorn replacements. On the other hand, the law of averages was now decidedly against even those battle-tested survivors. And besides, they knew they would have to put themselves at risk as they helped the inexperienced troops learn the ways of the enemy.

Throughout the last two years of the Pacific War, casualities, with only a few exceptions, rose on each island. In the Mariana Islands the battles at Saipan and Guam proved to be as horrid as the darkest predictions. Only Tinian surprised the Allies with relatively low casualties. At Saipan the Second and Fourth Marine Divisions, as well as the army's Twenty-Seventh Infantry Division, invaded what some strategists called the "gateway to the Japanese homeland" on June 16, 1944. Twenty-three days later, on Sunday, July 9, the island was secured. In the final analysis, because of the ferocious determination of the Japanese to hold the island, plus some debatably costly offensive tactics of Marine General "Howlin' Mad" Smith, as well as some less than timely and overcautious movements of Army General Ralph Smith, American casualties were inordinately high. Total U.S. servicemen killed on Saipan were 3100, with 13,099 wounded and 326 missing.[40] When nearby Tinian was invaded on July 23 and secured nine days later, the casualties were considerably lower. Total figures show 328 killed and 1,517 wounded.[41]

But, alas, casualty rates on Tinian were not indicators of what Americans would experience on Guam. This American territory, which had fallen to the Japanese on December 10, 1941, was retaken from America's enemy on August 9 after twenty-one days of grueling struggle. Almost 1400 men died in the fierce battle and another 377 died of wounds incurred in the fight. Another 5,970 men were wounded.[42] As official Marine Corps historians phrased it, "By any rational standard, the most devastating cost of war is the lives of the men it kills and maims. In these terms, the price of Guam came high."[43]

THE DEMAND FOR chaplains in the slaughter pens of the Marianas turned out to be much greater than the supply. Some regiments had only five or six chaplains, despite the Navy Department's designation of sixteen as a full complement. In some cases, however, an occasional sky pilot distinguished himself to be worse than none at all. An event that took place on an LST (landing ship, tank), part of a flotilla of five hundred ships zigzagging their way to the Marianas, is a case in point. The massive armada carrying supplies for war included precious cargo of 250,000 fighting men whose assignment was to capture the islands destined to become the launching pads for the invasion of Japan. Saipan was the most heavily defended of the group because it was, as the Japanese and the Allies knew, the main gateway to the Japanese homeland.

Father Donald F. Crosby, who wrote a historical account of this journey, related the story of one chaplain's badly chosen remarks: "Late in the evening on the day before the [Saipan] invasion, a Catholic chaplain spoke over the ship's loudspeaker and delivered what may well have been the most inappropriate announcement made by a chaplain during the war: 'Most of you will return,' he said, 'but some of you will meet the God who made you. . . . Repent of your sins. . . . Those of the Jewish faith repeat after me. . . . Now the Christian men, Protestants and Catholics, repeat after me.'" Father Crosby opined that "if he had set out deliberately to panic the men, he could hardly have done a better job. Officers aboard the ship complained angrily," and four decades later they were still protesting the chaplain's inappropriate behavior.[44]

On Saipan chaplains went to work as soon as the troops hit the beaches. Chaplain Emmett Thomas Michaels was ministering to several wounded and dying marines. He remembered only too well that "I had just stooped over to console a Marine on a stretcher when a bullet penetrated my collar bone and shoulder blade leaving them both broken." Only thirty-one years old, this otherwise healthy and eager to serve young minister was out of combat for the rest of the war.[45]

Chaplain John Harold Craven, a Missourian who had served since 1942, remembered the utter busyness of the Saipan battle. During "combat our main action was to go from place to place, unit to unit and start out early in the morning and go till dark, just visiting one unit after another and many times having a brief service." As a Baptist, Craven was less concerned about taking Holy Communion to the men than he was in finding a few minutes to sing a hymn and read from the Bible. Rather than a portable Communion set he had "some very small hymn books from some mission up in New York—they were very thin—and some Testaments I could carry in my map case, and we would just gather a few men together in a bomb crater or defilade." Wherever they could get "a little protection—I would have one service after the other. Sometimes we had twelve, thirteen or fourteen of those in one day, especially on Sunday," when possible.[46]

Craven made it clear that sometimes he had to take leave of the men on the front because "we had to take our turn at the cemetery. Each chaplain from different units would go down and take turns for burial." With the heavy losses on Saipan "we had a brief committal service for each one as they brought the bodies in."[47]

KEEPING CAREFUL RECORDS of the men who were killed each day and ministering to others in tent hospitals became an arduous task for Craven. "I worked closely with a sergeant major and it was amazing how we were able to keep up with men, and when they were killed and when and where they were buried." Obviously devoted to the men, Craven said, "I kept a notebook on all the casualties and we would keep that up from day to day and then we would compare notes each evening with the sergeant major for the regiment." Craven noted that this record keeping not only made for the accurate data required of chaplains, it enabled him to find the wounded and killed men's friends and work with them.[48]

Because keeping track of all the battalion and regimental combatants, visiting the wounded, burying the dead, and then writing condolence letters became more work than one or two men could handle, the army and the navy tried to assign one enlisted man to each chaplain as an assistant. An army chaplain serving on Saipan with the Twenty-Seventh Infantry Division, Rabbi Max Vorspan, certainly needed help, because added to his usual duties there were special tasks. One of the most macabre involved the task of handling the case of "a body washed in from the sea." The remains were "in an advanced state of decomposition," yet after making attempts at finding anything to identify the man, "proper Catholic, Jewish and Protestant rites were observed."[49] Chaplain Vorspan's reports reveal that his duties were lightened by his assistant and because he had excellent interaction with Christian chaplains. All the chaplains shared burdens, even between the army and the navy. Vorspan even arranged some joint services with a Jewish chaplain serving the Second Marine Division. But typically, until hostilities ceased on Saipan, most of Vorspan's ministry was among Protestants and Catholics, who greatly outnumbered Jewish men, who comprised only 2.75 to 8 percent of the troops at any given time.[50]

That all chaplains were available—indeed required and expected—to serve men outside their traditions was not always understood by the troops. Chaplain John Whalen, a young priest who would be awarded the Purple Heart before hostilities ended, related this story: Just before the Saipan invasion a Jewish corpsman inquired if a Catholic priest could serve a wounded man who was not Catholic. Whalen assured the corpsman this was no problem. Ironically, the Jewish man died less than an hour later on the beach and Father Whalen attended him: "He was failing fast. I went over to the boy, knelt beside him. I had a prayer book in my pocket which had prayers for the dying for Catholics, Jews, and Protestants. I read the Jewish prayer. Shells were still bursting around us. Men were cringing around the boy when he died."[51]

Ministering to dying men was never easy, but Chaplain Joseph Gallagher, a thirty-five-year-old who had earned degrees from Holy Cross College, two seminaries, Fordham University, and Oxford University in England, confided that two types of tasks were even more difficult. The first was merely revolting to the eyes and sense of smell. The Japanese seldom bothered to bury their dead. Americans, on the other hand, not only buried their own, but the enemy's remains as well. Because the Japanese often left their dead behind as they retreated, Gallagher described the repulsive scenes: "the enemy's bodies bloated and festered in the sweltering tropical heat. When it came time to bury them, the worst cases attracted thick clouds of flies, and their burial became a test of will for both the Marines and their chaplains."[52] The second most burdensome task, according to Gallagher, was to minister to a young man who discovered that a dead man was his close friend. One situation he remembered came while he was preparing to bury a lad and another young man came up and cried, "Oh my God, Father, that's my best friend." It seems that some years earlier the two men, both Georgians, had agreed to join the Marine Corps together. They enlisted together, took physicals at the same time, and spent as much time in each other's company as possible until the Marine Corps put them in different units. Because of separation the young marine "had not seen his friend again until that moment in Saipan." It was a most difficult task to help the lad pull his broken soul together.[53]

AS DREADFUL AS conditions could be on Saipan, there were bursts of humor that helped keep fighting men sane. Rick Spooner vividly recalled a chaplain scene on Saipan that quickly spread among the combatants and is still being talked about more than sixty years later. Spooner, a young enlisted man in World War II who went on to make a career in the Marine Corps, said that people are often told that chaplains did not carry firearms. To the contrary, Spooner claimed that every chaplain he met carried a .45-caliber automatic pistol. A committed Christian, Spooner sought out fellowship with chaplains when he could. One event he remembered involved two Holy Joes: one Protestant and the other Catholic. The names have been long forgotten, but the incident permanently marked his memory. The Protestant chaplain was checking his .45 with the clip removed, but he had failed to remember that one round had already entered the chamber. While he was checking out the piece, it unexpectedly fired and hit the helmet of the Catholic chaplain who was standing nearby. The innocent victim was not hurt, but the careless chappie was continually chided as the Protestant chaplain who tried to kill the Catholic priest.[54]

TESTIMONIES FROM CHAPLAINS and combatants in the Marianas suggest that conditions were similar on all the islands. There simply were too few chaplains. Chaplain John Craven argued that there were not enough chaplains at the outset of the struggle for the Marianas, and the situation grew worse with the explosion of casualties. On

Tinian Craven was flagged down by Colonel Louis Jones, who called out: "Hey, Chaplain. I don't have a chaplain now." Under the best of conditions, most regiments had only one chaplain from each of the three faiths. Craven had to inform the regimental commander that both his Catholic and his Protestant chaplain had been wounded. Nevertheless, Craven said he promised to "help him all I could."[55]

On Guam, where battle casualties were quite high, the shortage of chaplains became still more critical. One Marine Corps enlisted man, Tommy Wilson, a devout Christian from Birmingham, Alabama, who saw much combat, suffered severe back and arm wounds that left one arm partially debilitated for life. He sadly recalled that he never saw a chaplain on Guam—despite the fact that he certainly wanted to.[56]

It is doubtful if Tommy Wilson would have counted the experience of another marine on Guam as a legitimate chaplain sighting. A marine in the jungle on the island had a Japanese soldier in his rifle sight. He was preparing to shoot when the unarmed man with hands raised said in perfect English: "I am a priest." The flabbergasted rifleman responded: "All right. Just walk ahead of me, Father. I won't hurt you." Later, once the prisoner was inside the wires of a small prisoner cage, this Japanese Catholic priest celebrated Mass for some astounded Marines.[57]

Chances are this Japanese priest, who no doubt was conscripted to serve his nation's army, agonized over the way his fellow combatants wantonly destroyed lives and property among civilians in the wake of their conquests. Particularly offensive to Japanese Christian soldiers (a tiny percent to be sure) must have been the way their troops desecrated Christian houses of worship. Invariably when Japanese troops entered a chapel or church belonging to the people they occupied, they would destroy altars and riddle with bullets every crucifix and every face of Jesus Christ they could find on statues and paintings.[58]

* * *

AFTER THE STAGGERING casualties in the Marianas, and in the face of increasingly fanatical Japanese opposition, no one looked forward with optimism to the next steps that had to be climbed in order to invade Japan. In the Hawaiian Islands and especially on Maui, where Marines were preparing for the next invasion, men became increasingly interested in religion. There was a keen sense that accounts with God must be settled soon because this time the Sword of Damocles threatened to fall on every man.

Chaplain John H. Craven told an interviewer thirty-five years after the fact that before the invasion of Iwo Jima he baptized numerous men—even using irrigation ditches to handle the crowd. One of the reasons Craven had so many men to care for was that he had been assigned six battalions to serve and there were only two chaplains.

When asked about the morale of the veterans who had survived Saipan and Tinian, Chaplain Craven replied that "the morale was pretty good, but they became rather cynical." After all, they had survived two campaigns, and a third one seemed one too many. In an attempt to turn their concerns into humor, a chart referencing the $10,000 life insurance policy on each man could be heard in the tents at night:

> *Ten thousand dollars going home to the folks!*
> *Ten thousand dollars going home to the folks!*
> *Oh, won't they be excited!*
> *Oh, won't they be delighted!*
> *Ten thousand dollars going home to the folks!*[59]

Chaplain Craven said that cynicism and fatalism notwithstanding, the men faced battle with a longing for God. Sunday school,

Sunday morning and evening services, as well as midweek prayer services and two weekly evening Bible studies were well attended. Furthermore, local Christians provided still more activities to encourage the men and bolster morale. Craven was quick to point out that these were not just men going through the motions. Lives were changed permanently and "some of these young men are pastors around the world and we still hear from some of them."[60]

In early 1945 a fleet embarked from the Hawaiian Islands to join marine and army units in the Marianas. Eventually 495 ships moved an expeditionary force of 111,308 men. According to the calculations of historians George W. Garand and Truman R. Strobridge, "If one adds the crews of [Admiral Richard K.] Turner's ships . . . more than 250,000 men on the American side were involved in the Iwo operation."[61]

This task force comprised the largest convoy in the Pacific War, and it stretched seventy miles long. On the four-day voyage from the Marianas to Iwo Jima, the men played ball, wrote letters home, and attended worship services on deck because it was much cooler than down below. Everyone aboard the ships knew this would be a horrendous fight, but the officers and NCOs who studied maps and were briefed on the way recognized this to be an almost indescribably fortified stronghold where Imperial Japan's elite marines were ready and waiting. Consequently enlisted men and officers manifested an air of seriousness, and chaplains were faced with unprecedented demands for consultations, blessings, and prayers.[62]

Fifty-eight army and navy chaplains accompanied these warriors. Among them were four Jewish rabbis, nineteen Catholic priests, and twenty-five Protestant ministers. Most of these chaplains went onto the island with the invaders, but some remained on ships nearby off the coast, to care for the sailors, as well as the wounded and dying who would be carried out to the floating hospitals.[63]

One Protestant chaplain, who had been on Saipan and Tinian, explained that Iwo Jima was a different experience in several ways. First, there was less terrain to cover than on Saipan and therefore he could get around to the men more quickly. Second, there were so many wounded and dying men that it became almost impossible to break away from the aid stations and be among the troops.[64]

No wonder it was difficult to get away from the aid stations. On Iwo Jima there were 2400 casualties on D-day alone, with 600 killed and more than 1800 wounded. Between February 19 and March 17, the Japanese threw 21,000 defenders against the Americans and fewer than 200 survived. This slaughter pen of volcanic ash located 700 miles from Japan eventually cost the Americans 4,189 KIA, 15,308 wounded, and another 441 missing.[65] The Marine Corps historians who wrote the official history of Western Pacific operations included this report of the scene one man saw the morning after the invasion began:

> The first night on Iwo Jima can only be described as a nightmare in hell. About the beach in the morning lay the dead. They died with the greatest possible violence. Nowhere in the Pacific have I seen such badly mangled bodies. Many were cut in half. Legs and arms lay 50 feet away from any body. All through the bitter night, the Japs rained heavy mortars and rockets and artillery on the entire area between the beach and the airfield. Twice they hit casualty stations on the beach. Many men who had been only wounded were killed.[66]

One Baptist chaplain, Edgar Hotaling, a twenty-nine-year-old graduate of Brown University and Andover Newton Theological Seminary, averaged one hundred burial ceremonies a day—something he never trained for in seminary. He confessed that "most jobs you can get used to. But this one is different. Every man you bury is a fresh tragedy."[67]

Father Charles F. Suver, almost forty years old when he landed on Iwo Jima with a company of marines on D-day, overheard a young infantry officer say that he would see to it that the American flag would be hoisted atop Mount Suribachi if someone could secure a flag. Another young officer promised to find a flag. Suver did not want to be outdone by these young men, so he said, "You get it up there and I'll say Mass under it." Six days later Father Suver kept his promise. In a moment of ecumenical triumph, Suver realized a flag was going up. He donned a camouflage vestment made for him by a Protestant. Then he summoned his assistant, who grabbed the field Communion kit, and off they ran. Partway up the mountain Chaplain Suver asked for permission to hold Mass. The commander agreed as long as the men did not congregate and become a mass target. The agreement might not have been precisely obeyed when about fifteen men, most with helmets still on and rifles ready to fire, gathered around Father Suver's altar made of ammunition boxes so lopsided that the chalice and crucifix nearly slid off.[68] Suver had kept his promise, and he also distinguished himself as the first priest to celebrate Mass on Iwo Jima.

A Congregational minister, Alvo Olen Martin, who at forty-five trumped Suver in age, determined not to be outdone by his Catholic comrade. Martin, who began his ministry in Nebraska after graduating from Northwestern University and Garrett Seminary, pulled together a little band of brothers and officiated the first—if very brief—Easter service held on Iwo Jima just a few days later.[69]

THE QUESTION AROSE in 1944 and 1945, as it does today—what was so important about Iwo Jima that the Americans would sacrifice twenty thousand casualties to take it? General A. A. Vandegrift helps answer this question. He wrote that the Joint Chiefs of Staff chose Iwo Jima, albeit the decision was difficult. The island was described "as a barren rock of volcanic ash defended by a strong force" superior to that of any place already encountered. Despite massive Japanese defenses, "the Army Air Corps wanted it. Curtis LeMay's heavy bombers were currently striking Japan and particularly Tokyo from the recently acquired Saipan and Tinian airfields." Vangegrift pointed out that "radar located on Iwo Jima warned Tokyo of approaching B-29s and fighters based on Iwo attacked the returning bombers. We also needed an interim airfield for aircraft damaged over target, many of which were going down at sea."[70]

After World War II a Japanese admiral offered his assessment of how the Americans were able to destroy twenty-one thousand well-trained, highly disciplined, and almost impregnably entrenched Japanese defenders on Iwo Jima, where only two hundred Japanese men surrendered. Admiral Ichimaru concluded that it was American "material superiority as opposed to Japanese fighting spirit" that finally won the campaign. The United States did prove to have superior material support, but as historians George W. Garand and Truman R. Strobridge concluded, the Americans possessed factors that the Japanese admiral chose to ignore. "Not the least among these were the outstanding leadership and discipline of the men who came to take Iwo Jima or die in the attempt; the physical stamina and mental power of endurance of these men, both tempered in months or years of thorough training; and the intangible indefinable something known as esprit de corps or morale, that induces men to give their last in a common cause."[71]

Garand and Strobridge were correct. The Japanese admiral stubbornly refused to see beyond the material might of America and acknowledge the "intangibles"—the esprit de corps and morale. But the historians' analysis should be complemented by the credit Admiral Chester W. Nimitz gave the military men of the cloth: "By their patient, sympathetic labors with the men, day in and day out and through many a night, every chaplain I know contributed immeasurably to the moral courage of our fighting men."[72]

One of those chaplains was a thirty-five-year-old Jewish rabbi from Long Island, New York, with academic degrees from Western Reserve University, Columbia University, and Hebrew Union College. Rabbi Roland B. Gittelsohn, who had been serving with the Fifth Marine Division, delivered his division's Memorial Address on Iwo Jima in March 1945. He spoke to the courage and spirit of the men whose sublime sacrifice was manifested in a secured island that now cradled a massive field of white crosses and stars of David. Gittelsohn's address at once memorialized the dead and offered words of encouragement and hope to the survivors, who looked at the seemingly endless rows of graves and in their grief and weariness asked questions about the purpose of this sacrifice. The rabbi rose to the occasion and called the onlookers to envision again the freedom they were fighting for and to carry on to victory "the struggle" these buried men so ably began.[73]

MEMORIAL ADDRESS - FIFTH MARINE DIVISION CEMETERY-IWO JIMA - MARCH 1945

CHAPLAIN ROLAND B. GITTELSOHN
Hdq. Co. Hdq. Btn.
Fifth Marine Division
c/o Fleet Post Office
San Francisco, California

This is perhaps the grimmest, and surely the holiest task we have faced since D-day. Here before us lie the bodies of comrades and friends. Men who until yesterday or last week laughed with us, joked with us, trained with us. Men who were on the same ships with us, and went over the sides with us as we prepared to hit the beaches of this island. Men who fought with us and feared with us. Somewhere in this plot of ground there may lie the man who could have discovered the cure for cancer. Under one of these Christian crosses, or beneath a Jewish Star of David, there may rest now a man who was destined to be a great prophet—to find the way, perhaps, for all to live in plenty, with poverty and hardship for none. Now they lie here silently in this sacred soil, and we gather to consecrate this earth in their memory.

It is not easy to do so. Some of us have buried our closest friends here. We saw these men killed before our very eyes. Any one of us might have died in their places. Indeed, some of us are alive and breathing at this very moment only because men who lie here beneath us had the courage and strength to give their lives for ours. To speak in memory of such men as these is not easy. Of them too can it be said with utter truth: "The world will little note nor long remember what we say here. It can never forget what they did here."

No, our poor power of speech can add nothing to what these men and the other dead of our Division who are not here have already done. All that we even hope to do is follow their example. To show the same selfless courage in peace that they did in war. To swear that by the grace of God and the stubborn strength and power of human will, their sons and ours shall never suffer these pains again. These men have done their job well. They have paid the ghastly price of freedom. If that freedom be once again lost, as it was after the last war, the unforgivable blame will be ours, not theirs. So it is we the living who are here to be dedicated and consecrated.

We dedicate ourselves, first, to live together in peace the way they fought and are buried in this war. Here lie men who loved America because their ancestors generations ago helped in her founding, and other men who loved her with equal passion because they themselves or their own fathers escaped from oppression to her blessed shores. Here lie officers and men, negroes and whites, rich men and poor— together. Here are Protestants, Catholics and Jews,—together. Here no man prefers another because of his faith or despises him because of his color. Here there are no quotas of how many from each group are admitted or allowed. Among these men there is no discrimination. No prejudices. No hatred. Theirs is the highest and purest democracy.

Any man among us the living who fails to understand that will thereby betray those who lie here dead. Whoever of us lifts his hand in hate against a brother, or thinks himself superior to those who happen to be in the minority, makes of this ceremony and of the bloody sacrifice it commemorates, an empty, hollow mockery. To this, then, as our solemn, sacred duty, do we the living now dedicate ourselves:—to the right of Protestants, Catholics and Jews, of white men and negroes alike, to enjoy the democracy for which all of them have here paid the price.

PART THREE

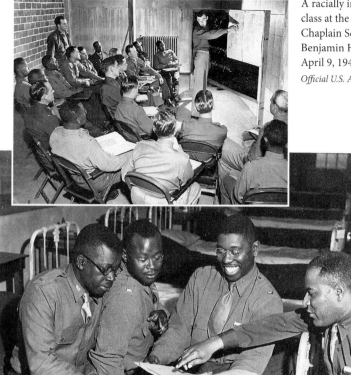

A racially integrated class at the Army Chaplain School, Ft. Benjamin Harrison, April 9, 1942.
Official U.S. Army Photograph

ABOVE: Students at Ft. Benjamin Harrison reviewing class notes at the Chaplain School, April 9, 1942. These men ordained in the African Methodist Church are (L to R): Walter S. White, George W. Williams, John R. Wesley, and John A. Deveaux.
Official U.S. Army Photograph

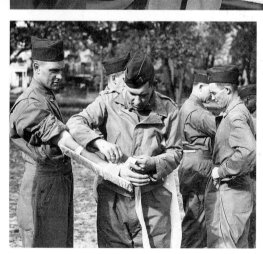

LEFT: Chaplains learning to minister first aid at Chaplains School, Harvard University, October 29, 1943.
Official U.S. Army Photograph

Chaplain Joseph B. Boggins, S.J., saying Mass somewhere in New Guinea, August 1943.
Official U.S. Army Photograph

ABOVE LEFT: Chaplain L. C. Lemons baptizing several marines and Seabees in the ocean off Munda. Rendova Peak is in the background, October 6, 1943.   *Courtesy of Dr. J. Stanley Lemons*

ABOVE RIGHT: Chaplain Lemons, October 6, 1943, off the coast of Munda.
Courtesy of Dr. J. Stanley Lemons

LEFT: Chaplain L. C. Lemons on New Georgia in his Jeep with his chaplain's assistant, C. K. Casteel, 1943.

Courtesy of Dr. J. Stanley Lemons

BELOW: Worship within the shadow of danger. While some of their fellow marines were mopping up Japanese patrols not far away in the Matanikou fighting on Guadalcanal Island, these Americans kneel in worship during a Catholic service conducted by Father Reardon, October 11, 1942.

Official U.S. Marine Corps Photograph, courtesy of the Norfolk, VA Naval Station archives

ABOVE: Parachuting "Sky Pilots." Parachuting with their men, these army chaplains don their equipment in New Guinea. (L to R): Robert Herr, Protestant chaplain; John J. Powers, Catholic chaplain; and chaplain's assistant, Charles E. Reagan.

Official U.S. Signal Corps Photograph

RIGHT: Chaplain L. Curtis Tiernan, European Theater Chief of Chaplains, cycling in England.

Courtesy of the Harry S. Truman Library, Independence, MO

Protestant Christmas Eve service in Italy, 1943

Official U.S. Signal Corps Photograph, courtesy of the Ft. Jackson, SC, Chaplain Archives

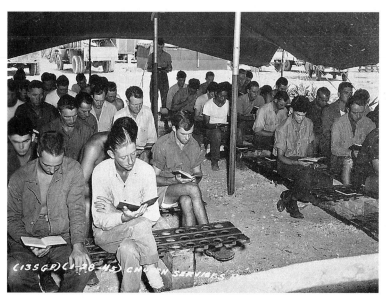

A chapel in Anguar, Palaus. Worship service led by Chaplain (Lieutenant) Jack Cooper. Note the pews made of airplane landing mats.

Official U.S. Marine Corps Photograph, courtesy of the Norfolk, VA Naval Station archives

Marines attend Catholic Mass before their assault on the front lines of New Georgia.

Official U.S. Marine Corps Photograph

Chaplain Harold Hirsch Gordon with the "Flying Torah."

Official U.S. Signal Corps Photograph

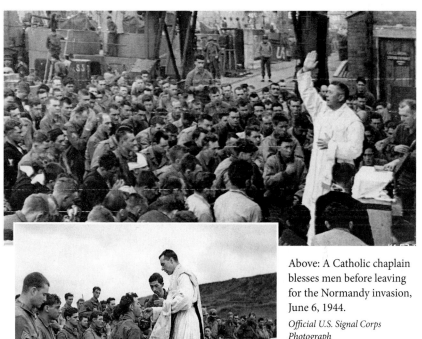

Above: A Catholic chaplain blesses men before leaving for the Normandy invasion, June 6, 1944.

Official U.S. Signal Corps Photograph

Left: A Catholic chaplain serving Holy Communion on Normandy Beach, June 1944.

Official U.S. Signal Corps Photograph, courtesy of the Ft. Jackson, SC, Chaplain Archives

American and enemy dead are received at Graves Registration Company for processing and burial in France, July 21, 1944. *Official U.S. Army Photograph*

Chaplain Johnstone Beech leads a worship service for WACs, army officers, and enlisted men in an apple orchard in France, July 8, 1944.

Official U.S. Signal Corps Photograph, courtesy of the Ft. Jackson, SC, Chaplain Archives

France, summer 1944. Note the field organ played by the chaplain's assistant.

Official U.S. Signal Corps Photograph, courtesy of the Ft. Jackson, SC, Chaplain Archives

Protestant battlefield service in central Europe, autumn 1944.

Official U.S. Signal Corps Photograph, courtesy of the Ft. Jackson, SC, Chaplain Archives

The flag-draped coffins of American dead are prepared for burial after a funeral with full military honors in England, November 4, 1944.

Official U.S. Army Photograph

Chaplain Vananty Szymanski hearing confession in Germany in early 1945.

Photo courtesy of Bernard Ciolek

Chaplain Stanley Brzana, early 1945 in Germany.

Jewish soldiers gather with their chaplain at the Siegfried Line, late 1944.

Official U.S. Signal Corps Photograph

LEFT: Chaplain Bernard King at the grave of one of his men somewhere in western Europe. His assistant took this and similar pictures so that Chaplain King could send copies to the families of KIA soldiers.

Photo courtesy of Janet Kuhns Howard

BELOW: Christmas Mass held in a warehouse at Antwerp, Belgium, on December 25, 1944. Note the piles of food rations that have arrived for the Yanks at this port.

Official U.S. Signal Corps Photograph, courtesy of the Ft. Jackson, SC, Chaplain Archives

Field worship on the move during the Battle of the Bulge.

Official U.S. Signal Corps Photograph, courtesy of the Ft. Jackson, SC, Chaplain Archives

Jewish service in the Pacific theater.

Official U.S. Signal Corps Photograph, courtesy of the Ft. Jackson, SC, Chaplain Archives

Passover in Europe, 1945.

Courtesy of the Ft. Jackson, SC, Chaplain Archives

A chaplain teaching songs to Japanese prisoners of war, 1945.
Official U.S. Signal Corps Photograph

Chaplain L. C. Lemons leading worship services on the U.S.S. *Manila Bay* in 1945.
Courtesy of Dr. J. Stanley Lemons

Marines at Saipan attend Mass near the front lines, June 1944.

Official U.S. Marine Corps Photograph, courtesy of the Norfolk, VA Naval Station archives

LEFT: Burial at sea. Chaplains aboard the U.S.S. *General M. M. Patrick* prepare for a sea burial of a KIA comrade.

Official U.S. Navy Photograph

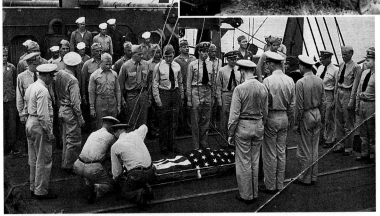

Corporal Cleaveran Bryant, an ordained minister in civilian life, conducts worship for men at an advanced base of the 7th Army, Army Air Force Headquarters on Saipan. These men were without benefit of a Protestant chaplain. Laymen like Corporal Bryant conducting worship services for troops was common among African Americans where there was a shortage of chaplains.

Official U.S. Signal Corps Photograph, courtesy of the Ft. Jackson, SC, Chaplain Archives

Above: V-J Day service, August 19, 1945, led for servicemen by Jewish chaplain Daima on Saipan.

Official U.S. Signal Corps Photograph, courtesy of the Ft. Jackson, SC, Chaplain Archives

Left: Worship service on Guam.

Official U.S. Marine Corps Photograph, courtesy of the Norfolk, VA Naval Station archives

Marine chaplain L. W. Meadhum serving communion to marines in the Pacific theater from the tail gate of a truck in October 1943.

Official U.S. Marine Corps Photograph

TOP RIGHT: Chaplain (Captain) Edgar H. Stohler, receives the silver star for heroic action in France from Brigadier General James A. Van Fleet, October 29, 1944.

Official U.S. Signal Corps Photograph

RIGHT: Lieutenant Colonel Harry B. Leversledge, commander of the 3rd Raider Battalion on New Georgia in 1943, is pictured in the center and is flanked by Catholic chaplains serving the Raiders: Paul J. Redmond on the left and John P. Murphy on the right.

Official U.S. Marine Corps Photograph

BELOW: Catholic Mass on Mount Suribachi, Iwo Jima. Notice that two marines are holding ponchos to shield the service from the effects of the wind.

Official U.S. Marine Corps Photograph

CHAPTER SEVEN

BREAKING HITLER'S FORTRESS EUROPE

EUROPEAN AND MEDITERRANEAN THEATERS, 1942–1944

A chaplain's role in war is largely what he makes it, and every good chaplain has ways of increasing his usefulness beyond the work prescribed in the book.

JACK ALEXANDER[1]

WHILE Allied forces in the Pacific battled the twin enemies of Japanese warriors and jungles infested with reptiles and insects, from New Guinea and Guadalcanal to the black volcanic sand of Iwo Jima, the United States and her allies were simultaneously engaged in a deadly struggle to roll back the Axis nations in Europe and the Mediterranean. It was the strategy of President Franklin D. Roosevelt and Prime Minister Winston S. Churchill to break Hitler's Fortress Europe and then send the victorious Allies out to Asia to help Pacific Theater combatants force Imperial Japan to surrender unconditionally.

The United States, although strongly partial to Britain and her Western European allies, chafed under the yoke of neutrality legislation imposed by acts of Congress that manifested the post–World War I isolationist mood. Consequently, while Hitler's armies overran and occupied Western Europe, and while German bombers continually ravaged London and England's industrial cities, the most America's interventionist-minded president could do to help British survival was "lend" war material through various "lend-lease" agreements and send U.S. Merchant Marine ships across the North Atlantic laden with supplies for the beleaguered British Isles.

The Germans, of course, were not fooled by the American ruse. Therefore they unleashed their navy—and especially their submarines, or Wolf Pack—on U.S. Merchant vessels that eventually were armed for "self-defense." This meant that months before the Pacific Harbor attack, the United States and Germany fought an "undeclared" naval war in the North Atlantic.

Despite ever-growing naval confrontation at sea, America's full fury and strength would not be committed until December 1941 when President Roosevelt could—with neither restraints nor apologies—untether the nation's industrial and military giant to bolster Britain and join her to liberate the nations of Europe from Axis control.

WITH UTMOST URGENCY the army began its daunting task of turning tens of thousands of lads in their late teens and twenties into fighting men despite their knowing nothing of war beyond what they'd learned from Hollywood and World War I veterans. As quickly as the drill instructors toughened their young bodies for endurance and bridled their attitudes for discipline, the army tested, sifted, sorted, and finally assigned these twelve-week-boot-camp warriors to various camps across the United States. There they would learn how to kill Axis enemies with the expertise of the specialties for which they were selected. From California to New York, and Washington State to the Deep South, in divisions as diverse as armor and artillery, infantry and intelligence, paratroops and engineers, ordnance and communications, these basic training veterans were put through many months of specialized preparedness. Once these khaki- and olive-drab-clad troops had reached a modicum of combat readiness, they were shipped out to Britain for still more advanced training and preparation for invasions in North Africa, Italy, and the coasts of France.

ONCE THE WORD came down from divisional headquarters, most personnel were given brief leave time before embarking for unknown destinations. At every embarkation location, those deploying overseas scurried to say their good-byes to loved ones and tend to last-minute personal matters. As would be expected, battalion and regimental chaplains assigned to these troops had their own families to part with and personal obligations to settle. But invariably the sheep of the military flocks inundated their chaplains with cries for help of all kinds. Enlisted men, in particular, found themselves short of funds to get sweethearts to the port cities for personal farewells. Some missed connections and were not able to rendezvous at the planned destination, and desperately needed someone to meet a loved one with words of explanation. There were always men who had forgotten to sign the form for their $10,000 life insurance policy—given free to all troops but still requiring the insured person's signature and information about beneficiaries. The most administratively astute of chaplains had a checklist of these things, which they distributed to all personnel under their care. Nevertheless, some soldiers still failed to tend to these responsibilities on time, if at all. Consequently, long lines of careless men implored their chaplains to intercede on their behalf and get the impossible done at the eleventh hour.[2]

Chaplains managed to see their families and tend to their own personal needs yet still care for the emergency requirements of their charges. Letters were mailed, telegrams sent, money delivered, and ambassadors dispatched to stand in the gaps and explain why a loved one could not be there. One case involved a young wife and her baby who were left in a dingy rented room in New York with almost no money. Her soldier husband could not get there. She had traveled to New York from the camp where her husband had been stationed. The plan was for him to meet his wife and baby, and of course pay for lodging. But he was put on alert and given an assignment that would prevent him from seeing his wife and baby before shipping out. The chaplain went to see the frightened wife and explained why her husband had left her stranded and unnotified for two days. Then the chaplain arranged for the Red Cross to care for the destitute family and help them get back to their lodging several states away.[3]

Some incidents did not end so well. Army chaplain B. L. Bowman recalled his helplessness in one case, that he described as

characteristic of the type of service the Chaplain is called on to render in a staging area. A rather young soldier came into my office in great excitement. He, too, had been "alerted." He lived in New York but for months had been at a camp in a distant state. He had been in the staging area several days and had been allowed to leave Camp one time to see his wife. Through a friend, who belonged to the permanent party of the Camp, he had just learned that his wife had been taken to the delivery room of a hospital not more than thirty minutes ride from the barracks. His officer would not give him permission to go to be with her. Could the Chaplain help him out? The Chaplain tried, but could not. "That settles it" he said with great finality. "I haven't gone over the hill since I have been in the army, but I am going to the hospital to see my wife." Did he go? I do not know. What concerned me most for the next few minutes as I sat there thinking about him was what I would have done under the same circumstances.[4]

After the farewells were said and the mountains of problems solved, hundreds of officers stepped up the gangways, followed by thousands of enlisted men and women burdened down like pack mules with duffel bags full of gear.

Chaplain Arnold T. Olson, assigned to an infantry battalion, was in first-rate physical shape by the time his division "set sail for 'parts unknown' out of New York harbor." The Minneapolis native, by now in his middle thirties, recalled their days zigzagging across the North Atlantic to avoid Germany's dangerous Wolf Pack of submarines. Aboard the troop transport *George Washington* "the troops slept in narrow canvas bunks stacked three and four high. The enlisted men were served two meals every twenty-four hours. For example, if you had one meal at 1 p.m. your second would be at 1 a.m." The troops were given cards with their eating assignments. And despite the fact that "many were sea sick," you would take the food at the assigned hours or miss your meal. No exceptions. Olson remembered that "the chaplains conducted services every evening in a large lounge room which were well attended. Later in the evening some of us got together for a prayer meeting."[5]

Chaplain Clyde E. Kimball of the 1128th Engineer Combat Group admitted that despite a relatively calm sea, his stomach turned inside out. But as a spiritual leader of men, he had to tighten his belt and keep at his duty post. For him that post at sea was a little stateroom. At night the young soldiers would gather in his room "for a talk about forty eleven things. At thirty-five I am an 'old man,' so they love to question me, if only to argue with me."[6] Talking with the "old men" helped alleviate the homesickness, and friendly debates with their Holy Joe made the soldiers feel closer to home and perhaps closer to God.

Most chaplains on the troop ships helped conduct worship services, and they spent what could have been leisure time listening to and praying with people. One chaplain remembered giving out hundreds of New Testaments to Protestants and prayer books to Catholics. And he took advantage of the few days at sea where troops had plenty of discretionary time. To him anxious soldiers were not actually a captive audience, but at least they were bored enough to listen to his talks about God and his warnings about sexually transmitted diseases that lurked in every port and community where men went on liberty. For the most part the men were attentive and open to spiritual subjects. But by far the most spiritually hungry and alert to his counsel were the African-American troops.[7]

This chaplain never mentioned details of talks because as a minister he could not divulge such confidences. But years later he wrote, "I felt highly honored that The Great Judge of the Universe should have arranged it" that he could hear confessions and even "minister to a brother chaplain in distress." Priests, rabbis, and ministers, after all, needed spiritual care, too.[8]

CERTAINLY THE MOST famous and celebrated event in the history of the chaplaincy in World War II is the case of four army chaplains who served the soldiers and seamen on the troop carrier *Dorchester* in early February 1943. This story is replete with unusual gallantry and self-sacrifice, involving four courageous chaplains, including a rabbi, a priest, and two Protestant ministers (one a sacramentalist and the other a low churchman). If a person encountered this story in a novel, it would be dismissed as overly contrived.

But the events surrounding the sinking of the *Dorchester* did not come from the Cooperesque imagination of a second-rate novelist. On the contrary, this story reveals that history is often more captivating and inspirational than fiction.

The *Dorchester*, an army troop transport of 5,252 tons, was en route from Newfoundland to Greenland. She carried 751 army passengers, 1,000 tons of cargo, and a Merchant Marine crew of 130 men, plus a navy armed guard of 23.[9] During the late hours of February 2, the ship encountered such severe weather that Captain Hans Danielsen ordered all passengers to fully dress in their warmest clothes, put on their life jackets or belts, lie on their bunks, and be prepared to abandon ship, if necessary. Before midnight the *Dorchester* sailed into calmer waters, and the captain urged everyone to keep life belts and jackets on because "this will be the most dangerous part of our mission. [The German submarines]. . . can really spot us out there. I want you to go back to your quarters, lay down on your back with your life jacket and even your parka. We're not here for a beauty contest. It's going to be a dangerous thing."[10]

Some survivors of the imminent disaster remembered that the Catholic chaplain, Father John Washington, held services in the mess hall for men of all faiths. And all four chaplains "followed up with visits to the staterooms to raise the spirits of the men."[11]

At just a few minutes past midnight on February 3, only one hundred miles from Greenland, a torpedo ripped through the hull of the ship, which sank within twenty minutes in near freezing water and air temperatures. Of the 904 men on board, 678 perished. Among the lost were the four chaplains: Alexander D. Goode (Jewish), John P. Washington (Catholic), George Fox (Methodist), and Clark V. Poling (Dutch Reformed).[12]

The four chaplains—men from three faith traditions yet united in a holy mission—came from strikingly different backgrounds. George

Lansing Fox, born in 1900, in Lewiston, Pennsylvania, attended Moody Bible Institute in Chicago and Illinois Wesleyan University. A highly decorated World War I medic, he married and fathered two children and received ordination in the Methodist Church.

The birthplace and early home of Alexander David Goode was New York, where he was born in 1911. He earned a bachelor's degree from the University of Cincinnati and next went to Hebrew Union University, where he studied for the rabbinate. Goode eventually earned a Ph.D. in 1940 from Johns Hopkins University. He and his wife had one child, and he became a chaplain early in the war, applying to serve before Pearl Harbor. The Catholic chaplain, Father John Patrick Washington, was born in Newark, New Jersey, in 1908. A New Jersey man most of his life, he attended Seton Hall, as well as seminary in his home state, where he was ordained in 1935. Clark Vandersall Poling, a Dutch Reformed Church pastor, grew up in the home of a well-known pastor and writer. Born in Columbus, Ohio, in 1910, he received his undergraduate education at his denominational school, Hope College, and his divinity schooling at Yale. Like Goode and Fox, he was a family man, blessed with a wife and one child.

Forty men from among the 226 survivors provided testimony that outdid any legend. According to an official army historian, "they told of the round-the-clock ministry of faithful shepherds who visited the sick, led worship, and sang with men aboard ship in informal gatherings before that fateful night." Quoting a Red Cross source, historian Robert Gushwa wrote:

> They also told how "with utter disregard of self, having given away their life jackets to four men with them, the chaplains stood hand in hand, praying to the God they served for the safety of those men who were leaving the stricken ship on all sides of them."

Survivors told how all four chaplains not only gave away their life jackets, they quieted panicked men by offering words of encouragement and prayers while they distributed life belts from a box. One soldier said he would never forget that Chaplain Goode took off his gloves and gave them to him—saying not to worry because he had another pair. The last scene—a picture engraved forever in the minds of those who made it off the *Dorchester* and could see the chaplains just as the ship went down—was four men, hand in hand, praying to their God who had called them to serve.[13]

Pictures of the four chaplains and the story of their ministry on the *Dorchester* became ubiquitous during the war and after. Chaplain H. H. Heuer in the Office of the Chief of Chaplains was instructed to "make a big thing of it." But as Chaplain Gushwa noted more than thirty years later, Heuer did not need to do anything because "the American public made a big thing of it, for the story of the immortal four captured the imagination of the nation."[14] The news media understood what people on the home front hungered for—stories of heroism in combat undergirded by reverence for God and unity of purpose among the major religious traditions of the nation—so they kept the story alive. The military establishment also fanned the flame of this story because it reassured the folks at home that their loved ones were ministered to by faithful chaplains right up to the moment of death.

NO DOUBT THERE were other heroic actions by chaplains on troop ships, but their stories were never reported. Indeed, Rabbi David Max Eichorn related an event that took place in December 1942. Chaplain Eichorn, while he was stationed at Camp Croft, South Carolina, had developed a close friendship with Rabbi Goode and Father James M. Liston. One evening while the three men were playing pinochle, "Both Alex and Jimmy had a premonition that the ships carrying them to their respective overseas destinations were not going to make it." Rabbi Eichhorn said that "Jimmy told me that he had contributed $50 to a Boston church for masses to be said for the repose of his soul if he should be lost at sea." On the very same night that the *Dorchester* was sunk, another troop carrier bound for Ireland and part of the same convoy was torpedoed and lost. "Chaplain James M. Liston was on that other ship and went down with it," Eichhorn wrote. "I am very glad to have this opportunity to let it be known that not four but five heroic chaplains died for God and country in the cold waters of the North Atlantic on the night the *Dorchester* went down."[15]

Fortunately for the Allied war effort most transports reached their destinations as the U.S. and British navies became increasingly successful in challenging the German fleets. The bulk of the transports safely deposited their valuable human and war-materiel cargo where it would do the most good. Consequently, in concert with the British, America could equip and train troops to prepare for invasions of Europe while simultaneously taking the war to the continent with almost round-the-clock bombing raids.

Once American personnel and supplies safely arrived in the United Kingdom, chaplains faced new responsibilities and challenges serving the men and women in uniform who were placed under their care. Almost every U.S. military installation in Britain had at least one chaplain. Although not every battalion or air base had a chaplain representing each of the three traditions, all chaplains made a valiant effort to travel as needed to other camps and bases, making certain that all men and women in the U.S. Army had access to at least one worship service a week.

In England, Scotland, and Northern Ireland most chaplains were issued a jeep with a trailer, and they were assigned an enlisted man as a chaplain's assistant. These assistants did everything from drive

the jeep, type letters and orders of worship for services, to help prepare chapel facilities for meetings. The availability of jeeps helped
chaplains cover a lot of territory, and with a trailer they could bring
along cases full of the 194-page maroon hard-bound *Song and Service
Book*, as well as a fold-up field organ and field Communion set.[16]

Chaplain Captain Clyde E. Kimball, who would die in combat
in the Battle of the Bulge in December 1944, left behind a diary
that provides a glimpse of a chaplain who willingly made rounds
in England to serve as many troops as possible. In December 1943
this chaplain, who would be posthumously awarded the Silver Star
"for gallantry in action . . . displaying great personal bravery, volunteered to pass through fierce enemy machine gun fire in an effort to
render treatment and evacuate the wounded." Kimball blessed
many men by tirelessly traveling, speaking, and passing out Bibles,
stationery, and other useful items he would purchase in the PX
(post exchange).[17] During his brief stint in England, he visited and
served paratroops and men in hospitals and guardhouses. He
recorded that he traveled "a hundred cold wet miles today" where
"I visited men in bivouac" who "hiked seventeen miles, then as rain
fell, set up pup tents, and lined up for 'C' rations."[18]

Kimball, who was married and the father of two sons, served on
training maneuvers with the 1128th Engineer Combat Group.
"These troops are scattered and it is a hard job visiting them," he
wrote. One day he returned from his itinerating ministry "too late
for our hardening up exercises and my absence was commented
upon."[19] In January 1944 he wrote that "I'm tired tonight. However,
we must learn to do with little sleep, food, warmth, etc. Last night
it was about eighteen degrees and I froze all night long."[20]

Sandwiched into marching and maneuvers, Chaplain Kimball
managed to prepare sermons; he "took a man to town to see the Red
Cross Field Director about family troubles," and he purchased three

books on the English countryside because "they will give a number of officers and men pleasure. I'm afraid we'll not see much of the country, but can at least read about it."[21] He helped a U.S. sergeant cope with red tape surrounding his desire to marry a WREN (Women's Royal Naval Service) from Scotland, and helped another enlisted man who chose to go AWOL and suffer the consequences. Then on another night that typified his counseling ministry: "After dinner, officer hours. A long visit with a rather lonely new officer. Jewish, well-educated. His hobby being minerals, I gave him some specimens I'd picked up and put him in raptures. Then another man to see whose father had dropped dead."[22]

Chaplain Kimball typified many Americans stationed in England inasmuch as he enjoyed meeting English children. Recounting some of these moments of joy in his diary, he wrote that he experienced delight when "a child came up to me and said, 'Are you a real Yank?'" and he found much pleasure when being "besieged by kids asking for American gum and candy."[23]

If some of the Americans offended the British because the Americans were, as the English said: "overpaid, oversexed and over here," good chaplains helped build bridges of goodwill between local English and Scottish communities and the U.S. military. Hundreds of chaplains visited British clergy and took up donations to help rebuild public buildings and parish churches damaged by German bombs. The Yanks generously pooled their dollars to buy toys, Christmas trees, and food in order to provide Christmas parties for local children—especially those thousands who had been placed out from their city homes to live in towns and villages less vulnerable to Luftwaffe bombing raids. In the same vein, even small gestures made by Americans went a long way in promoting goodwill. For example, Colonel L. Curtis Tiernan, who would become army chief of chaplains for the European Theater of Operations (ETOUSA) later in the war, made a profoundly positive impression on the British by riding all over on his English bicycle, complete with wicker basket on the front handlebars to carry his briefcase. Petrol was rationed in Britain, and local civilians often resented all the Yanks who rode around in jeeps—even for weekend excursions. Tiernan, of course, had a jeep and a driver, but he rode his bicycle often enough that it endeared him to locals who had no choice but to ride their bikes or walk down the roads he traversed.[24]

CHAPLAIN GORDON COSBY, a married man in his late twenties when he became an army chaplain, was born and raised in Lynchburg, Virginia. A graduate of Hampden Sydney College and the Southern Baptist Seminary in Louisville, Kentucky, Cosby attended chaplain school at Harvard and went directly from there to Fort Bragg, North Carolina, where he trained with the 101st Airborne Division. While training with his 327th Glider Infantry Regiment in England, Cosby proved remarkably energetic and became an unusually able ambassador of goodwill among the English, while at the same time keeping many of the men he served out of trouble and engaged in good deeds. Cosby helped men build relationships with local churches—even organizing a soldiers' choir that performed for various English churches on Sunday nights. He started a Christian club for local boys, eventually gathering forty-five regulars for weekly meetings. This seemingly anointed chaplain tried to plug each man in his unit into a Sunday evening service with an English church, and he opened the way for his Yanks to have access to one or more of the forty-eight civilian homes that English clergy had helped open to offer hospitality. By December 1943 nearly a hundred soldiers in his regiment had found their way into English homes.

As a way of thanking the hospitable English, Chaplain Cosby organized a Yank-sponsored Christmas party for 254 English children, and some of his men put on a New Year's Eve celebration in a local church, where 73 locals and a group of American soldiers observed the turn of the year.[25]

Chaplain Gordon Cosby was an evangelistic Protestant—a Baptist by tradition. Therefore, during the weekly Bible studies, he organized and encouraged enlisted laymen to lead the groups where soldiers were taught about the life and claims of Jesus Christ. In the same vein, some of his occasional "Devotional Services" were pointedly evangelistic.[26]

Cosby's evangelistic endeavors, however, did not keep him from serving men of all traditions. When he led Sunday morning worship, the services were traditional but appropriately generic enough to encourage Protestants of most denominational persuasions. Catholic soldiers usually found access to priests and masses in the 101st training area, as did most Catholics deployed throughout Britain. But the small percentage of Jewish officers and men (Cosby estimated them at 1 percent) were neither ignored nor proselytized in areas where there were no rabbis. With the help of Jewish laymen, Chaplain Cosby arranged Friday evening services for the Jewish men in the 101st. And he was by no means unusual in his care for Jewish troops. Chaplain A. E. Autrey, a Baptist who served 8th Air Force personnel, regularly coordinated Friday night services and he located a rabbi to conduct a Seder service.[27]

In early 1944, as all officers and enlisted men began to sense that invasion and combat were imminent, Cosby's monthly reports reflected growing attendance at worship services and Bible studies, as well as men seeking one-to-one conferences. Typically during such times, men decided to get right with God. In Cosby's tradition this might be described as praying to "receive Christ as Savior," or a prayerful event referred to as being "born again," and then typically followed up with baptism. Although openness to such opportunities grew before invasion or when units were preparing to move up to "the front," in retrospect neither Cosby nor other evangelical Protestants could be certain if such experiences were genuine. Years after the war, Cosby wrote that his experiences in Europe caused him to be careful about the enduring effects of personal conferences:

One incident I recall took place in England. One night a young man came into my chaplain's office. He was from the same company as that of a man whom I had recently baptized. I asked, "How is so-and-so getting along in his Christian life?" He asked what I meant, and I said, "Just what I said, how is so-and-so getting along in his Christian life?" He replied, "I don't know what you mean." So I said to him, "Well, just a week or so ago, after several conferences with him concerning the meaning of the Christian life, I baptized him. I would like to know what progress he is making, what sort of witness he is making in his company." The young man, a faithful Christian and a good friend, put his head back and started laughing. He said, "If old so-and-so is a Christian, no one in the company knows it."[28]

Chaplain Cosby's incident notwithstanding, no one can quantify or qualify the ultimate effects of religious experiences that took place during wartime. But what is evident is that men and women in the armed forces were eager to acquire prayer books, New Testaments, Missals, and other devotional literature published by their respective traditions. These materials distributed by every chaplain were designed to foster encouragement during time away from home and during those agonizing weeks and days before entering combat. And given what these combatants, as well as the doctors and nurses who accompanied them, were about to experience, everything that would feed souls and strengthen wills for the firestorms ahead was considered invaluable.

* * *

AMONG THE FIRST Americans to invade Hitler's fortresses in Europe and the Mediterranean were those led by General Dwight D. Eisenhower. Between November 8 and early December 1942, the U.S. joined British troops in a major invasion of North Africa. While British General Bernard L. Montgomery was driving German General Erwin Rommel out of Egypt, Eisenhower and British Admiral Sir Andrew Cunningham landed forces at Casablanca, Oran, and Algiers. By mid-November Allied troops had advanced toward Tunisia, setting the stage for a gradual and costly advance against the Germans. U.S. General Lloyd R. Fredendall, who led the army's II Corps, was put on the defensive by Rommel's Africa Korps at Kasserine Pass in mid-February 1943. Although the Americans gradually regained the offensive, they would not decidedly break Germany's hold on North Africa until U.S. General George S. Patton replaced Fredendall as commander of the II Corps.

Beginning in March 1943, the American First Army and II Corps under Patton and the British Eighth Army under Montgomery battled in concert to surround the Germans, take the strategically vital gateway to North Africa—Tunisia—and force the Germans to surrender 250,000 men. It proved to be a costly victory. American casualties alone approached 20,000 men.

The siege of North Africa was the first test of American strength, character, and resilience outside of the Pacific. To the surprise of the German high command, who had assumed Americans were too soft to endure months of a bloody war of attrition, U.S. leaders and troops were willing and able to make the incredible sacrifices necessary to drive the Germans out of Africa.

American chaplains in the Pacific had been dragged through avalanches of blood, fire, forests, and rain with the troops, on island after island, beginning with Guadalcanal. Now these untried chaplains assigned to Europe and North Africa would slog through deserts pelted with rains of artillery, mortar, machine and rifle fire that would unleash a bloody flood of human bones and flesh. No one could have imagined the devastation they would face.

IN A PORTRAIT of U.S. Army chaplain Albert J. Hoffman, written for the *Saturday Evening Post*, April 26, 1945, Jack Alexander astutely observed that "a chaplain's role in war is largely what he makes it, and every good chaplain has ways of increasing his usefulness beyond the work described in the book." The book to which this journalist referred is the *Army Chaplain Technical Manual*, which army chaplains were required to study and apply.[29] The book might have been the skeletal outline of the chaplain's calling, but each man gradually developed his own muscles and flesh.

Chaplain Albert Hoffman, who inspired Jack Alexander's story, is remembered as one of the twelve thousand army and navy chaplains who brought life to the chaplain template each in his unique way. On one level Father Hoffman served similarly to all of his fellow chaplains. He traveled with the troops, marched, ate, and slept with them, and held worship services as often as circumstances allowed. Born and raised in Dubuque, Iowa, he grew up in a middle-class family. As a lad he loved to read popular boys books such as *The Motor Boys, The Frontier Boys, Tom Swift,* and *The Boy Allies.* He enjoyed most sports but never excelled enough to earn a letter. Always an able student with a flair for writing, he won scholarships to Catholic schools—both high school and college, and his writing eventually provided part-time employment as a sportswriter for the *Dubuque Tribune.* During college this able young man experienced a divine call to the priesthood. Always a first-rate scholar, he graduated magna cum laude from Loras

College in 1931 and became one of two men in his diocesan seminary selected to pursue his theological education in Rome.[30]

The scholar-priest, who served as an assistant pastor in a Dubuque parish beginning in 1935, entered the army in early 1941, to answer the call for priests to serve men and women in the armed forces. Assigned first to North Africa, then Italy, Father Hoffman was obsessed with caring for lonely and isolated men who had gone out ahead of their units to scout enemy lines. Such a man, if wounded, would likely be in a place no one could see. Furthermore, these soldier scouts would probably have donned camouflage and crawled in crevices, ditches, and shrubs. Disguised to fool the enemy, such a warrior would be hard for his own men to find, especially if he had been wounded.

It boosted the morale of infantrymen to know that there was someone in the regiment who was an expert at "crawling rescues." In the 133rd Regiment of the Thirty-Fourth Infantry Division, everyone agreed that the expert was Chaplain Hoffman. The priest became fondly know as their "bird dog." No wounded and hidden man was beyond his dogged sense. The warriors in his unit boasted that "the priest bird-dogged the wounded with the skill and persistence of a setter pointing and retrieving quail. Even the medics who were old hands at bird-dogging, willingly deferred to him "because he frequently 'got there first.'"[31]

The singular Chaplain Hoffman became a highly decorated sky pilot, being awarded the Silver Star for crawling into the line of enemy fire to pull a wounded man from the field of battle. Hoffman pulled scores of men to safety, taking no apparent thought to his own life. And if saving the wounded was not important enough, he was known to drive a jeep right into enemy territory, pile the dead and wounded onto it, and roar away to safety. If he seemed impervious to injury, he proved otherwise in Italy. His left leg was blown off by a German mine, and his right one was horribly mangled. But this did not slow him down for long. After several surgeries, and becoming adept on crutches and in a wheelchair, he traveled the rehabilitation units of hospitals to minister to men with wounds similar to his own. "Like them, among them, to show them God's love" became his mode of operation on and off battlefields.[32]

OTHER CHAPLAINS TAILOR-MADE their service to meet the needs of their environment. Historian Mac Davis provided a cameo portrait of Louis Werfel, whom he dubbed "the flying rabbi." According to Davis, "Louis Werfel was a Holy Joe." A studious rabbi in New York before the war, he wanted to be a soldier after Pearl Harbor. "But the Army declared him not physically fit."[33] Never easily discouraged, this brilliant Jewish intellectual eventually met the physical qualifications to become an army chaplain. After finishing chaplain school at Harvard, he begged his superiors to place him with men who were in areas of gravest danger, so they placed Werfel in the Twelfth Air Force, with assignments to fly from place to place where Jewish soldiers were at risk and without benefit of a rabbi. "Chaplain Werfel covered enormous distances by plane to be with Jewish troops fighting in remote parts of the world." As Mac Davis phrased it, "To them he brought hope and spiritual peace." Werfel did his utmost to encourage Jewish troops. Even in areas "with cannon fire and shrapnel slugs singing an ugly requiem around him, the flying rabbi would hold religious services." He would preach, if possible. If not, he spoke softly and briefly to each man, bringing the peace of God into some of the least peaceable environments imaginable. "One day he would be at some distant fighting front, and the following day he would be hundreds of miles away, serving his God," according to his biographer and his fighting comrades. The man who had failed the physical to enter the U.S. Army died serving the fighting forces of that army, when his plane crashed in Algeria.[34]

IF ARMY TECHNICAL manuals for chaplains contained no informtion on bird-dogging, crawling rescue, and puddle-jump flights from one front to another, they likewise failed to prepare men like Rabbi Earl S. Stone for instantaneous flexibility. Assigned to an army unit in Tunisia, Stone made plans and spread the word for an upcoming Passover Seder. But less than twenty-four hours before the holiday, he was taken aside and sworn to secrecy about a plan that their entire division would begin an all-night mobilization to attack the German line. According to historian Albert Isaac Slomovitz, because of the precise timing of the all-night march, ". . . it would be impossible to hold the seder meal. Consequently, Rabbi Stone assembled his Jewish troops in the desert and offered a fascinating service."[35] He remembered it this way:

> *In an open field that night, I stood before some 300 hardened veterans of six arduous months of battle. . . . I asked them to sit on the ground and to conjure up in their minds the memory of seder at home. . . . I recited the Kiddush [the prayer over the wine] with an imaginary cup of wine in my hand and had everyone break an imaginary matzo [unleavened bread]. . . . At the end of the service man after man, with tears flowing down his checks, bade me Gut Yontif [Happy Holiday].[36]*

As the imminence of battle nudged the Jewish troops with Rabbi Stone to find strength and solace in their ancient religious tradition, other men discovered that there was nothing like immediate brushes with death to awaken a latent belief in God. Philip H. Oxnam, a

Methodist minister from New England, observed that his battalion in North Africa included several men who often used foul language, displayed slight or no interest in worship services, and sometimes belittled and argued with men who expressed their faith by worship, Bible reading, and prayer. Chaplain Oxnam recalled that soon after the battalion had hunkered down for the night in an area presumed to be relatively safe from German attacks, everyone was awakened by "deafening noise. It was our first real air raid." The building where Oxnam and his assistant were sleeping had been hit. "The windows were shattered. The walls tottered." The Yankee Methodist said, "My clerk was blown through the door."[37]

All the survivors gathered outside, mingling in confusion with local Arabs. Then another wave of bombers came over, and everyone sought shelter in an abandoned sewer streambed that still retained the nauseous stench of its original purpose. Captain Oxnam said, "That night the men there experienced their first air raid." Many "grew up" during those early morning hours.[38]

The next morning Chaplain Philip Oxnam received a steady stream of visitors. From then on men attended worship who confessed they had not done so for years. One of the Catholic lads, whom Oxnam had been urging for several months to go to Mass celebrated by their Catholic chaplain, decided he needed God and made his way to the office of the priest. Oxnam credited that bombing raid for awakening faith in many men. "Church attendance has almost doubled since that day. The men's language has improved a thousand-fold."[39]

AMERICA'S MOST POPULAR war correspondent, Ernie Pyle, had a knack for ferreting humor out of frightful situations. He acknowledged that German aerial attacks were serious business, and no WACs or soldiers viewed them with anything but utmost respect.

Nevertheless, in the wake of these tension-filled assaults, humorists always emerged. Pyle particularly enjoyed the way one soldier comic made fun of himself:

> One morning I sat in a tent with a dozen airplane mechanics and heard Sergeant Claude Coffey of Richmond, Virginia, say:
>
> "I hear there's one man who says he was not scared last night. I want to meet that man and shake his hand. Then I'll knock him down for being a damned liar.
>
> "Me, I was never so scared in my life. As soon as those bombs started dropping I started hunting a chaplain. Boy, I needed some morale-building. A big one came whistling down. I dived into the nearest trench and landed right on top of a chaplain. Pretty soon, I had an idea. I said, 'Chaplain, are you with me?' He said, 'Brother, I'm ahead of you.' So we went whisht out of the ditch and took off for the mountains.
>
> "Anybody who says a scared man can't make fifty miles an hour uphill doesn't know what he's talking about. Me and the chaplain can prove it. Now and then we'd slow down to about thirty miles an hour and listen for a plane, and then speed up again. But in the moonlight the Jerries picked us out and came down shooting. I dived into an irrigation ditch full of water and went right to the bottom. After a while I said, 'Chaplain, you still with me?' And he said, 'With you? I'm under you.'
>
> "It never occurred to me till this morning what . . . fools we were to get out of that ditch and run in the moonlight. It won't happen again. After this, from six P.M. on, my address will be the top of that farthest mountain peak."[40]

Humor aside, the constant Luftwaffe bombing raids, complemented by days on end when the artillery and mortar barrage almost never stopped, took a massive toll on American and British forces. Of the nearly twenty thousand U.S. casualties in the North African campaign, 25 to 35 percent of all nonfatal casualties were psychiatric.[41] While medical doctors and experts in military psychiatry disagreed then and now about factors that might predispose a man to breakdown during combat, the truth is that even the best of men cannot survive long without a minimal amount of sleep required to restore the mind and soul. Some front-line men spent weeks in the center of uninterrupted roaring, whining, and deafening explosions accompanied by dust, flying debris, and tremulous earth. Screams, hideous wounds, and death became constant companions in this hellish environment.

Historians of the psychiatric effects of World War II wrote that during the Tunisian campaign and especially in the battles for Faid Pass and Kasserine Pass there was "a flood of psychiatric casualties, overwhelming the scant facilities for treatment hundreds of miles to the rear, and for a while evacuations exceeded theatre replacement capability."[42] Chaplains as well as doctors and nurses were asked to help with these wounded souls. The problem for chaplains was that fighting men needed their presence on the front lines. As one combat historian phrased it, "I hold it to be one of the simplest truths of war that the thing which enables an infantry soldier to keep going with his weapon is the near presence or presumed presence of a comrade."[43] And the evidence from testimonies of combatants is replete with observations of the encouragement men had when chaplains were near.[44]

That camaraderie proved to be a major ingredient in mental and emotional stability during combat is evident from the experiences of men in such divisions as the Eighty-Second and 101st Airborne, where massive stress had been placed on developing the "Band of Brothers" mentality. Only Army Rangers and U.S. Marines equaled these airborne units in inculcating loyalty to and interdependence upon one another. Men in these divisions manifested far fewer breakdowns because they hung on and fought on, not out of unusual bravery or hatred for the enemy, patriotism or fear of appearing cowardly. They carried on out of loyalty to their brothers. In brief, anything—even death—was preferred to letting down the brothers. What the military learned along the way was that "battle fatigue" was neither an aberration or cowardice, it was normal. Therefore, "supportive relationships" became a higher priority.[45]

That chaplains were as essential to caring for "battle fatigue" cases behind the lines as were nurses and doctors was generally acknowledged. But most chaplains who had joined combat battalions in training camps in the United States, then continued with them for invasion preparation in Northern Ireland or England and invaded enemy-occupied territory with these "sheep of their flock," were seldom inclined to leave their men for the hospital tents and ships miles behind enemy lines unless urged to do so by their superiors. A Lutheran pastor with a division under General Patton provided a glimpse of the significance of his presence during the fight. Chaplain William R. Thierfelder wrote, "today I'm crawling from foxhole to foxhole, and the men gobble up every word of encouragement. Some were reading their Bibles, others their prayer books." Thierfelder went on to describe how he helped a young man with a compound fracture of both bones in the lower leg. After the chaplain had helped take him back behind the line, Thierfelder "knelt down on the ground at the head of the litter and began talking to him very quietly. I took one of his hands in each of mine and told him to squeeze my hands hard whenever the pain got real bad." As the medic put the damaged leg in a splint to immobilize it, the chaplain held the young man's hands and asked him, "Phrase by phrase . . . repeat after me the Lord's prayer." The wounded lad squeezed hard, and by the time they finished the prayer, his leg was set and he was ready to be evacuated.[46]

The same chaplain was called to another soldier lying "on a litter

shaking so violently he could not stand up." He had received no physical wounds, rather he had been laid low from "battle fatigue." In a letter to his wife, the chaplain stressed that every physical and emotional
case is unique. In this case, however, he helped the shaking man stand
up and then had him look at men on litters with shell fragment wounds.
The fellow did not want to look, so his chappie "took him by the lapels
of his jacket and raised him to a standing position and held him up and
asked him if he were a Christian and did he believe in God's help for
those who believe in Him? Then, after a few minutes talk . . . I told
him to repeat my words, and we recited the 23rd Psalm together."
Thierfelder wrote to his wife that "these things made quite an impression on him. He had learned the Psalm, I could tell that he knew it.
Recalling it to his mind now renewed his faith in God. The power of
God's word is wonderful. . . . This lad . . . has since returned to duty."[47]

LITTLE IN CHAPLAIN school, technical manuals, or words of wisdom
from World War I veterans could equip chaplains for the problems they
would encounter with Jewish refugees. Already in North Africa, the
first German-occupied territory to be liberated, a prelude to what they
would find in Central Europe sounded through the ranks. As Judah
Nadich wrote, "The conditions obtaining among the Jewish survivors
of the holocaust varied from the liberated countries to the *Vaterland*
that had spawned the evil. Consequently, the problems that demanded
the immediate attention of the Chaplain in North Africa, Western
Europe and Italy were unlike those in Germany and Austria."[48]

Whenever possible chaplains assisted all displaced persons to find
safe shelter, food, and medical attention. They remained among these
refugees long enough to give them hope as well as some material support. But they could never remain in one place long enough to do
more than stand in the gap until Red Cross workers could come along

and provide more substantial care. In North Africa, however, liberation uncovered large Jewish communities with problems beyond those common to other civilians suffering the ravages of war.

Jewish chaplains in North Africa discovered entire Jewish communities still together, but they had been incarcerated in concentration camps. Their synagogues were destroyed by the Germans and the Vichy French who cooperated with the Nazis. The Jewish chaplains were implored by these newly liberated people to help them find Torah scrolls and functional facilities in order to reestablish religious and education life. Chaplain Louis Werfel, the famous "flying rabbi," managed to find fourteen Torahs and disperse them among refugee congregations. He also contracted American congregations and through them acquired Hebrew textbooks for the schools.[49]

The Nazi infrastructure designed to destroy all Jewish people with deadly efficiency remained underdeveloped in North Africa. The wretched situations chaplains encountered shocked and disgusted them to be sure, but conditions in Africa turned out to be almost minimal in comparison to the atrocities they would uncover in Central Europe and particularly Germany.

IN MAY 1943 German resistance in North Africa collapsed, and by July the Allies under General Eisenhower sat poised for an all-out invasion of Sicily and Italy. Beginning in July 1943, and continuing for twenty-one months, Allied forces tramped, skied, marched, crawled, and rolled through ingeniously constructed German defenses. American GIs loathingly referred to the campaign that would cost them and the British tens of thousands of casualties as the campaign of "mud, mountains, and mules."[50]

Because of press attention given to several major battles in the Pacific, and the obsessive focus on the invasion of France in 1944, the carnage, courage, and downright heroism that marked the Italian campaign attracted little attention. In fact, Americans heard little about the devastating battle up the so-called "underbelly" of German-occupied Italy that proved to be as strong as any part of the anatomy of Hitler's Fortress Europe. Chaplain Karl Wuest labeled the men of the U.S. Fifth Army in the Italian campaign as "the men of the 'forgotten front.'"[51]

A correspondent for the *Chicago Sun* reported in 1944: "It may surprise many Americans to learn that their Army Chaplain Corps has won more distinctions in proportion to its numbers than any other branch of service, including the air forces." H. R. Knickerbocker went on to say that "the chaplains have won such coveted medals as the Distinguished Service Cross and the Silver Star, never for killing but for saving lives, and none can count the number of souls they have saved. They have saved them from the actual hell of despair." The correspondent wrote that the chaplains' record "should make the clergy of America proud and should comfort the mothers of America."[52]

Regardless of how American home front clergy and mothers reacted to the work of these priests, rabbis, and ministers, the troops on the front and the doctors and nurses in the tent hospitals behind the lines celebrated the presence of the Holy Joes who followed the troops—fierce and treacherous fighting notwithstanding. A high percentage of the decorations awarded chaplains came during the campaign to liberate Sicily and the "Boot" of Italy.

ONE OF THE most highly decorated chaplains of World War II was Delbert Kuehl. Awarded two Bronze Stars while serving with the Eighty-Second Airborne Division in Italy, this graduate of the University of Minnesota (1941) went on to receive the Silver Star for heroic action in Holland, at the Rhine River. Born on a farm near Alexandria,

Minnesota, Kuehl claimed he never did anything that any brother in the Eighty-Second did not do or would not have done. In an oral history interview, this gutsy clergyman recalled that his unit embarked on an all-night assault on the German line over a mountain ridge in Italy. Then at dawn the U.S. troops pulled back. No sooner had they reached their pull-back position than one of the men cried out that some Yanks had been left wounded and lying immobilized on the German side. Kuehl said, "I talked to some of the medics and we got a couple of folding litters and found an old tattered Red Cross flag. You couldn't hardly tell what it was. I put it on a stick and said, 'We're going after them.' We all knew that if they were the more fanatical type Germans we wouldn't come back . . . .We started down the ridge. It was all open at the top and the Germans were down in cover below. They opened the machine gun. They hit right alongside of me and I got showered with little bits of stone and I thought, 'Well, this is it?' And they stopped. We gathered our wounded. I put one right over my shoulder and we climbed back over the ridge." Kuehl remembered that as soon as they brought the wounded into American lines, "they opened up again with everything."[53]

Another chaplain rewarded for his heroic performance was Israel A. S. Yost. He grew up in Eastern Pennsylvania and became accustomed to suffering as a child when his father was killed in an auto accident caused by a drunken driver. He published a memoir of his time as a combat chaplain in World War II and remembered that only "a few months after my twenty-seventh birthday, an association with a remarkable group of men was suddenly thrust upon me: I was assigned to the 100th Infantry Battalion (Separate) as a chaplain. These men were Americans of Japanese ancestry (AJAs), and all save a few of the original unit were from the Territory of Hawaii. Their officers, both Haole (Caucasian) and Nisei (AJA), were also from Hawaii. Committed to combat with the Fifth Army in southern Italy in September of 1943, the 100th soon distinguished itself. It earned the title of 'The Purple Heart Battalion.'"[54]

Israel Yost received a lot of ribbing during training. After all, why would the army send a Jewish chaplain to a battalion of Japanese-Americans who were predominantly Buddhist and Christian? He protested that there had been no SNAFU because he had been baptized, confirmed, and ultimately ordained in the Lutheran Church.[55]

Growing up in the upper Midwest, Yost had no experience with Japanese-Americans. Nevertheless, he bonded with these men of the 100th who would distinguish themselves as the most decorated and honored of all infantry battalions in World War II. His memoir, edited by his daughter, based on the copiously detailed letters he wrote to his wife during the war, reveals how he and the troops under his care battled almost impregnably fortified and determined Germans, as well as freezing weather and mountainous terrain, for nineteen months from Salerno, to Anzio, and on up to France. Ministering like other battlefield chaplains, this Lutheran pastor from rural Minnesota climbed into foxholes with infantrymen, helped medics retrieve the wounded, and spent countless hours burying American and German dead. When there were lulls in fighting, he visited the wounded, held worship services for men of all faiths, wrote condolence letters to families of the men killed, and finally did anything else he could to bolster the sagging morale of the men, whose KIA and WIA rates escalated with each major battle.[56]

Chaplain Yost proved dedicated to his men, and they held him in high esteem. In 1945 a soldier paid tribute to him in this way: "Chaplain Yost gave the impression not of a hero, shining with bravery in the midst of threatening danger, nor of the coward cringing with fear as the enemy fire ranged about over his head. Rather he seemed a faithful minister among his flock, moving about with loving unconcern, as though there were no more danger than in a parish in peacetime."[57]

Yost appeared unconcerned about danger, yet he knew it lurked everywhere. Indeed, he received the Purple Heart with a cluster during the Italian campaign. This admired sky pilot also received the Legion of Merit. His monthly reports reeked of carnage on every hand. But self-pity never slipped into the reports given to his regimental commander. With details of work most of his fellow chappies experienced, Yost wrote: "Troops in combat all but one Sunday, made group worship difficult, but men were visited and reminded of the day." "Organized litter squads when members of two regular litter squads were wounded or killed. Assisted Battalion Surgeon at forward aid station. Evacuated 14 men, killed in action, from hills by mule train. My assistant was wounded 10 January 1944, while acting as litter bearer in a forward position."[58]

Not everything done between Yost and his men entailed danger or was shrouded in woe. There were many interludes of joy. Because of the paucity of Jewish chaplains, during a quieter time Yost wrote: "Two nights, Wednesday and Friday, I took a few Jewish officers we have to Passover services in town [at Pisa]. . . . For tomorrow, Easter, I have some candy for the eleven or so children nearby . . . [and] while writing this soldier from our A and P platoon . . . brought me about 20 chocolate bars since he heard I was planning something for the kiddies."[59]

This sensitive and purposive man, whose ministry flowed from strong personal faith, quietly and without pressure urged men without religious life to consider becoming Christians. Most men respected the chaplain but showed little inclination toward Christianity. But some men did receive instruction and baptism, and thereby became members of the Lutheran Church. On Easter 1945 Yost conducted a 6 A.M. service to celebrate the Resurrection of Jesus Christ. He paid a local Italian to strew wildflowers around the makeshift altar that supported his field Communion set, complete with a cross and his Christian chaplain flag, dark blue with a white cross, which he draped as an altar frontal. His letter explained that "we read the Easter story responsively from [a] pamphlet. Six soldiers were baptized: the font was my helmet placed in between three rods stuck in the ground." Yost drew a sketch of his altar, flag, and baptismal font to accompany the letter.[60]

There were few Jewish chaplains among the Fifth Army troops in Italy, but Chaplain Aaron Paperman did arrive at Salerno soon after the beachhead was secured. In his capacity as the only Jewish rabbi with the Fifth at that time, he conducted a service "for the observation of the High Holy Days" in September 1943 and had the privileged distinction "to bring the first Jewish services held within the limits of the anti-Jewish empire, that Hitler had expanded to include the farthest limits of Europe."[61]

Among the Catholic priests who served the troops in Italy, none was as famous as Father Albert Hoffman, mentioned earlier during his tour of duty in North Africa. It was in Italy, however, where his leg was blown off near the village of Santa Maria Oliveto but not before he had distinguished himself by being awarded "the Distinguished Service Cross, the Silver Star, the Bronze Star, the Purple Heart, and the Italian government's Medal of Valor, making him the most highly decorated American chaplain of World War II."[62]

Father Hoffman might have been the most highly decorated chaplain, but he maintained a humble sprit. "In combat," he said, "no one stands out as doing anything heroic. Out there acts of heroism are commonplace. Probably the only reason that anyone gets a medal is that his deeds happen to be noticed and reported."[63]

DISPLAYS OF COURAGE in Italy appeared in places other than on the battlefields. A young lieutenant, Cleo W. Buxton, who engaged in heavy combat at such places as Santa Maria Oliveto, Mount Marone, Cassino, and Alban Hills, served as an infantry officer not a chaplain. But whenever possible he encouraged and assisted chaplains, doing all he could to gather enlisted men into small group prayer meetings and Bible studies when there were lulls in the fight. Like chaplains of all faiths, he attempted to provide wholesome opportunities for men with liberty passes, or a few days' rest in a town behind the line. In some of the towns and small cities where troops rested to restore minds, bodies, and souls before the next battle that "our experience told us . . . was going to be rough," Buxton would talk with local Italians and organize dances with folks in the community. He paid for "lots of good food, followed up by one of my favorites, ice cream." Whenever he could pull off one of these gatherings, "everyone had a good time, and not one man got drunk."[64]

Other choices open to these battle-weary men were not as wholesome or healthful. Women whose lives had been decimated by war and German occupation offered their bodies to men in exchange for money, American cigarettes, or food. Besides these war-ravaged women, there were the professional prostitutes who followed the armies in pursuit of their livelihood. Buxton remembered that "in each of those big R & R [rest and recreation] centers the army provided supervised houses of prostitution, which were certified free of disease." To this lieutenant's mind, "the brass seemed to care a lot more about the soldiers' health than they did about their morals. I was given to understand there were MPs inside that would take your dog tags and you wouldn't get them back until you had a cleansing treatment. But I never knew how they could be sure, unless the doctors checked the girls between each customer. Those poor women might have sex with seventy or eighty men a day."[65]

In the face of much criticism and ridicule from many officers and enlisted men, Buxton and the chaplains urged the men to refrain from these sexual encounters for reasons of health and morality. Some chaplains, on the other hand, urged the men to take army-provided prophylactic kits with them when they went on liberty just in case they succumbed to temptation. Such counsel infuriated most chaplains.[66]

Problems escalated in the wake of sexual promiscuity in Italian R & R centers. The venereal disease rate skyrocketed among soldiers during the Italian campaign, as it would again in France and Central Europe in late 1944 and 1945. STDs placed an added burden on medics, doctors, and nurses, and caused otherwise able-bodied men to be out of combat for days or even weeks. As well, chaplains found a marked upturn in numbers of men suffering from spiritual depression—many of whom sought their chaplain's counsel in the darkness of guilt.[67]

A few officers like Cleo Buxton, as well as some courageous Jewish, Catholic, and Protestant chaplains, aggressively confronted the obvious problems manifested by sexual encounters outside of marriage. Army doctors and chaplains had always given lectures in camps on the home front. And these exhortations to refrain from promiscuous sex were repeated in every base overseas. Chaplains tucked the message into their sermons, and their personal consultations, but some officers took still bolder steps. Buxton claimed he saw "lines three or four blocks long of guys waiting for a prostitute. In the military we were used to waiting in lines all the time, but my mind boggled at standing that long just to have sex like an animal." He labeled it "mass copulation."[68] In the fashion of a biblical Jeremiah, Buxton and other officers and chaplains sometimes walked the long lines of soldiers who were bored, battle-weary, and intoxicated. They urged men they knew and those they did not to consider the consequences. "Do you want this on your conscience when you next see your wife or girlfriend?" "Do you want to take this tawdry memory on your honeymoon when you get home?" "Do you realize this is a sin against God and the woman you use?"[69]

Most soldiers in the lines ignored the challenge to walk away, but some stepped out. Chaplains and officers got plenty of criticism for being "holier than God" and "guilt-peddlers." And men who walked away from these sexual temptations common to all healthy men were verbally chided for being "Puritans" or "emasculated men."[70] In the face of ridicule most men merely followed the biblical precept to "turn the other cheek." Some, on the other hand, offered to cleanse the temple of the morally corrupt if they did not remain quiet. One chaplain, Father Ignatius Maternowski, "a tough, energetic little Pole" from Maryland, "had been extremely well liked and respected by the men of his regiment." According to a fellow chaplain, "On more than one occasion he had volunteered to put the gloves on with officers who interfered with his work, tried to wise-crack about the Church, or made smart remarks about confession."[71]

CHAPLAINS LIKE MATERNOWSKI, whether in Europe or the Pacific, knew men well enough to understand that their ability to fight well was inextricably interwoven with the health of their souls. And the health of men's souls seemed closely related to the presence of men sent by God to minister to them. Chaplain Edward K. Rogers, a Lutheran minister who served from North Africa to Sicily and on into France, Belgium, and Germany with soldiers of the Eighteenth Regiment, First Infantry Division, described his understanding of the combat chaplain's ministry this way:

> When some come to inquire of their religious needs, which they have never cared for, he is happy to try and meet those needs—or show how God can meet them. . . . There are a host of subjects on which the soldiers from time to time will consult the chaplain.
>
> A lot of innocent kidding may keep many away from seeing the chaplain when problems come. . . . Some soldiers perhaps get the idea that only the "crybaby" goes to the chaplain. . . .

But the chaplain is there to help and many appreciate his being there. Others don't care about him, for they have had no religious faith and contact with the church, or have lost faith and broken those contacts since getting into the army. Nevertheless, the chaplain wants to be where some may need him. If they avoid him and the message of God which he offers, that is their misfortune. They can't say that the church forgot them, when they were called into service and henceforth in their lives they will forget the church. They may forget the church and God, but the church and God's pastors or priests did not forget them.

The psalmist once wrote: "If I make my bed in hell, behold, thou are there." The chaplain, I guess, leaves his parish so that when the soldier gets into the hell of war it will be true that God is there, through his ordained ones, to help, encourage, forgive and bless.[72]

Probably nothing during the Italian campaign did more to bring these words from the psalmist into the hearts and minds of soldiers than an event early on Easter Sunday 1944. The 349th Infantry of the Eighty-Eighth Division had dug in near a German front about halfway up the Italian peninsula and below Rome. As soon as word went out that the 349th would be on the line, the regimental commander and regimental chaplain executed a bold plan for the men at the front. A forward observer wrote: "Originally the idea was to set up loudspeakers to make Catholic and Protestant services audible to all. However, since some of the companies were directly in front of enemy positions, it was impossible to get the services over to them without being heard by the Germans. What would be their reaction?" After a brief discussion it was decided to open the worship service in German because "the Christian Religion is for all races and nations, for enemies as well as friends." The chaplains, some of whom spoke fluent German, "determined to hold a short German service for the enemy soldiers at the very start."[73]

On Easter eve regimental soldiers laid wire and set up loud-speakers. Rear echelon personnel, including nurses, made their way to the front to worship and observe. Early on Resurrection day Chaplain O. H. Reinboth, a Missouri Synod Lutheran minister of German descent, began to read the traditional service in German and English. Words of scripture and praise "broadcast by loud-speakers across the four hundred yards of devastated no-man's land to enemy lines." After reading the Gospel in German, Reinboth cried out: "Should not all Christendom be jubilant this day? Should not all people rejoice—now that Christ died and rose again for all men—for Germans and American alike—therefore, I wish you also today in the name of my soldiers a Happy Easter."[74]

A United Press correspondent stood among that singular congregation and witnessed that "through powerful telescopes there could be seen no sign of movement in the German lines. Their guns had not spoken since the ceremonies began." James E. Roper continued: "The doughboys had been told to lie low in their foxholes" and listen to the service over loudspeakers. Gradually, however, men began to slowly move forward and gather around a small altar that had been carried up by mule pack in the early dark hours of the morning. Then First Lieutenant Charlotte Johnson, a nurse from Ohio, sang "I Know That My Redeemer Liveth," composed by German-born George Frideric Handel.[75]

Thanks to some God-fearing American chaplains and a supportive regimental commander, hundreds of soldiers on both sides of the battle line learned with the psalmist: "If I make my bed in hell, behold, thou are there."[76]

CHAPTER EIGHT

THE FALL OF THE THIRD REICH

1944–1945

The chaplains have all taken courses in first aid and frequently they reach and bandage the wounded before the medics. But that's not their chief value. Their greatest work is in healing fear-torn hearts and giving hope to the hopeless. Most boys dying on the battlefield would rather see a chaplain than anyone else.

H. R. KNICKERBOCKER[1]

D URING the torturous campaigns in North Africa, Sicily, and Italy, U.S. troops in the European Theater were making preparations to invade Nazi-occupied Western Europe along the coast of France. Indeed, Rome fell totally into Allied hands on June 4, 1944. Two days later, the massive Allied invasion of Normandy, France, Operation Overlord, began.

In preparation for this inevitable assault on France's coast, the British had been raining explosives from the air on German installations since 1940. Starting in late 1942 and early 1943, the American Eighth Air Force, with its ever-growing bomber groups of B-17s and B-24s, plus the U.S. Tactical Ninth Air Force, with its continuously improved and expanding fighter planes, became a welcome complement to the British Royal Air Forces.

Beginning in January 1944 the Allies prepared for the land invasion with an accelerated air assault unlike anything ever seen in the history of air warfare. Day after day and night after night, British and American bombers dropped tens of thousands of tons of explosives designed to cripple German factories, rail lines, airfields, shipping yards, and communication centers. During early 1944, the Allied air forces were dumping a storm of fiery destruction on German cities and military installations. On March 6, 1944, the American contribution to the air war reached its peak. That day alone more than eight hundred U.S. planes made strategic strikes on targets all over Germany and surrounding areas.

Germany burned and bled, but by no means did she break. Nazi antiaircraft artillery units were widespread, well equipped, and superbly trained. America's B-17s and B-24s were legendary in toughness, but as Stephen E. Ambrose wrote, the Germans brought them "down in staggering numbers."[2] In the Eighth Air Force 6,537 B-17s and B-24s were lost in Europe during the war, and 3,337 fighter planes went down in flames as well.[3] The per capita casualty for Army Air Force crews earned the dreadful distinction of being the highest of all units in both European and Pacific theaters in World War II. And because casualties were so extensive, bomber crews originally retired after twenty-five missions. But a shortage of experienced crews forced the air force to extend the requirement to thirty-five and at times even higher.[4]

Because German tenacity and resilience appeared to know no limits until early 1944, despite the uninterrupted airborne pounding, some observers feared the Germans were supernaturally invincible. Certainly Nazi resourcefulness encouraged some of Germany's leaders to hope for a peace settlement rather than unconditional surrender.

*   *   *

MOST ARMY AIR bases in England had regular chaplains assigned to one or more locations. Since these chaplains typically had a jeep and an assistant, there were Protestant and Catholic worship services offered every Sunday, and sometimes meetings were offered during the week. Jewish rabbis were not on as many bases as Protestants, but mobility was not a problem, especially in England, where most bases were located. Jewish chaplains made their rounds quite efficiently. Consequently, most Jewish crew members and base-support personnel were at least provided with regular Sabbath services, even if they could not find a rabbi for one-to-one counsel as easily as Christians.

Protestants comprised approximately two-thirds of the chaplain force at any given air base location, and as a result of their numbers air force personnel had ample access to counselors, as well as worship services. But Catholic officers and enlisted personnel, in particular at bomber bases, seemed to be especially well cared for. A common theme that emerged from interviews with World War II air force people was the splendid care given to bomber crews. Typically flight crews were informed of a private room open to Catholics just prior to a bombing mission. There a priest would hear confession, offer Holy Communion, and anoint the crews. In the same vein, when bombers returned from missions, a priest would almost always be available to perform last rites on KIA crew members, as well as anoint and pray for the wounded fortunate enough to have made it back to base. Nearly sixty-five years later, Lee Watson, the pilot of a B-24, recalled, "Oh how we were strengthened by having Holy Communion before a mission." He said the chaplains "were great for us." Just knowing they would be there "to give last rites when the plane landed, and to care for the wounded" bolstered morale enormously.[5]

*   *   *

PHOTOGRAPHS ARE LEGION of chaplains of Catholic, Protestant, and Jewish persuasion blessing air force crews, paratroopers, and glider crews as they prepared to make the initial assault on France, D-Day 1944. Equally common are pictures of chaplains blessing ship crews and their precious cargo of army officers and men who were about to storm the beaches of Normandy.

On June 6 more than 176,000 Allied troops were packed into 4,000 invasion craft, supported by 600 warships and air cover of 11,000 planes. And this massive armada would be preceded a few hours in advance by the descent of thousands of British and American parachute and glider troops behind and inside German lines.

DURING THE INITIAL invasion by sea, Chaplain George R. Barber found himself crammed into an invasion craft with thousands of men pumped so full of adrenaline that every noise or movement alerted their senses. About four miles from the Normandy beach, Chaplain Barber, who stood six feet tall and towered over most of the troops, took off his helmet, allowed his totally shaved head to show (he said he shaved it because he wouldn't be able to wash his hair for a long time), and asked the men who could hear to join him in prayer. Many men removed their helmets and bowed their heads as the chaplain, only two months shy of his thirtieth birthday, asked God to bless "this great event so we could bring freedom to the world."[6] Barber's ordination had been in the Christian (Disciples of Christ) denomination and on D-Day he carried nothing but a backpack with a few personal items and a Bible. He had given away piles of pocket-sized Testaments, so now he traveled light, with little but "the Armor of God."[7]

Between June 4 and June 6 Chaplain Barber had managed to deftly board eleven invasion crafts floating at anchor in the harbor. In each vessel he spoke a brief message of hope and the importance of reliance upon God, followed by a general prayer. Now at approximately 2 P.M. he stood in the midst of anxious men on one craft, trying to lift the burden of their fears that were much heavier than their packs, rifles, ammo, and gear strapped to their strong but tremulous bodies. At the sound of a horn and the words of leaders, Barber and about thirty men climbed over the side and down a rope ladder into a rocking Higgins boat. As soon as all were aboard, the little landing craft surged forward and then rolled and swayed its way toward Omaha—one piece of a sixty-mile beach the Allied forces had been hitting since the break of dawn.

Although initial landings at Omaha had begun about seven hours earlier, the fighting along the strip of coastline designated Omaha Beach was still heavily besieged by German artillery and machine guns. Barber remembered that as soon as they hit the water, "I first saw death by seeing bodies in the Channel." He asked, "Are we going to pick up those bodies?" An officer told him to keep moving forward: "They'll be picked up later on."[8] Barber spent the next few hours helping medics bind up wounds. He prayed with dying and wounded men, saying: "I'm your chaplain and I'm here to help you. God is going to see us through. God knows you. He loves you." He recalled that the beach seemed a noisy and chaotic glimpse of Hell.[9]

Not all the wounded and dying men had chaplains nearby. William Nesbitt, a young medical doctor assigned to the Seventh Naval Beach Battalion, landed on Omaha several hours ahead of Barber. He never saw a chaplain on his troop carrier or on the area of beach where he cared for the wounded and dying. On the contrary, this devout Christian and graduate of Duke University's medical school "conducted religious services for those who were on board both during the invasion and on the return to England."[10] His task as a medical officer "was to provide temporary care for the wounded and prepare them for evacuation to military hospitals in England." On D-Day he carried out his duty while enemy bullets, mortar, and artillery fire pummeled Omaha Beach. He wrote that "the vision of hundreds of casualties lying quietly in rows, lonely, in pain, silently pleading for someone to comfort them, lingers in my mind." Decades after the unforgettable event, Dr. Nesbitt grieved that he did not have time "to go down those rows and kneel beside each man, say a prayer, offer an encouraging word, take a message for a loved one."[11] But as he and Barber both experienced, the noise of battle was so loud that many of the wounded could not hear words of comfort and prayer.

UNIT HISTORIANS, VETERANS, and chroniclers of troop movements debate trivia such as who landed first in various invasions. Students of World War II argue about chaplains as well. Indeed, several men have been honored as "the first army chaplain to wade ashore on bloody Omaha Beach." One historian asserts that Ralph Haga, a Virginian who pastored a Methodist church before the Pearl Harbor attack, served as chaplain of the Sixty-First Medical Battalion in the Fifth Engineer Special Brigade Group, was the first chaplain on Omaha Beach. It is quite possible that Chaplain Haga, who distinguished himself by ignoring his own safety and working tirelessly to aid battle-torn combatants, and went on after the cessation of hostilities to help establish the American cemetery at Colleville-sur-Mer, indeed put his boots on the sands of Omaha Beach before any other sky pilot.[12] Nevertheless, a month later *Stars and Stripes* suggested that Captain Julien Ellenberg, of Greenwood, South Carolina, was "perhaps the first chaplain to land with the troops." According to *Stars and Stripes*, by July 4, 1944, less than a month after D-Day, Ellenberg had "been awarded the Silver Star for his work in the initial operations. According to the citation, Captain Ellenberg came in with his unit about 39 minutes after the first landing craft touched and immediately began to aid the wounded." The article celebrated this dedicated chaplain who "stuck with his men at an aid station while it was almost completely demolished by German 88s."[13]

It is doubtful that either Ellenberg or Barber cared who hit the shore first. Like thousands of survivors on that day when more than 49,000 casualties were estimated by 10 P.M., they probably thought the most important thing was that Germany's vaunted "Atlantic Wall" had been broken.[14] By July 2 the Allies would pour approximately 1 million troops, 172,000 vehicles, and more than a half million tons of supplies into Normandy.[15]

This costly but massive victory did not end the war with Germany. It would require eleven more months of destruction and death to bring the stubborn Third Reich to its knees. But after June 6, 1944, the final outcome of the war in Europe was never in doubt.

DURING THE BATTLES to establish beachheads on the code-named beaches Utah, Omaha, Gold, Juno, and Sword, sustained ministry of the kind chaplains had been trained for disintegrated. Sometimes it took days for combatants to reunite with their companies and battalions, and chaplains also became separated from their units as they struggled to survive and help the wounded with emergency care. It could also take several days for chaplains to find their battalions. But once reunited with them, the chaplains went to work, with some providing Holy Communion even if a mess kit served as a paten until portable Communion cases could catch up to the fast-moving troops. Others simply led prayer among small clusters of worshippers huddled under trees, or jumped fox-hole-to-foxhole to offer words of encouragement to the men.

One veteran, Ernie Denk, a devout Christian who attended chapel services faithfully on the home front and in England before D-Day, remembered that in the battles of Normandy, Northern France, the Ardennes, the Rhineland, and Central Europe—the five engagements where he served as a sergeant with the 462nd AA, he never saw a chaplain unless his battalion happened to encamp or hunker down near a local church. Then the word sometimes circulated that a chaplain would hold a service, allowing a few of the men to find their way to a house of worship.[16]

European theater chaplains who served with units in combat from June 1944 until May 1945 tell the same story. Burt Biddulph, who served with a battalion of combat engineers, in peacetime served as a Protestant minister in the Free Methodist Church. Under the offices of the Methodist denomination, he bemoaned the paucity of chaplains available to care for so many battle-weary men. By January 1945, he said, "We were so short of chaplains. There were two of us— one Catholic and me—to care for over five thousand who were added to our 1159th Engineer Group. While we sometimes had sustained ministry in the days prior to crossing the Rhine River, after crossing in early 1945 I was always looking for my men and seldom found them. We went looking for engineers but seldom got to the place before they had moved out." Consequently, he had his assistant offer ministry to little clusters of troops along the way, holding services in barns, beer halls, or any other fairly safe and enclosed location.[17]

Improvisation became the rule of ministry. Chaplain Biddulph's jeep broke down, so he walked alongside the troops. One-to-one counseling became almost impossible except for a brief talk on the move. While assigned to the Ninth Armored Division, Biddulph provided no formal worship service with music because without a jeep he could haul neither a fold-up field organ nor cases of songbooks. "Our biggest contribution was encouragement. Our own officers depended upon us to give encouragement to the troops, and it was not unusual to have a company commander point to some men scattered along the line and beseech one of us chaplains to go and just talk to the men."[18]

The diary of Chaplain Bernard S. King reveals a similarly chaotic environment. Although he was assigned to an infantry unit several months after D-Day, and therefore did not serve in the chaos of the invasion and early days and weeks in Western France, this thirty-one-year-old married man from Minnesota learned that his ministry across Central Europe and on into Germany would seldom consist of regular Sunday worship, let alone a service complete with music, songbooks, and preaching. Chaplain King, an ordained minister in the Christian and Missionary Alliance, sometimes traveled by jeep. But like Biddulph he walked or rode and became a pastor constantly on the move—dodging enemy artillery flak, taking shrapnel on his helmet, and exulting in an occasional barn or other local structure where he could pull in a few men for a simple service of Bible reading and a brief message of exhortation and hope. Men of the 355th Regiment of the Eighty-Ninth Infantry Division sought out Chaplain King because they knew chaplains were not required to be on the front lines, and yet their chaplain, according to his official citation, stayed with them: "Chaplain King throughout the entire campaign accompanied lead elements of the battalion despite frequent heavy opposition. Under most adverse conditions Chaplain King administered the needs of his men performing his duties with zeal and unflinching faith."[19] As they came under regular fire from the Germans, King's presence offered comfort to these soldiers who wondered if they would see another sunrise. Simply having their chaplain nearby suggested God's hand rested upon them in an environment haunted by death.

AMERICAN CHAPLAINS IN Europe after D-Day did more than stay with their units during heavy combat; like their counterparts in North Africa, Italy, and the Pacific, they worked alongside medics to care for the wounded and became able litter bearers. Chappies also fulfilled the important responsibility of keeping records of the dead, marking on hastily drawn maps locations of temporary graves, holding proper burial services whenever possible, and finally writing condolence letters to the next of kin for every soldier killed under their care.

An example of how a good combat chaplain stayed abreast of killed and missing men can be seen in the records of Chaplain Henry Wall. A Catholic priest, Father Wall was assigned to the Eighty-Second Airborne Division, 325th Glider Infantry, Company C. The padre was given a company roster on March 14, 1944. It contained the names of 154 men and identified their religion, serial number, as well as the name and address of nearest of kin. In the immediate wake of the unit's landing inside France on June 6, 1944, Father Wall gathered reports from platoons, examined the dead, and made notes by each name if that man was KIA, WIA, or MIA. Of the 154 infantrymen, one was Jewish (H), forty-six were Catholic (C), and 107 were Protestant (P). It seems incredible that of the 154 men, 20 were KIA, 47 WIA, and 30 MIA. In brief, 97 of 154 men were dead, wounded, or missing. And of course the mortality rate would rise because some of the wounded would die and invariably some of the missing combatants would be found dead.[20]

Father Wall's notes were clearly made from a well-used and rather blunt pencil. And he carefully noted that one man killed that morning, Staff Sergeant Sam Marinos from Birmingham, Alabama, was Greek Orthodox. Although he was not a Roman Catholic, this caring priest embraced Marinos as his own, performing last rites, overseeing a proper burial, and finally notifying the deceased man's closest survivor.[21]

* * *

ANOTHER CATHOLIC CHAPLAIN, Francis L. Sampson, who served with the 101st Airborne Division, dropped into France on D-Day along with Father Wall and the Glider Infantry of the Eighty-Second Airborne. Father Sampson wrote that arrangements were made for him and his fellow Protestant chaplain "to fly back and forth between the airports so that we could see all our men prior to D-Day and H-Hour." Before this last-minute circuit flying ministry, Chaplain Sampson "had each man write his name and put it in a box beside my tent when he went to confession so that I might be able to check up later to make sure all the Catholic men received the sacraments. Though confessions took more than three full days, it was a great satisfaction to know that all the Catholics of the regiment had fortified themselves in the sacrament of penance." On the eve of departure, it took Father Sampson an hour to distribute communion at the two Masses. Consequently, "I could later write with certainty to the parents of men who did not return from Normandy that their sons had been well prepared for death."[22]

All of the 101st men were loaded with extra gear along with their rifles, ammo, four boxes of K rations, and blood plasma. The planes caught heavy flak flying into their drop areas, and at least one soldier on Sampson's plane had shrapnel in his leg before jumping. The Germans were ready for the Yanks, and they cut parachutes and men to ribbons as they descended toward the ground through semidarkness. Sampson landed in a deep stream, and it took ten minutes that seemed like an hour to get him disentangled from his chute and harness. Once free, the sacramentalist chaplain realized he had lost both his medical and Mass kits. More medical supplies could be found, but his Mass kit, with its sacred contents, was another matter. Father Sampson dove five or six times into that deep, cold stream and "miraculously"—as he put it—recovered his religious kit.[23]

Chaplain Sampson's experiences during the first hours and days after the invasion epitomized the chaos of war and the singularity of most men's experiences in it. While Chaplain Wall prayed with the wounded and dying, and made copious notes on his company roster, Father Sampson, who had entered chaplain school in 1942 only a year after ordination, moved slowly with a few men under the cover of hedgerows, in search of more paratroopers. The first paratroopers they encountered were not from the same regiment, but they indicated the area where those men must be. "We went in the direction they pointed until we came under heavy enemy fire. We ducked into a nearby farm house where we found about twenty-five troopers, all wounded or injured from their jump."[24] It was a small, three-room house still occupied by the farmer, his wife, and their little daughter, who were doing their best to assist the Protestant chaplain care for the wounded.[25]

Sampson remained with the other chaplain. Together they cleaned wounds, sprinkled sulfa, and applied compresses. Later that afternoon a wounded soldier "came in and told us that he and his buddy had been shot a hundred yards or so from the house. His buddy still lay where he fell." Sampson and Chaplain McGee (Sampson never learned his first name) immediately set out to find the soldier. When they found him, "he was already dead. We dragged him back, rolled him in a blanket and put him in the shed. Then a mortar shell hit the back door of the house just as the French woman and her little girl were bringing in water from the well. Both were killed. As I knelt to anoint them, the farmer threw himself on their bodies and broke into agonizing sobs. When I put my hand on his shoulder, he jumped up, his hands and face smeared with the blood of his loved ones, and went yelling down the road shaking his fists in the direction of the Germans."[26]

The farmhouse carnage turned out to be a mere prelude to several horrific days for Sampson and the men he encountered. More shells hit the house and outbuildings and some of the wounded were killed. As a few German paratroopers approached the house, Sampson made a white flag and went out to meet them. His goal was to protect the immobilized Americans before the Germans leveled the house assuming it was a fortified trap. One of the Germans charged Sampson, put a Schmeiser (machine gun) in his stomach, and shoved him against a hedge, since he could not either understand or care less that Sampson kept insisting he was a chaplain. Just as the soldier stepped back and pulled the bolt of his weapon to shoot, a German enlisted man who spoke English fired a shot in the air to attract attention away from Sampson. He then consulted with the other Germans, who allowed him to take Chaplain Sampson to an officer who ordered his men to let the priest stay with his wounded comrades. In the midst of this nearly fatal encounter, it became apparent that the German who intervened was a Catholic. In fact, he even saluted his captive when he saw his chaplain credentials. Sampson said he then "made a slight bow, and showed me a religious medal pinned inside his uniform. . . . (I was so glad of the universality of the church)."[27]

The disputed area where Chaplain Sampson cared for his wounded American soldiers changed hands more than once. Only after much fighting did the Yanks push the Germans out, leaving Chaplain Sampson to spend several days at a division hospital set up in a French château. There he attended "between two and three hundred wounded . . . lying on the lawn [and] about the same number in the main building."[28]

Father Sampson arrived at a field hospital in dire need of doctors and medics. He found that the "hospital chaplain, Father Durren, looked completely washed out. He had had scarcely any sleep" for several days. "I told him to go to bed," said Sampson, and "that I would take over." Before Chaplain Durren agreed to rest, he showed the 101st chaplain that he had "tagged the men he had anointed and indicated on the medical tags of the other men those whose confessions he had heard." There were many Germans as well as Americans among the wounded and dying. Sampson learned that "about sixty percent of the Germans were Catholic, and they always made the Sign of the Cross when I took out the stole. They made acts of contrition and received Viaticum [Communion given to a dying person in danger of death] reverently as well-instructed and good Catholics. These, I later learned, were mostly from Bavaria. Many of them were in their early teens; some had not even begun to shave."[29]

Francis Sampson prayed with Protestant and Jewish soldiers, and he allowed the hospital chaplain to sleep for several hours. During this busy time he witnessed tenderness and a helping hand offered to dying Americans from a German lad who himself had only a few minutes to live. When Chaplain Sampson left this hospital unit a day and a half later, he set out to find his own regiment and serve them on the front. And despite the hardships he would endure with his men, he concluded that "front-line duty is not nearly as tiring, I think as hospital duty, especially when the wounded keep pouring in as they did those first few days."[30]

DURING JUNE, JULY, and August 1944 Allied armies battled tough and tenacious German armies all across France. British and U.S. forces continued to enter Europe through Normandy, and by August the Allies, including the Fifth and Seventh U.S. Armies, pressured the Germans in France from the south and west. Paris was liberated on August 25, and three days later General George Patton's Third Army reached the Marne River forty miles east of the city. By early September France, Belgium, and Luxembourg had been liberated and the Allies had landed nearly 2,100,000 men and 3,500,000 tons of supplies.

Besides the challenges of performing all their usual duties, army chaplains encountered some special problems. As soon as Paris was liberated and secured, thousands of U.S. troops were pulled off the lines and given a few days of R & R in Europe's most glamorous city, while others gradually marched eastward. Consequently, one chaplain who gathered his statistics from official army sources reported that "during our first three or four weeks in Paris our VD rate went up 300%." Chaplain Cornelius Van Schouwen wrote in his diary on Sunday December 10, 1944, that 105 soldiers attended his worship service. He also recorded: "We have 1,200 WAC [Women's Army Corps] under this command." He noted that the VD rate among WACs was 1 percent, while the rate among the 17,500 soldiers in Paris was 15 percent.[31]

Van Schouwen, ordained in the Christian Reformed Church and married, with a wife in Illinois, became increasingly occupied with servicemen who suffered with STDs. "The doctors told me," he wrote, "that Penicillin neutralized syphilis temporarily. Most of the cases the medics treat are for gonorrhea. They say that syphilis can be dormant for some time and reappear later."[32] The bespectacled, pipe-smoking Protestant suggested that part of the problem must be laid at the feet of chaplains who refused to "offend" anyone by calling the troops to live lives committed to Christ. Indeed, one soldier in Paris told him, "You are the second chaplain I have heard that dares to preach Christ and Him crucified." Whatever the underlying problems, this evangelical pastor celebrated hopeful signs when he saw them: "Our WACs, compared to the soldiers, have an excellent record as far as VD is concerned. Our biggest problems are French girls who solicit on the streets."[33]

Rabbi Morris N. Kertzer saw the situation from a different angle. He wrote: "The hazards of war were not all at the battlefront. Our men were granted a kind of dispensation from the fourth, sixth, and eighth Commandments [Sabbath, murder, stealing], and often they let the seventh [adultery] slip into the 'list of exceptions.' They attended chapel regularly, but their moral standards were far from puritanical. . . . G.I. Joe tended to be careless in his morals, yet more pious in mood and general behavior than he had been as a civilian."[34]

Chaplain Van Schouwen also saw that the men in his battalion needed to be steered away from more than sexual temptation. They became angry when criticized by French civilians and army officers for not providing more milk for French babies and food and cigarettes for everyone else. Heaping still more insults on their American liberators, the French demanded payment for every facility the Americans needed to conduct the war effort through France. In short, this busy chaplain had to pour a lot of water on the heated tempers of U.S. soldiers who were about ready to turn their weapons on the French as well as the Germans.[35]

Serving as a coolant to hot tempers and helping ameliorate causes and effects of a VD epidemic were only part of Van Schouwen's new duties in France. He also found time to minister to British troops who lacked the benefit of spiritual comfort. This chaplain felt a burden to care for the souls of all people within his range of influence. He passed out hundreds of New Testaments and Christian tracts. He also counseled U.S. soldiers and women (usually French) when they asked for army permission to marry. In order to protect both parties to a marriage, he refused to perform marriages until the couple had "a six month courtship." Frequently, if the soldier was sent to the front or assigned to a different unit, "that is the end of the courtship. During my stay in Paris," he wrote, "I interviewed a large number of applicants for marriage but did not marry a single couple."[36]

A CHALLENGE VAN Schouwen and almost all chaplains faced, once they got deep into France and on into Belgium and Germany, involved the plight of refugees. Father Jean P. Cossette, born in Massachusetts but educated by Dominicans in French-speaking Canada, was thirty-five years old when he was commissioned in the army and assigned to the Eighty-Third Infantry Division. Every bit as evangelistic as some of his fellow Protestant chaplains, he gave out thousands of Catholic Missals, Sunday prayer books, and pamphlets, as well as countless Rosaries and medals. Father Cossette also taught catechism classes, and he performed baptisms for new believers and organized "Army of Prayer" groups among soldiers. He even sent postcards to Catholic families who had soldiers under his spiritual care and encouraged them to join the "Army of Prayer" for protection of the men's bodies and souls.[37]

Father Cossette's fluency in French made him an invaluable asset to officers in his regiment. He frequently served as an interpreter when French displaced persons were being evacuated, and his fluency with the language enabled him to help the army build good relations with local authorities and townspeople when U.S. troops needed to occupy a town. This Canadian-educated padre conducted memorial services in French for local people and he celebrated Masses for French displaced persons who no longer had a parish priest. His linguistic skill worked equally well once the Eighty-Third entered Belgium. Although he did not speak Flemish, most Belgians knew French. Therefore the chaplain could build bridges with the Belgians almost as easily as he had done with the French. During his months in French-speaking regions, Chaplain Cossette became famous for taking the problems of local people to the military, and presenting requests from the military to local people. He also became an advocate for both French and Belgian people in dire need of medical and welfare assistance.[38]

Cossette did not forsake the soldiers under his care, despite his concern for civilians. Whenever possible, he visited the wounded, as well as men in "exhaustion centers" who suffered battle fatigue. But most of the time he was on the line with the men at the front. During the Battle of the Bulge, for instance, he reported that conditions were so horrid he could not conduct Mass. Nevertheless, he moved from one company area to another to encourage the men and offer prayer. Indeed, twice he was awarded the Bronze Star for "heroic achievement" in France.[39]

CHAPLAINS WHO SPOKE fluent German became even more important to the U.S. war effort. Pastor Oscar W. Schoech, for example, a Missouri Synod Lutheran, was forty years old when the war ended. Married with two children under ten years of age, Schoech had served as a chaplain in the Army Reserves since 1939. In summer 1940 he was called to active duty, and his fluency in German prompted his immediate assignment to Europe. Serving first with a field artillery unit and later with the Eleventh Armored Division, this man who had faithfully pastored a Lutheran Church in Parsons, Kansas, became an invaluable aide to his entire division as a translator. Schoech frequently helped with the interrogation of German prisoners. As his unit increasingly encountered displaced persons who had information to pass on to the Americans or who had needs that the ever-generous Americans tried to meet, Schoech proved to be invaluable.[40]

Chaplain Schoech's sensitivity to hurting refugees, especially ones with little children, became well known. Once when driving his jeep, he came upon a refugee of Polish descent with her two little girls. The woman's back was broken, and as the chaplain's report read, "no one was able to help her. I borrowed a litter and with my ¼ ton truck [jeep] placed her two small children in the care of other Polish people."[41]

BY DECEMBER 1944 the American high command believed that the German armies were broken and would soon surrender. Some of the British were less sanguine about Germany's imminent collapse. In any case the evidences of a German buildup on their western perimeter near the Belgian and Luxembourg borders were discounted by the American military. General Eisenhower confidently dismissed the evidence, arguing that not even Adolf Hitler could be audacious enough to attempt a counter attack.

On the morning of December 16 a German counter offensive erupted along an 80-mile front in the Ardennes. The Germans planned to split the Allied forces and capture Liege on the Mense River and then Antwerp. Even when news reached Generals Omar Bradley and Dwight Eisenhower, they did not immediately sense the gravity of the situation. An hour later, however, they learned that dozens of German divisions were involved in a massive breakthrough, including eight divisions that had not previously been spotted on the western front.[42]

Despite the valiant efforts of scattered American companies and platoons, the German assault could not be quickly repulsed. Because American commanders had been convinced the Germans were retreating into a totally defensive position, they had pulled thousands of men off the front. Furthermore, many of the most experienced U.S. combatants were on leave behind the lines— already enjoying what they expected would be a relatively quiet Christmas season in Paris or parts of Belgium and Luxembourg.

Their positions had been recently filled by inexperienced replacement troops who had never fired a shot at the enemy.

Although General Eisenhower would finally see the full picture of the German advance and ultimately reposition his armies to check the German drive, the cost of these intelligence and preparedness blunders was enormous. It took until January 21, 1945, to restore the original line of advancement. The Battle of the Bulge resulted in seventy-seven thousand U.S. casualties. Approximately eight thousand Americans were killed and nearly fifty thousand wounded. To make this disaster even worse, twenty-one thousand U.S. soldiers were captured or declared missing in action.

Chaplains, like all troops, paid a heavy price for the gross ineptitude of U.S. upper echelon leaders. Numerous chaplains, like the men they served, died unnecessarily in the line of duty. One instance began very early on the morning of the breakthrough. A company commander of the Ninety-Ninth Infantry Division recalled the initial assault that included an artillery bombardment lasting about one hour. "Time appeared to stand still. . . . My mind seemed to reject the reality of what was happening to say it was make believe. . . . One of our young lieutenants danced a rubber-legged jig as he twisted slowly, making the bullet hole between his eyes clearly visible. One moment our battalion chaplain and his assistant were kneeling beside their disabled vehicle. The next moment they were headless, decapitated by an exploding shell as if by the stroke of a guillotine."[43]

Another casualty in the Bulge was Captain Clyde E. Kimball, a Protestant minister whose civilian pastorate was in New Hampshire. He regularly wrote a diary designed to keep his wife, Ellen, informed of his experiences and reflections on the war. Kimball's last entry in a collection of nearly two hundred pages was recorded on December 18, 1944. This minister attached to 1128th Engineer Combat Group had been through much combat with his men. By early December his diary reveals a deep sense of sadness that he will not be at home on Christmas with his wife, but at least there is relative quiet and joy with the men. On December 6 he writes: "I guess our units have taken up a collection of their candy and gum for nearby [Belgian] kids, or will do so at the time of our Christmas. This company has some musical instruments captured by others at Aachen. I can hear men practicing on them now in another room." He also mentions looking at the picture of his two-year-old daughter whom he had never seen and wishing he had a "miniature fur jacket" to send to her.[44]

On December 8 Kimball tells his wife that holiday festivities are beginning for all the men: "I came into my own camp last night. I held a Jewish service, the first since Normandy. It was an appropriate coincidence that it was the anniversary [of Pearl Harbor]. Part of the service is the sipping of a little wine to remember the feasts at home. I've been carrying some they bought months ago. They had a revenge on the Jew-persecuting Nazis by using a captured swastika-marked cup. I preached from Proverbs and gave them copies. In autographing them, one boy turned out to be a Catholic man who had driven some men. I autographed his copy as having been used by a Roman Catholic at a Jewish service conducted by a Protestant. We read in unison from them."[45]

December 18 was Chaplain Kimball's last diary entry. He informs his wife: "I am, as is so often the case, with a unit. Sort of roughing it for a few days. I am supposed to be a prince's guest, hunting in a couple of days, but may not be able to keep the date. This unit is very busy." To be sure, they were busy. Kimball always downplayed the dangers so as not to alarm his wife. But his unit was scrambling because the Germans were breaking through several lines in the forest of the Ardennes. The next day Kimball would distinguish himself "for gallantry in action on 19 December 1944. . . . When medical personnel were not available to render aid to a unit suffering heavy casualties . . . Chaplain Kimball, displaying great personal bravery, volunteered to pass through fierce enemy machine gun fire in an effort to render treatment and to evacuate the wounded. While on his courageous mission, he was ambushed by infiltrating Germans and received severe wounds which resulted in his death. Chaplain Kimball's conspicuous valor and unflinching devotion to the welfare of his men reflected credit on himself and the military service." These words appeared on Kimball's posthumously awarded Silver Star citation.[46]

CHAPLAINS NOT ONLY died in the Battle of the Bulge, many were captured by the Germans and became part of a massive throng of American PWs who experienced much suffering during the last five months of the war. In the Bulge, German troops captured nearly 21,000 Americans, adding a burden to Germany's already large PW population. Prior to December 1945, 26,000 U.S. airmen were captured, and another 10,000 Americans had surrendered in Northern and Western Europe. All totaled, approximately 56,000 American officers and men in Germany lived behind barbed wire. The biggest haul of prisoners at one time came when two entire regiments of the 106th Infantry Division, 7,500 officers and men, surrendered at one time.[47]

From one angle of vision, these soldiers who comprised the German catch of 21,000 prisoners were lucky. At least they survived. Others were less fortunate. Some German units—in particular the vicious SS—refused to take prisoners during the Bulge. Indeed, during the SS race through the Ardennes, they slaughtered at least 350 U.S. soldiers who raised their arms or waved a white flag. The most infamous incident occurred near Malmédy, a Belgian village just a few miles above Luxembourg and west of the German border. Early one afternoon the Germans overran a U.S. field artillery battalion—

all of whom promptly surrendered. After the Germans briefly interrogated more than 100 officers and enlisted men, including medics wearing red crosses, they lined up the men and then gunned them down with machine guns, rifles, and pistols. Almost ninety men perished. The few who escaped into the woods during the slaughter or pretended to be dead in the blood-soaked pile of bodies, quickly reported the atrocity. Word of the massacre spread like a virulent infection, causing Americans to stiffen their defenses, eliminate surrender as an option, and determine to destroy Hitler's army.[48]

Jesuit historian Donald F. Crosby discovered that U.S. troops in the Bulge no longer viewed SS troops as well-trained elite fighting men; they now saw the storm troopers as evil animals deserving extermination. One Catholic chaplain who had the responsibility of attending American and German wounded in a field hospital found himself praying: "From the SS, deliver us, O Lord." This same priest discovered he could not turn the other cheek when an SS prisoner who was laid out on a hospital cot sat up and "in haughty Hitlerlike fashion and language broke into an insulting tirade against the Americans for my benefit until I rapped him across the teeth."[49] Most men who fought the SS would have applauded the chaplain. And another man of the cloth, Chaplain Leo Weigel, argued that the SS was "a menace that should be exterminated now because it will not be checked any other way." Father Weigel's conclusion about the SS took form in part after learning about the massacre near Malmédy, but he and the others were also well aware of the unarmed Belgian civilians—at least a hundred—who were slaughtered by the diabolical SS during their blitz through the Hürtgen Forest.[50]

AMERICANS WHO ESCAPED the fury of storm troops but found themselves as PWs during the December 1944 breakthrough did not fare well. It is true that the German Luftwaffe operated all prison camps for Allied airmen, and it is generally accurate to describe the treatment of U.S. Army Air Force prisoners as reasonably humane. The Luftwaffe prided themselves on being urbane gentlemen, and this posture poured over into the PW camps. If the records of First Lieutenant Jesse Marlow Williamson, whose P-47 plane was shot down in late 1943, are typical, he and other airmen PWs in Stalag Luft 1 near the Baltic Sea were treated humanely. His papers reveal that he was allowed to mail a postcard or letter home to his mother at least twice a month. His living conditions were spartan but clean, and the Red Cross parcels were dispensed to all the officers in his area. Food rations did not offer a balanced diet, but until early 1945 (he was in from December 1943 until May 1945) there was at least stale brown bread and potato or pea soup enough so that the men lost a minimal amount of weight.[51]

By early 1945 conditions for all American prisoners had drastically deteriorated. There were few camps large enough to accommodate the massive influx of prisoners, and many functional camps had to be evacuated as the Americans, British, and Russians began to push the retreating Germans into ever-decreasing portions of land. Consequently, even airmen were placed in nearly uninhabitable locations. William Turner's experience beginning February 21, 1945, was common. Turner served as the bombardier on a B-24. His bomb group, based in Italy near the Adriatic Sea, made a bombing mission over Vienna. After they had dropped their bombs, both inside engines were knocked out and the pilot knew they could not return to their base. Outside of Vienna the crew bailed out. They were captured and forced to subsist in truly terrible conditions. After being marched miles to a transit PW camp, Turner received a bath, an overcoat, a pair of gloves, and a scarf. He did not have another bath during his sixty-nine days of confinement, and for eighty days he never slept without all of his clothes on. He and about three hundred other men were marched to their first "permanent" PW camp at Nuremberg. "After arriving at the camp, we were processed and assigned barracks. We walked in and saw one empty room about eighty feet long and twenty-five feet wide. An American captain was inside to greet us. We asked him where the beds were and he said: 'Men, there is absolutely nothing here.'" The captain did not exaggerate. Only a bare room: "no bed to sleep in, no baths, no fire wood, nothing." The food proved to be almost as sparse as the camp. A "slice of bread in the morning, and some watery soup in the afternoon. That was all."[52]

William Turner recalled that they were also without benefit of a chaplain. An American major had a Bible and led Sunday morning and Wednesday evening services. He read Scripture and the men sang hymns from memory such as "The Old Rugged Cross" and "Rock of Ages." For the men who knew only one verse of a hymn, they all sang the same verse two or three times. While the Protestants sang hymns, read from the Bible, and prayed, "the Catholic boys read their Rosary every morning and had their own service." On Easter Sunday morning 1945 the German guards permitted a British chaplain PW to make the rounds into all the compounds. "He had words of encouragement for us and prayed for our loved ones at home."[53]

On April 6 all the PWs at this camp were marched into Southern Germany. They covered 140 kilometers in fifteen days, to a camp a few miles north of Munich. There they remained in even poorer conditions and on short rations until the Yanks liberated them on April 29.[54]

Turner's difficulties proved to be minor compared to thousands of other Allied prisoners. Chaplain Burt Biddulph remembered liberating a PW camp of American airmen. He recoiled in horror at what he saw. The Americans had been "treated horribly. They slept on damp and cold floors on nothing but straw. They had been given almost nothing to eat for months." These conditions did not exist because their captors had nothing more to offer. The liberators discovered a building filled with food for the prisoners and denied to them by the camp commandant. Chaplain Biddulph, serving with a combat engineers unit of the Ninth Armored Division, grieved most when his regiment had to push on after only a day. It broke his heart to leave these men who so desperately needed physical care and spiritual nurture.[55]

In another PW camp, at Hammelburg, near Schweinfurt in Northern Germany, 435 American officers were imprisoned in a facility once used as a Serbian PW camp. Official investigations of this camp and several others by the Swiss Red Cross documented how crucial spiritual care was to the imprisoned men. At Hammelburg, with more than four hundred officers, there were nine chaplains: seven Protestants and two Catholics. Despite wretched living conditions and food rations causing malnutrition, the spirits of the men were relatively good. Protestant and Catholic worship services were held regularly and often, providing spiritual nourishment to men who were losing weight on the average of four to five pounds per man per week. U.S. officers begged the German guards to place some of these chaplains in the enlisted men's areas because they had no chaplains. Finally in March 1945 two chaplains were pulled out and sent to an enlisted men's compound, but the Germans generally frowned on placing officers (even chaplains) with men in the ranks. This so distressed chaplains, who felt constrained to offer spiritual care to all prisoners, that some were known to write sermons, tie them on rocks, and heave them over fences so they could at least be read among the enlisted men.[56]

Living conditions in the enlisted men's compound were equally dreadful but without benefit of clergy. A Red Cross report done on the Hammelburg camp revealed in March 1945 that for three months men lost "at minimum 5 kilos" or eleven pounds. These prisoners were being worked in coal mines—sometimes seven days a week. In one PW camp farther east and beyond Nuremberg, at Weiden, the U.S. workers, who put in ten-hour days had no day off for a month, found some solace when a British PW chaplain finally secured permission to get outside of his compound and visit the working parties.[57]

The Swiss Red Cross sent their workers to German Catholic priests, hoping the organization's good offices could open the way for local priests to get Communion supplies and Bibles into the camps. There is no evidence in the National Archives revealing the extent of their success, but Catholic Chaplain Francis L. Sampson's memoir mentions that "the Swiss failed to help the prisoners very much, but one thing they did do that I appreciated was to obtain for me an outside *Ausweis* [identity card] that allowed me to leave the camp to visit American working groups within a radius of a hundred miles." Father Samspson, serving with the 101st Airborne Division and captured near Bastogne during the Bulge, traveled by bicycle with a German Catholic guard, and as a consequence he was able to secure more favors—including reduced work days—for the enlisted men in labor gangs outside the main camp. Sampson was also able to meet and develop a relationship with the Catholic priest at Neubrandenburg and through him get small favors for the prisoners in the camp and among the labor groups.[58]

Chaplain Sampson also secured favors in food and medical supplies for Allied Prisoners when German guards came to him seeking pastoral help. About a quarter mile from the camp "the Germans had a large army hospital. . . and it was packed with wounded." As a faithful priest who willingly served suffering men, he wrote: "At the request of the guards I had gone there on several occasions during the preceding months to anoint dying Catholic German soldiers."[59]

* * *

PROBABLY THE MOST heartrending assignment undertaken by Sampson during his time as a PW came when the Russians "liberated" Stalag II-A in Eastern Germany. In late April all the PWs knew liberation was imminent as the thunder and earth-shaking from Russian artillery grew closer each hour. On the night of April 28 German guards fled as the Russian tanks and infantry rolled into the region. Sampson shuddered as he recalled that "the events of the next few days were to be among the most terrible I have ever seen." He observed that "these Russians soldiers seemed to be wild men."[60] These soldiers from the east—drunk on vodka and victory, put the torch to the entire city of Neubrandenburg. They burned the hospital where Sampson had anointed and prayed for German soldiers, and it seemed obvious that as the building became engulfed in flames, all the wounded patients met their end in a raging inferno. Even more devastating to the eyes and mind of this sensitive American chaplain was what he found as he and a friend PW, also a chaplain, arrived at the local Catholic Church rectory. "The house had been partly destroyed by fire and two sisters, both nuns, and [the priest's] mother and father had come to him for protection. The priest and his father were sitting on the steps, obviously in a state of extreme shock." The three "women huddled together on a couch." One of the sisters spoke to the French priest and confessed that "the three women had been violated by a group of Russian soldiers while their brother and father had been forced to watch." Sampson and his chaplain friend asked if they could do anything. "They shook their heads. I judged that they were on the verge of losing their minds; they were certainly beyond tears and beyond receiving any expressions of sympathy. A rosary hung from the fringes of the old woman. As she sat there with her eyes closed, I couldn't be sure that she was alive."[61]

What those two stunned chaplains had witnessed became just one glimpse of what Allied soldiers and their chaplains uncovered as they battled their way across Hitler's crumbling Third Reich.

AS MUCH AS possible, Jewish, Catholic, and Protestant chaplains served the refugees they encountered along their way across France, Belgium, and the Netherlands. While they offered assistance to people whose dwellings had been demolished, and trying to place an ever-growing line of orphans in the care of Red Cross workers and Catholic nuns in convents along the way, the first signs of Nazi oppression quickly appeared. Chaplain David Max Eichhorn, a tall, thin, and erect man in wireless spectacles, maintained a neatly trimmed mustache that conspired with his receding dark hairline to make him appear ten years older than his age. Only in his early thirties when the United States entered the war, Eichhorn had grown up in a small industrial city on the Susquehanna River, near Lancaster in Eastern Pennsylvania. Privileged to be raised in a prosperous family that encouraged him to develop his alert mind, Eichhorn grew to be a lover of books. His pursuit of religious education led to Hebrew Union College in Cincinnati, Ohio, where he became a rabbi in 1931.[62]

Early in his career, Eichhorn served a Jewish congregation in Texarkana, on the border of Arkansas and Texas. This Pennsylvanian whose parents had emigrated to American from Germany in the 1890s soon moved farther south, to direct the Hillel Foundation at the University of Florida and later to serve as rabbi of Tallahassee's Temple Israel.[63] By the time Rabbi Eichhorn volunteered to be an army chaplain, he was married and had four children under the age of ten.[64]

Because the U.S. Army assigned Eichhorn to the XV Corps, he moved continually—serving nearly a year in areas of heavy combat, with parts of the First, Third, and Seventh Armies. During his duty across France, Belgium, and on deep into Germany, he had the privilege of ministering to scattered Jewish soldiers who sometimes were gathered from rather far-flung lines in order to receive ministry from a rabbi.[65]

One practice that distinguished Eichhorn from Catholic and Protestant chaplains was his constant search for Jewish people who had managed to secure shelter and evade the searching eyes of the Gestapo's men, who were determined to carry out Hitler's "Final Solution" to the "Jewish Problem." In a report Rabbi Eichhorn wrote to the Jewish Welfare Board on August 14, 1944, he offered a glimpse of the horrors he discovered that only grew worse during the next nine months:

August 14, 1944
France

[Report to the Jewish Welfare Board]

Today I have come to the end of a search, a search which lasted five weeks and covered many a blood-bathed mile. Because of the military censorship I cannot tell you the exact name of the village where I am at the time writing this. Let it suffice to state that it is not too far from the French village of Le Mans and that it is a little rural town which only days ago was filled with the sounds of war and now is quiet in that strange sort of way in which all towns and countrysides are quiet after the sights and noises of warfare have proceeded on their fearsome way. A beautiful sunset fills the evening sky as I sit on a bench in the middle of a grassy pasture, balance my typewriter on two sawhorses and recall a period of my search—my search for French Jews who have escaped the keen eye of the Gestapo and the crazy wrath of Hitler. Ever since landing on Omaha Beach July 10, I have been ask-

ing people in the various cities and villages through which we have passed, "Are there any Jewish people here?" Invariably, the reply has been a sad shaking of the head and a "Non, messieur, there are no Jews left here." Once, when I inquired at a Norman farmhouse near Perriers, a grave peasant woman (after giving me a welcome gift of two precious chicken's eggs) told me a gruesome tale. The Jews of that part of Normandy had been gathered together last April, with a number of Christian hostages, and had been transported to Germany. There the Jews had been placed in specially prepared vans and had been literally boiled to death by being exposed to jets of live steam that spurted at them from the inside of these vehicles of destruction. The Christian hostages had been forced to bury the bodies of their Jewish friends. The hostages had been told that they were to return to Normandy and tell their neighbors what they had witnessed. They were to tell their neighbors that they would meet a similar fate if they aided the Allied troops if and when these troops invaded their country. This tale had been told my informant by a woman who had been one of the hostages. Today I had come to visit an evacuation hospital, to contact its Jewish personnel and to seek to comfort its wounded patients. Later I visited the 647th Medical Clearing Company which was nearby. When I returned to the hospital, I was met by my assistant, Corporal Irving Levine of Chicago, beaming as only Irving can beam. "Chaplain," he cried excitedly, "while you were gone the most astounding thing happened. A lady and two children came into the area with a basket filled with eggs and pears to give to the wounded (the French have been wonderfully generous in sharing their pitifully small possessions with their American liberators, especially in their gifts to the wounded and their flowers showered upon the heads of the living and the graves of the dead). When this lady passed our jeep and saw the Magen David on it, she became very excited and ran up and asked in the purest Yiddish, 'Bist du a Yid?' Chaplain, you could *have knocked me over with a feather. I told her I sure was and we've been chewing the fat in her French Yiddish and my best Chicago Yiddish ever since. She is waiting for you at the jeep."*

Yes, there she was, standing by the jeep, holding in her hands a Jewish Welfare Board Siddur which Irving had given her. She was trying to read the first Hebrew book she had seen in five years. She was about 35 years old, prematurely gray (as were all the other adult refugees I was yet to meet, save one), but very alert looking and supremely happy. Her children, a boy of twelve ("I hope now he will be able to become Bar Mitsva," she said) and a darling girl of nine, looked quite typically French. She had been born in Poland but had come to France when she was four years old and she regarded herself as almost native-born French. Her husband, a Polish citizen, had been in a concentration camp in East Prussia for two years. She had not heard from him in seven months. She had left Paris when her husband was arrested and had come with her mother and children to a village eight kilometers from the hospital. Her family had been protected by the mayor and the villagers, all of whom knew that they were Jewish. Only once had she been in danger. An English warplane had bombed the village by accident. A woman, whose home had been destroyed and whose child had been killed by a bomb from this plane, threatened in retaliation to turn the helpless Jewish family over to the Vichyites. The villagers told the grief-crazed mother that, if any harm were to come to the Jewish strangers in their midst, her own life would be forfeit—and that ended that. Later we met our refugee's mama, a haggard old woman of 69, very poorly dressed, who cried when we talked to her and, in very fluent Yiddish, assured us that not one day, during all her troubles, had she neglected to say "Krishma"—and now God had answered her prayers.[66]

Jewish Chaplain Morris N. Kertzer had countless experiences with Jewish refugees similar to those of Eichhorn. Serving with the Fifth Army in North Africa and Italy prior to 1944, he encountered Jewish refugees, but the Germans had not been able to do much more than segregate and humiliate them. Once Rabbi Kertzer entered France in 1944, however, he found that the few Jewish survivors were in dire need of food, medical assistance, and personal care. One of the most painful parts of his calling as a chaplain involved Jewish orphans. In France, for instance, he recalled that "often soldiers expressed a desire to adopt an orphan, some child they had run across, whose parents had disappeared into Germany." The soldiers asked their chaplain's help in bringing the children home to America. Rabbi Kertzer himself met "a winsome girl of nine" who implored him for help. "To me, her small sad voice carried centuries of anguish. I would have taken her back to America, if I could." But "the stumbling blocks against adoption in France were formidable. The question 'Is this child really an orphan?' was nearly always unanswerable."[67]

According to Kertzer, no Jewish underground warrior or American Jewish soldier had "to be enlightened on 'why we fight.' They saw in this war an elemental struggle for survival, a battle against physical annihilation."[68]

BECAUSE JEWISH SOLDIERS were scattered in small numbers among thousands of non-Jewish troops, finding a Jewish chaplain for counsel was often impossible. Finding a Jewish religious service could be difficult, too. Of course Catholic and Protestant chaplains offered bare-bones services, but it was never the same, even if a Jewish soldier could serve as a lay leader. On rare occasions a rabbi would be discovered among the combatants, and sometimes he could be persuaded to serve as a regular chaplain. Harry Skydell, for instance, had trained as an Orthodox rabbi at Yeshiva University before the war. Serving with the Twenty-Ninth Infantry Division in Europe, this native New Yorker, who had been employed as an accountant in the Big Apple before the war, agreed to set aside his rifle and put on a tallith [prayer shawl] to serve the Jewish troops as their chaplain.[69]

The demand for Jewish chaplains could be seen when word spread among the troops that a Jewish chaplain would be in the area to hold a service. Chaplain Eichhorn could always attract from fifteen to seventy-five men from one or two regiments on short notice.[70] And it was not only the soldiers who longed for a Jewish service. Indeed, whenever the Americans liberated a city, cleaned out the debris from a desecrated synagogue, and spread the word that a Jewish service would be held, if there were Jewish refugees they joined American soldiers and went on pilgrimage from far and wide to receive the blessing of which they had for too long been deprived.

Just before Rosh Hashanah 1944 Rabbi Eichhorn made it to Verdun, and he soon discovered that the synagogue had been turned into a soup kitchen by the Germans. Later the building had been partially destroyed by a bomb and the Germans began to deliberately desecrate it and use it as a facility to store piles of animal dung for fertilizer. When American troops occupied the city, Eichhorn found the violated synagogue and impressed ten German PWs into service as cleaners and restorers. The rabbi delighted in what he called the "poetic justice" of assigning Germans the restoration project. To his surprise the Germans cooperated well and "did a good job. Without urging they scrubbed the walls and floors thoroughly and when they got through the place did not look too bad." Despite the demolished roof and a drenching rain that caused worshippers to be soaked, "500 American Jewish soldiers jammed into the place for the evening service and the next morning we had over 600." The chaplain wrote to his wife that the Eve Rosh Hashanah service "was very dramatic." And at a service the next morning, "since we had no shofar, an army bugler played the traditional notes on the bugle and, though we had no Torah, we opened the Ark and went through the entire Torah service just as though we had a Torah. Everyone was profoundly moved."[71]

JEWISH CHAPLAINS, AS well as Christian priests and ministers and the tens of thousands of troops who battled their way across France, Belgium, and the low countries and into the German fatherland, increasingly saw that they were fighting for much more than the liberation of German-occupied countries and the silencing of German guns. They were fighting to stop a well-planned and organized program of genocide designed to eliminate all Jewish people from the earth.

Rumors of Nazi atrocities against Jews, as well as eyewitness accounts of mass executions, had been circulating since the late 1930s. But people were reluctant to listen, let alone believe. Even among Jewish people a spirit of denial prevailed. Elie Wiesel, who as a teenager survived the horrors of both Auschwitz and Buchenwald, wrote in *Night*, his terrifying account of Nazi brutality, that people in his hometown of Sighet, Transylvania, denied the gruesome evidence until it was too late. Even when a man whom everyone in the town knew came in early 1942 and told them of his miraculous escape from a mass killing of fellow Jews by Germans—no one believed him.[72]

ONLY WHEN THE Allied armies plunged into the heart of Germany did they truly discover the shocking but incontrovertible evidence. The rumors, the passionate pleas of escapees from labor and extermination camps, were not exaggerated anti-German propaganda stories. On the contrary, the sights, stench, and mournful sounds encountered at dozens of camps liberated by Allied warriors proved to be worse than anything rumored or spoken of prior to early 1945.

Confronting the living and the dead, coming face-to-face with hideous evidence of the Holocaust in all of its dimensions, at such places as Bergen-Belsen, Buchenwald, Dachau, Ebensee, Flossenbürg, and Mauthausen, caused combat-hardened soldiers across the ranks to weep, vomit, and become enraged with hatred for Germans. Meyer Levin, a war correspondent who had been dedicating his work to raising funds from Americans for Jewish refugees who were discovered in ever-increasing numbers as the Allies advanced, was traveling with the U.S. Fourth Armored Division. Early on the morning of April 5, 1945, Levin and the Yanks "came upon cadaverous refugees . . . like none we had ever seen," Levin later wrote. These people were "skeletal, with feverish sunken eyes, shaven skulls." Barely able to talk, these scarcely alive refugees pointed the advancing army to a camp at Ohrdruf, a slave camp near Weimar. With some well-armed and cautious soldiers, Meyer Levin walked into the first of the Nazi concentration camps to be found by Americans. He wrote: "We had known. The world had vaguely heard. But until now no one of us had looked on this. It was as though we had penetrated at last to the center of the black heart, to the very crawling inside of the vicious heart."[73]

Actually, there were camps even more vicious and darker than this place. Ohrdruf served as a labor camp, enslaving approximately ten thousand men. Although workers who grew too weak or sick to dig the underground caverns designed to hide communications and transportation centers were killed, this was not an extermination camp. To be sure, the SS guards killed and burned bodies of those slaves who were too weak to march away from the approaching Americans. Nevertheless, more hellish sites were still to be discovered.[74]

Six days later men of both the Sixth and Ninth Armored Divisions found Buchenwald, a place of organized labor—complete with torture, rape, starvation, and medical experimentation. Buchenwald was an almost unbelievable prison city that housed more than fifty thousand men, women, and children by 1945. Filth, stench, death, and disease marked this camp where inmates were discovered lying and sitting naked in their own excrement, or clothed in everything from filthy striped prison uniforms to pieces of rough cloth sacks, which shrouded the shuffling, skeletal Jews, Gypsies, political prisoners, and sundry other people deemed "inferior" or "undesirable."[75]

Lieutenant Colonel Harold MacKenzie of the Ninth Armored Division was on an errand in his jeep when he and his driver came upon Buchenwald by accident. The gates had just been opened and an American army chaplain happened to notice MacKenzie. The chaplain knew MacKenzie and waved him inside, urging him to use all the influence he had as a member of the general staff to get immediate help to the wretched survivors. Timely and concerted efforts— overseen by chaplains and high-ranking general staff officers such as Harold MacKenzie—saved lives at Buchenwald, where sanitation and living conditions were improved as quickly as possible.[76]

During the next few days more camps—some of them massive extermination centers such as Dachau—were uncovered by the Americans and their allies. At each camp, Allied chaplains helped organize everything from assembly-line delousing, showering, shaving, and dressing of inmates, to segregating the contagiously ill and those in need of immediate and special medical care. Once sanitation and emergency care issues got sorted out, the liberators undertook the task of assigning Red Cross and nonessential military personnel to the task of gathering names and former residences of those men, women, and children who were at once free but unable to roam the still dangerous countryside.[77]

*   *   *

ALL AMERICAN CHAPLAINS with units that entered the concentration camps became involved with these demanding tasks, and their efforts required round-the-clock urgent care, as well as innovative procedures. Chaplain schools, like seminaries, had prepared none of these men for the formidable challenges that prior to 1945 would have been unimaginable.

By far, Jewish chaplains became the most taxed at every concentration camp, where at least 50 percent of the inmates were Jewish, and usually those numbers were much higher. Consequently, a unique and multifaceted challenge confronted the already overextended rabbis. A report Chaplain David Max Eichhorn wrote for the Jewish Welfare Board during the first week of May while at Dachau provides a context for the mission he faced. Rabbi Eichhorn reported that the XV Corps to which he was assigned took the concentration camp at Dachau, which lay nestled in beautiful Bavaria about a dozen miles northwest of Munich. On the edge of the camp they drove up on "39 boxcars loaded with Jewish dead in the Dachau railway yard, 39 carloads of little, shriveled mummies that had literally been starved to death." Their next ghastly discovery was the extermination center—gas chambers and adjacent crematoria "still filled with charred bones and ashes. We cried not merely tears of sorrow. We cried tears of hate."[78]

A few weeks earlier, on March 21, Eichhorn and his driver had crossed the German border in his "little jeep with its big Mogen David [Star of David]" proudly displayed. To celebrate the victorious occasion, they dipped into their crate of chaplain supplies so that as they entered "the land of the enemy, the chaplain is munching on a crunchy sheet of you-know-what [matzos]."[79]

But there was no celebration at Dachau. Instead, Eichhorn admitted that once they entered such depths of degradation and evil, "we stood aside and watched while these guards were beaten to death, beaten so badly that their bodies were ripped open and innards protruded. We watched with less feeling than if a dog were being beaten. In truth, it might be said that we were completely without feeling. Deep anger and hate had temporarily numbed our emotions. These evil people, it seemed to us, were being treated exactly as they deserved to be treated. To such depths does human nature sink in the presence of human depravity."[80]

After his initial paralysis of mind and soul, Rabbi Eichhorn set out to care for the survivors at Dachau and its various little sub-camps. He had been given a Torah in the town of Treuchtlingen as he drove toward Munich. The local mayor had hidden the Torah in 1938 when Nazis destroyed the synagogue and killed many of the Jews who had not already fled to the woods.[81] At the Allach camp the chaplain discovered that Jews and Gentiles were segregated. The Jewish prisoners appeared much more malnourished and debilitated than the Gentiles, and the camp conditions were also worse. Eich-horn wrote: "The comparative conditions in the Jewish and Gentile sections may be understood through one simple statistic: The first day I was there 40 Jews and 5 Gentiles died. In other words, the death rate was about 15 Jews to one Gentile."[82] But these conditions notwithstanding, on April 30 the rabbi presented the Torah from Treuchtlingen to the Jews at Allach camp and presided over a mag-nificent service. During the celebration "a Czecho-Slovakian rabbi, Dr. Klein, who spoke about a dozen languages . . . thanked me elo-quently for the Torah in English, German, and Hungarian." A cantor from Poland chanted the "El Male Rachamin" with "a very beautiful voice," and "after the service literally hundreds of people crowded around me, kissing my hand and begging for an 'autogram.' "[83]

Not all concentration camps had Torahs, rabbis, and cantors. Therefore the pressure mounted on rabbis like Eichhorn to stay in the camps and minister to these needy souls who had been without pastoral care for years. As a result, Jewish chaplains felt pulled in several directions. Jewish soldiers under their care, after seeing the camps, needed pastoral comfort and guidance now more than ever. Likewise, Christian soldiers needed counsel and care as well.

To further complicate matters, chaplains were pressured to meet the almost endless list of other human needs. Rabbi Lee Levinger said these liberated prisoners were suddenly "displaced persons" and the issues of "legal status, housing, clothing, food," as well as medical care and cries for help to find relatives, simply overwhelmed armies that were only equipped "to win wars."[84]

Some chaplains—both Christian and Jewish—were given permission to lag behind their regiments for a few days to meet these crushing demands. But whether they stayed on or continued deeper into combat zones, they suffered from knowing that someone somewhere else also needed their help.

Rabbi Abraham Klausner, according to historian Albert Isaac Slomovitz, "gave his all and risked his career to care for survivors."[85] When his outfit, the 116th Evacuation Hospital Unit, was ordered out of Dachau, he obeyed orders and accompanied it "to a resort area a hundred miles away." But soon he fabricated a story about receiving orders to return to Dachau, because in good conscience he could not stay away from people with such desperate needs.[86]

SOME OF THE intense pressures of choosing between serving men in combat or remaining to aid desperate camp survivors ended when Germany finally surrendered unconditionally on May 7. But new problems quickly sprouted in the garden of victory. Wherever Russian troops advanced, German civilians and women of any nationality met fates often worse than death. These barbarian atrocities prompted chaplains to lean on their commanding officers to move refugees to areas of safety within American or British zones of influence. Jewish and Christian chaplains were particularly keen on protecting women from the brutality awaiting them from the westward-advancing Russian troops. Chaplain Ernst Lorge, for example, served with the Sixty-Ninth Infantry Division. A twenty-nine-year-old rabbi, he assisted more than a thousand Jewish women survivors of Auschwitz. When he discovered these starving women in several camps east of Leipzig, "he requested . . . Major General Emil F. Reinhart, the commander of his division," to come to their rescue. General Reinhart immediately cut his division's rations by 20 percent. In the wake of this noble enterprise, Lorge organized a "mercy caravan" of jeeps—all ladened with food and medical supplies—that he carefully directed to deliver and distribute the bounty."[87]

Thanks to Lorge's tireless efforts, when word came that Russian soldiers would soon assume occupation and oversight of the region, rail transportation was arranged to move the women into the American zone. Rabbi Lorge's heroic efforts were not unique. Chaplains and their assistants from all traditions, with the hearty support and hard work of soldiers and officers from scores of units, did their utmost to protect survivors from the marauders. Indeed, historian Alex Grobman documented how Jewish chaplains Herschel Schacter and Robert Marcus secured supplies and protection for women refugees from Buchenwald who were frantically attempting to stay outside the reach of Russian troops.[88]

GERMAN CONCENTRATION CAMP commanders and guards seemed to hate Polish people as much as Jews. When the lid on Dachau atrocities was opened, it became evident that Polish prisoners were dreadfully tortured and special abuse seemed to be reserved for

Polish Catholic priests. The situation proved to be so dire that the Chaplain Corps put one of its men inside the liberated camp to minister full-time to the priests. Donald Crosby learned that "his orders were to see that their total rehabilitation (of body, mind, and spirit) proceeded as rapidly as possible for the Polish priests to celebrate Mass every day, something the Germans had relentlessly denied them—which meant they had to hold Mass in secret, often at great danger to themselves."[89] Consequently, just three days after Rabbi Eichhorn enabled the Jews in Allach, Dachau, to have their first Jewish service in the camp, on May 3, "the traditional day on which Polish Catholics commemorate their devotion to the Blessed Virgin Mary . . . the oldest priest at Dachau acted as principal celebrant, assisted by 200 others, and nearly 10,000 former prisoners participated in the first public Mass in the camp's twelve-year history." [90]

IN THE WAKE of Germany's surrender, not only were all concentration camps liberated, German prisoner of war camp gates opened wide in every place not already overrun by Allied forces. Twenty-one U.S. Army chaplains were freed. These incarcerated clergymen had ministered to prisoners of all traditions with an ecumenical and loving spirit. In the same vein, army chaplains who accompanied liberating units did their utmost to meet the needs of people freed from both military and concentration camps. As prisoners' shackles were broken, centuries of bondage from religious bigotry were smashed as clergy and laymen alike recognized that they had been fighting an enemy much bigger than the differences of their traditions.

As the victorious troops celebrated, rested, and bandaged wounds, they anxiously awaited orders that would tell them if they would be allowed to go home before being sent to the Pacific to help bring Japan to its knees.

CHAPTER NINE

A GLIMPSE OF
ARMAGEDDON

VICTORY IN THE PACIFIC

*The power of the Cross to inspire surpassed its power of
recognition. . . . Boys of all faiths would go anywhere if the
chaplain would go with them.*

CHAPLAIN JOHN T. O'CALLAHAN[1]

A S Western Europe thawed from the coldest winter on
record in late 1944 and early 1945, Allied troops slogged
and battered their way into the strongly defended heartland of Germany. Guns finally fell silent in May when Germany
surrendered. But victory celebrations were brief. While some troops
prepared to pack and go home to America, many warriors were
being reorganized and positioned for moving out to the Pacific.
They were needed for the dreaded invasion of Japan.

During early 1945, while Allied forces in Europe paid a heavy
price in human casualties and destroyed equipment, Allied advances
toward Japan were equally costly. And despite the fact that the
Japanese were on the defensive everywhere in the Pacific, their

resistance only stiffened. No one anticipated an early or easy end to the Pacific War. Indeed, it increasingly became evident that barring some completely unimaginable turn of fate, the Japanese would refuse to surrender. There were prepared for a last-ditch battle and would fight on until every man, woman, and child died trying to stave off the invaders.

BEGINNING IN AUTUMN 1944, combined American and British forces launched major offensive actions to retake Indochina and the Philippine Islands. On October 20, 1944, General Douglas Mac-Aruthur, with his inimitable flair for the dramatic, waded ashore with cameramen and radio microphones already planted to record his announcement: "People of the Philippines, I have returned." Quickly invoking the Almighty's hand in the celebrated event, he continued: "By the grace of Almighty God, our forces stand again on Philippine soil—soil consecrated in the blood of our two peoples. . . . The seat of your government is now, therefore, firmly re-established on Philippine soil. The hour of your redemption is here."[2]

The announced redemption proved to be prophetic, but thousands of lives and tens of thousands of casualties would be required before the entire Commonwealth of the Philippines could be liberated nearly nine months later. The American invasion of Leyte gave the Filipino people hope, but it was only the beginning of a horrid war of attrition. For nearly three-quarters of a year, the Japanese would stubbornly cling to the big islands and cities of the Commonwealth's 7,083 islands. Japanese and Allied artillery devastated the major ports and many of the nation's cities during seemingly endless bombing raids.

The Japanese military did more than tenaciously defend their strongholds, they systematically murdered Filipino guerillas, as well as civilians who aided the Allied cause with as much as a cup of cold water to a thirsty combatant. Japanese treatment of prisoners of war was particularly cruel. Beginning in 1942 when Americans ran out of food and ammunition and were finally forced to surrender, Japanese army guards, with some few exceptions, tortured, murdered, and brutalized all prisoners.

The infamous Bataan Death March in April 1942 proved to be only the beginning of more than three years of hell on earth for Allied and Filipino prisoners. In the death march alone, almost ten thousand of the eighty thousand captured men died on the sixty-five-mile forced march to Camp O'Donnell. Another twenty thousand died during the next two months. Seldom allowed to rest, the men suffered from lack of food and even water. They were beaten and bayoneted for stumbling or falling out of line—or simply because the guards wanted to display their contempt for soldiers who would rather surrender than die for their country.[3]

When U.S. General Jonathan Wainwright surrendered thirteen American soldiers on Corregidor in May 1942, his men received dreadful treatment as well. They were kept incarcerated in a tunnel for a week with no access to water, food, or medicine. Upon release, the weak and sick soldiers were paraded through the streets of Manila. Donald F. Crosby, S.J., wrote in his history of Catholic priests in World War II that the men were driven "like cattle through the streets" with the Japanese "bayoneting those who fell and bullying them whenever the whim struck," before being put on trains for a prison camp near Cabanatuan.[4]

INVASION FORCES DISCOVERED the horrors perpetrated on American prisoners when they landed in October 1944. American troops were shocked and infuriated by the condition of American and Allied prisoners whom they managed to liberate. Survivors, racked by malnutrition and sundry diseases, appeared skeletal. While freeing prisoners, the army learned that nearly 30 percent of the prisoner population had perished. In Germany, on the other hand, the death rate was only 4 percent.[5]

To make matters worse, the Japanese began to move prisoners as soon as Allied troops came within a few days of capturing an area. Prisoners were relocated to other places in the Philippines, and the least fortunate were massacred and many even burned alive after being doused with gasoline. Others were taken to ports and placed on troop and cargo ships destined for Japan or Taiwan, where they became slaves in mines or stevedores on docks.[6] The mortality rate on these "Hell Ships" was enormous and unnecessary. On one ship alone, the *Oryoku Maru*, approximately sixteen hundred American officers were dropped into three holds of the ship. With no ventilation or sanitary facilities and only minimal water and rice, each man had only about two square feet of space. In one hold, thirty men died the first night. This ship and others like it were strafed and bombed by American planes the crews of which had no idea that their own fellow countrymen comprised the precious cargo. Ultimately only 25 percent of the Americans survived the trip on the *Oryoku Maru*.[7]

Among the American prisoners in the Philippines were thirty-two army and four navy chaplains. There was the usual distribution of Protestant and Catholic chaplains among the thirty-six, but there were no Jewish rabbis. Many of the nearly two hundred Jewish prisoners at Cabanatuan, however, viewed a Russian Jewish emigrant who married a Filipina woman, Aaron Kliatcho, as their chaplain. Trained as a cantor in Russia before emigrating to the Philippines, Kliatcho donned a U.S. Army uniform and served as a liaison between the Filipinos and American soldiers who had escaped into the jungles. When captured and treated as an American, "Sergeant"

Kliatcho, who "could sing from memory seventy Jewish services," became the "catalyst for Jewish spiritual life at Cabanatuan."[8] He died on the "Hell Ship" *Oryoku Maru* in early 1945.[9]

SURVIVORS OF THE Philippine prison camps testify that the chaplains scattered throughout the camps performed valiantly as encouragers of all the prisoners—officers and enlisted men alike. All prisoners, according to a joint army and navy intelligence report "were without exception put to hard labor—chaplains, officers, and enlisted men alike." Although this practice violated Geneva Convention regulations, it did cause chaplains to be among all the prisoners and thereby allowed them opportunity to minister to everyone.[10]

Chaplain Alfred C. Oliver, Jr., a Methodist clergyman who was senior chaplain of the Philippine Department when the Americans surrendered, distinguished himself as one of the most respected leaders among the prisoners, from the time of his capture in spring 1942 until liberation in 1945. He repeatedly implored their Japanese captors to allow religious services, but for more than a year they refused. Chaplain Oliver, who held the rank of colonel when captured, explained that the "Japanese hated and feared all Americans, especially the chaplains as leaders of the people." The reason stemmed from the uses to which the Japanese put their own chaplains—who were as armed and dangerous as all combatants. According to Oliver, the Japanese chaplain's duty "is to arouse their troops to fanatic endeavor. They do not understand or believe that chaplains are used by Christian nations only to uplift soldiers spiritually. . . . Consequently, the American chaplains serving with troops in the Philippine Islands were treated with no respect but often used worse than other officers as they were held under suspicion of being dangerous army and navy propaganda agents."[11]

Chaplain Oliver suffered a broken neck and wore a neck brace for months after the war because a guard beat him with a rifle butt. Despite the pain and time spent in "hot house" isolation on several occasions, the spunky Methodist continued to cling to his dignity and did everything possible to care for the spiritual well-being and morale of the men. Eventually the Japanese camp commandant allowed religious services when the dead were buried. And this happened so frequently that the commandant gradually allowed regular worship services with sermons and singing, as long as the sermons were written in advance and censored by a bilingual Japanese officer.[12]

This Protestant minister became a father to the young prisoners, and they adored him when he and other chaplains and officers "participated in every camp activity," including performing "such details as cleaning out Japanese latrines, then spreading this fecal matter over some of the farm area."[13]

Oliver and the other chaplains at Cabanatuan implored the Japanese commander to send a chaplain along each time a group of the strongest prisoners were pulled out and sent to Japan or Manchuria to repair bomb-damaged airfields. Numerous groups of prisoners—sometimes as many as eight hundred at a time—were sent away. But the commander always refused to send a chaplain. Therefore, Chaplain Oliver, as well as some other chaplains and devout Christian lay leaders, began "training laymen for spiritual leadership through Bible study. One man in each outgoing group was appointed religious leader. He was furnished with as many copies of the New Testament as could be spared, a supply having been sent from Manila by the American Bible Society." Oliver recalled that there were not nearly enough Testaments to go around, but at least there were enough to place in the hands of each leader, along with handwritten copies of baptismal and burial services.[14]

Chaplains in other PW camps were equally enterprising in their determination to care for men's spiritual needs. Sacramentalist chaplains bartered valuables to smugglers in order to get wine for Holy Communion. And if all else failed, they acquired raisins and prunes through their dangerous but efficient underground network to the outside, thereby making their own wine for sacramental purposes.[15]

Because Roman Catholic priests were still ministering among civilian Filipinos, albeit underground most of the time due to Japanese occupational forces' hatred of all things Christian, wine and even small crosses could be smuggled into the camps with medicines, food, and other contraband. In some parts of mainland Japan, sacramentalists fared even better. Navy Chaplain James E. Davis, who was captured on Guam in December 1941, was taken to Japan in early 1942. He spent all but the last few weeks of the war at the Zentsuji Prisoner of War Camp, Shikoku Island. He recalled that religious services were not prohibited in his camp, although the Japanese viewed it with suspicion because of their own understanding of the duties of a chaplain. Davis said that "religious interest was high, largely as a result of the harrowing experience of war." He admitted that "many of us felt that we were living on borrowed time and were thankful to God for our preservation. We also felt the need of divine support in our time of trouble." Therefore, "as soon as we secured the necessary permission from the Japanese, we expressed our thanksgiving and praise to God in worship."[16]

Although the prisoners on Shikoku Island had access to a Bible, there was no hymnal. So the men pooled their memories of hymns and Gospel songs, enabling them to eventually write out what they labeled the Zentsuji Hymn book. The freedom to write a hymn book and make a wooden cross and pulpit distinguished this prison camp from the horrid conditions American and Allied prisoners experienced throughout the Philippines and most other parts of the

Pacific. Indeed, at Zentsuji the commander allowed a Japanese Anglican priest to send communion wine to the prison, and an Australian Catholic priest prisoner, Father Turner, "secured some vestments from the Roman Catholic bishop of Japan." The bishop not only provided vestments and supplies, he received permission to pay a pastoral visit to the prisoners.[17]

Chaplain Davis, who was born in Venice, California, in 1911 and earned a B.A. from UCLA in 1933 and Th.M. and master of arts degrees from the University of Southern California in 1936 and 1937 respectively, was ordained in the Congregational-Christian denomination and was the only chaplain at Zentsuji for many months. Davis provided spiritual oversight to more than five hundred men for nearly a year. He did his best to care for the men of all faiths. Therefore he celebrated the arrival of a new prisoner, an Australian Catholic priest, as a great source of comfort and support. Davis admitted that "it was very difficult to do business through the Japanese army," so the opportunity to have one visit from a Japanese Catholic and one more call from a Japanese Anglican became two celebrated "stones of remembrance" during his captivity that lasted from December 1941 until September 1945.[18]

IF EXPERIENCES OF imprisoned military chaplains were quite varied, one thread of continuity is woven throughout their stories: enlisted men and officers alike unanimously sang the praises of chaplains as unselfish servants who devoted their energy to keeping men alive both physically and spiritually.

Robert Preston Taylor proved to be one of the most effective soul doctors in the prison camps of World War II. Born in Henderson, Texas, in 1909, he sensed God's call on his life to go into ordained Christian ministry while still in his teens. After earning a B.A. from

Baylor University in 1933, and then a master's and doctorate in Theology from Southwestern Baptist Seminary in 1936 and 1939 respectively, Preston Taylor served as a pastor until he entered the army as
a chaplain in 1940. Assigned to an infantry regiment in Manila in
spring 1941, he found his place of service on the front lines while the
U.S. Army tried to defend the Bataan Peninsula from the Japanese
invaders. Taylor became famous for staying near the men he preached
to, prayed with, encouraged, and counseled. He was awarded the Silver Star for his bravery before the Americans surrendered in 1942.[19]

Chaplain Taylor became a prisoner of the Japanese, a survivor of
the "Death March" through the streets of Manila and on to the
prison on the outskirts of Cabanatuan. A close friend of Chaplain
Alfred C. Oliver, Taylor provided nursing and pastoral care to more
than ten thousand Allied patients. He helped administer medical
and spiritual care; prayed with the wounded, sick, and dying; and
became a spiritual father to thousands of boys in their late teens
and early twenties—some of whom he helped nurse to recovery and
others he buried in the black soil of the jungle near a filthy building
that served as a makeshift hospital.

Refusing to watch his "congregation" die from starvation, vita-
min and mineral deficiencies, and sundry infections and diseases,
Taylor continually risked his life to smuggle food and medicines into
the prison hospital. In summer 1944 the courageous and defiant
minister, who at six feet in height towered over his Japanese captors
and most of his fellow Americans, withstood severe beatings and
fourteen weeks of solitary confinement in the infamous and dia-
bolically cruel "Heat Box," when he was caught smuggling supplies
for his men.[20]

Much to the dismay of his vicious captors, Taylor defied all odds
by remaining alive for more than three months in the Heat Box.
When word got out that he was in a coma and on the brink of death,

an American doctor risked his own life, angrily confronted the Japanese camp commander, and demanded the release of his dying friend so that he could be cared for in the camp hospital. Every American agreed that a miracle took place when the camp commander agreed to Taylor's removal from solitary confinement. And the miracle took on added momentum when Chaplain Oliver organized a nonstop, twenty-four-hour-a-day intercessory prayer chain for the healing of the pastor so greatly loved by all the wretched prisoners in what many spiritually depressed men assumed to be a God-forsaken camp. Within a few days, Preston Taylor came out of his coma; he gradually regained his mental and physical strength, and began to hobble around on an ugly bamboo stick that became his trusty cane.

The effect of Chaplain Taylor's recovery inspired a spiritual revival in the camp. Spiritually comatose soldiers became enlivened; doubters embraced hope and faith in Jesus Christ, who they believed had healed their pastor and friend. Even the Japanese commander and guards were affected. Consequently, the Americans were allowed to hold worship services in the open compound, where the Japanese captors surrounded these praise gatherings with ever-growing interest.[21]

To the minds of many Christian officers and enlisted men who were ministered to by Chaplain Taylor, and to many of those soldiers who requested prayer and baptism in the wake of his miraculous recovery from the Heat Box–induced coma, it seemed God's hand had spared the Texas Baptist's life because there were still more missions for him to fulfill. The chain of miracle-like circumstances grew when Taylor was "selected" by the Japanese to take a "Hell Ship" voyage to Japan. Twice Americans bombed the ship on which Taylor sailed. More than one thousand men lost their lives from heat, starvation, dehydration, or shrapnel from American

bombs. Although Robert Preston Taylor slipped into unconsciousness and was presumed dead on more than one occasion, this iron-
willed Texan defied all odds, survived the war, returned home to
his faithful wife, and served as a chaplain in the U.S. Air Force until
1966, when he retired with the rank of major general.[22]

CHAPLAIN ROBERT PRESTON Taylor proved to be one of the
fortunate ones because, as Father Donald F. Crosby succinctly
showed, "as the Americans began their assault on Luzon, Catholic
and Protestant chaplains, as well as hundreds of other prisoners,
continued to perish in ships taking them from Manila to Formosa
and Japan. Three more chaplains would die at sea, and the same
number would fall in the campaign for Luzon itself."[23]

Men like Chaplain Taylor were dubbed "survivors" by military
men who enjoyed labeling people. Father William P. Cummings
nearly earned that label as well. An army chaplain who seemed destined for the longevity title, Cummings impressed people as a ten-
der and soft-spoken priest. Ordained in the Maryknoll order and
already balding and gray-haired in 1941, this bespectacled American distinguished himself first as a deeply caring pastor in the wake
of Japan's senseless bombing raids on Manila two days after they
had already captured and secured Clark Field and subdued the
entire area. Jesuit historian Donald Crosby described Father Cummings's energy and pastoral concern in the immediate aftermath of
what one periodical described as a "barbaric act" inflicted on a
people "utterly unable to defend themselves" this way:

*Cummings worked day and night at the army's Sternberg Hospital
in Manila, which had started receiving civilian as well as military
casualties. In one especially hectic week, he visited over 800 patients*

in the hospital, sent hundreds of telegrams to relatives at home, and
assisted the Red Cross in its efforts to bring relief to the victims of
the bombings.[24]

Cummings left the hospital only when the army ordered evacuation of the city. From early in the war, this American priest could always be found among the fearful and wounded, manifesting courage and strength that made him seem indestructible. Parenting the troops wherever they were marched, Chaplain Cummings endured a long line of ordeals. Captured by the Japanese in 1942, he suffered beatings, starvation, and all the physical and mental agony that vicious men could devise. He not only maintained his dignity and pastoral posture during a time at Bilidad prison in Manila, he emerged through the fires of mental and physical tortures at Cabanatuan and continued to be a sensitive and long-suffering shepherd to men of all faiths and none. Scores of survivors pointed to Cummings as a catalytic presence who engendered hope when everything seemed lost. Finally herded onto a Hell Ship that was bombed once in Manila Harbor and then again at a harbor in Formosa, Father Cummings brought light to the darkest places. A small group of prisoners who survived the Hell Ship ordeal recalled their spiritual father's death. They reported stories of his "nightly talks to the men deep in the confines of the ship. One night as they squirmed for space in their fetid quarters, fought for air, screamed for food and water, and stumbled over the bodies of the dead, the sound of their cries rose higher and higher."[25] Just when the crowd of broken men seemed on the verge of uncontrollable hysteria, Father Cummings's "voice rang out over the clamor." An officer in the hold said, "Father Cummings began to speak. The sound was clear and resonant and made me feel he was talking to me alone. The men became quiet." Then the charismatic priest began praying, "Our Father, who art in heaven, hallowed be Thy name . . ." In a few moments, the officer recalled "strength came to me as I listened to the prayer, and a certain calmness of spirit." He remembered that sanity began to come to him and others for a while. Gradually some men slipped back into their various degrees of lunacy, "but some of us continued to be held by the strength in that voice, the voice of a man who believed and who wanted us to believe."[26]

Chaplain Cummings did not survive the monthlong seagoing ordeal. He so totally spent himself pastoring others that some men said he never slept or ate. Although not a physical "survivor," his spirit imparted life to others who did survive the Hell Ship voyage and lived to see the Japanese surrender.[27]

ON JANUARY 28, 1945, a company of 121 soldiers from the U.S. Army Sixth Ranger Battalion liberated the prison camp at Cabanatuan. On the twenty-five-mile walk toward the American lines and freedom, a rugged, barefoot, shirtless, and hatless soldier in tattered pants drew alongside Chaplain Oliver and said a few words that summed up rather well the great impact of POW chaplains: "You know, Chaplain, I lost everything back there in that hell hole of a prison camp, every earthly thing including my health—but I didn't lose God."[28]

Of course it would be wrong to give military chaplains all the credit for helping bring light to the dark nights of men's souls in World War II. It became absolutely necessary to have laymen lead worship services and Bible studies. Without them, the spiritual lives of combatants would have suffered greatly, and consequently the war effort would have been substantially weakened. No soldiers understood this better than Jewish and African-American troops. Throughout the conflict and in all theaters they often made do without benefit of regular chaplains. To be sure, Protestant and Catholic warriors were frequently without benefit of clergy, too. Most of the veterans I have interviewed over the last decade or more admitted that they seldom or never saw a chaplain after they left their training camps and stations in the United States. In fact, the presence of a chaplain in combat areas—unless it was on board a ship—served as a surprise rather than a presence to be assumed. (Medics and corpsmen, on the other hand, were readily available to care for the wounded, and they were almost universally admired.) Indeed, many soldiers attested to the fact that one of the greatest assets they could carry into combat was their personal faith that provided essential sustenance when the going was tough.[29]

The main reason for the paucity of chaplains was the fact that there were not enough rabbis, priests, and ministers to meet the demand that increased each year. Sometimes, too, chaplains were deterred from going to the front lines by senior officers who argued that they were too important to the men's morale to be lost on first invasion waves, and in initial front-line infantry charges the mortality rate almost invariably skyrocketed above the average, even for men in heavy combat.

Certainly some military chaplains lacked courage and lagged behind the lines only to appear among the combatants after the heaviest fighting subsided. Some evidence of this comes from letters sent home from the front. Chaplain Russell Cartwright Stroup, a thirty-seven-year-old pastor of the prestigious First Presbyterian Church of Lynchburg, Virginia, when the war began, left his pastorate and volunteered to serve with the army infantry. He made it clear that he wanted to serve men in combat. He got his wish because throughout the war, from 1942 until the end of hostilities in the Pacific, this man with a receding hairline and a Clark Gable–like mustache, who was old enough to have fathered many of the men he served, continually managed to be where the soldiers were under fire. Assigned to the 1112th Engineer Combat Group, he accompanied his men on initial assaults at Hollandia, Biak, and Sansapor in New Guinea and Lingayen Gulf in the retaking of the Philippines. But his combat presence notwithstanding, some of his letters home alluded to one or two of his fellow chaplains who never appeared on the front until hostilities subsided.[30]

Despite the shortage of chaplains, and even given the less than gallant efforts on the part of a few sky pilots during the war, in the last analysis the spiritual ammunition given out by chaplains during the last months of the Pacific conflict proved to be indispensible. As vicious as the Japanese resistance had been all the way from the American invasion of Guadalcanal in 1942 on down through battle after battle in 1943 and 1944, it grew worse by early 1945. During the thirty-six-day battle for Iwo Jima in February and March that year, almost six thousand Americans were killed and seventeen thousand more were wounded. After this bloodbath, no one, including seasoned combat veterans who'd had plenty of previous contact with the Japanese—expected that the savage disdain for life encountered on Iwo Jima could get worse. Japan's willingness to destroy the lives of any and all combatants—including their own troops—surpassed expectations of even the most cynical, negative, and battle-hardened prognosticators in the next island battle on the way toward Japan.

OKINAWA IS A sixty-mile-long island with a land mass of five hundred square miles. Its widest place is eighteen miles and its narrowest two. In early 1945, the Japanese boasted a strongly entrenched defense force there of one hundred thousand men, complemented by the largest concentration of artillery located anywhere in the Japanese-controlled Pacific. This military citadel served as home to half a million civilians, and the long, narrow island bristled with Japan's four state-of-the-art air bases, replete with hangars, fuel dumps, and service facilities for a significant portion of the Imperial Air Force. Among the planes stationed on Okinawa were hundreds of kamikaze (suicide) planes. This strategically important island supported more than artillery and air power; there were numerous anchorage locations all along the coastline, as well as the major seaport of Naha.[31]

If the U.S. military prior to early 1945 bypassed a few Japanese-controlled islands as strategically unimportant, this island was never even considered for such a list. Okinawa loomed as one of the supremely important final steps up the ladder to the heart of Japan. General A. A. Vandegrift labeled it "the last redoubt before Japan proper, and the enemy seemed as determined to hold it as we were to take it."[32]

For military reasons, the U.S. high command chose Sunday, April 1, 1945, to launch the invasion. Ironically, April Fools' Day that year also coincided with Easter Sunday—the highest holy day of the year for Christians who celebrate the Resurrection of Jesus Christ and look with hope to the resurrection for all faithful Christians. In retrospect, the irony proved to be greater than the convergence of April Fools' Day and Easter. On the day Christians celebrate life, a battle began that became the bloodiest and most costly engagement for Americans in World War II. The U.S. Tenth Army, in concert with the Marine Corps Third Amphibious Corps made up of the First, Second, and Sixth Marine Divisions, launched the first assault on April 1. By the time Okinawa was finally secured on June 21, 11,260 Americans had died and nearly 34,000 had been wounded. Furthermore, the U.S. Navy suffered nearly 10,000 killed and wounded when 30 ships and other craft were sunk and 368 damaged.[33]

Never before in the history of American warfare had so many chaplains served in one engagement. And at no time before or after have so many men of the cloth been needed. This is understandable only by considering the staggering numbers of U.S. Naval vessels (more than 1,200) and a combined army and marine invasion force of 183,000, plus more airplanes and their crews placed into action than had ever before been assembled in a single Pacific operation.[34]

THE INVASION OF Okinawa began April 1, but the U.S. Navy began assaulting the enemy on March 18. The big guns from the ships of the Fifth Fleet started shelling Okinawa and the small islands on the Ryukyu Island chain for two weeks before the land invasion. Fighter planes from the aircraft carriers constantly patrolled the air to protect U.S. ships from Japanese air attacks, and U.S. dive bombers targeted enemy air bases and ships in order to soften up Japanese defenses and draw the enemy planes out for a fight before the land attack.

Chaplains on all ships held regular worship services, and they made their rounds throughout the vessels to encourage men during mealtime and at their duty stations. Father Joseph T. O'Callahan, in his memoir of World War II titled *I Was Chaplain on the Franklin*, wrote that a week before the fighting began he devoted "several hours each day . . . to hear confessions." The men were growing anxious, and by scores they sought out their chaplain to pray and get right with God.[35] With 1200 Catholics on this 3300-man carrier, O'Callahan kept busy, but this was only part of his work. On March 18, the first day of combat, he also went down to the pilots' "ready rooms to say a short prayer with the boys before they take off." He needed to encourage them yet be careful to neither "scare . . . nor delay them."[36]

The sea battle that began in earnest on March 18 became much more problematic and dangerous than earlier battles because of the added element of kamikaze planes. The Japanese had hastily trained at least two thousand young pilots. Each man had one task: fly his airplane laden with a five-hundred-pound bomb into an American ship. Some of the suicide planes had been used sporadically already, but the tempo escalated enormously in the waters near Okinawa. As U.S. Marine Corps historian Allan Millett explained it, "Eventually the Japanese launched ten large-scale *Kamikaze* attacks on the 5th Fleet with almost 1,500 planes." This new dimension of air warfare accompanied the continuous air assaults by conventional bombers.[37]

The men who lived through these attacks experienced an unusual kind of horror, and some of them tried to describe it. A. M. Lusk, the Protestant chaplain aboard the cruiser *Astoria*, recalled that the general alarm sounded in the early afternoon and the gunnery officer calmly announced: "Some 40 enemy planes have just succeeded in getting through the Combat Air Patrol and coming in on the fleet." He remembered that the sky became "somewhat black with exploding shells as five suicide planes dived on our task group." All five were knocked down and a "lull" came in the battle. But then a sixth plane appeared, and as it was blown apart by antiaircraft guns, a machine gun slug from the plane "hit me in the back penetrating to a position near the kidney and the lining of the stomach." The thirty-four-year-old chaplain praised God for his deliverance and recalled, "I was able to go ahead with my work on the eighth day after being hit."[38]

Chaplain L. M. Cole on the attack transport *Henrico* suffered a less serious wound when several kamikaze planes flew toward his ship. One broke through. Chaplain Cole's left arm was burned and torn open from molten shrapnel, but many on the ships were not so fortunate. The chaplain organized a group of army soldiers, on their way to a land invasion and with no specific duties onboard ship, into stretcher bearer teams. Sixty men were killed in the attack and nearly eighty more were wounded and evacuated to other ships.[39]

Cole, a Protestant, prayed with dying men and took as many messages as he could for their next of kin. Soon thereafter this forty-five-year-old minister joined a burial party on a little island off Okinawa, "saying the burial service for the Catholic, Jewish, and Protestant dead, since chaplains of the other faiths were not available." Eventually Chaplain Cole "sent letters of condolence to the nearest of kin with a photograph of the burial plot."[40]

LIKE THE CLERGY who served on ships, army and navy chaplains who accompanied soldiers and marines invading Okinawa were involved in a flurry of activities. On some parts of Okinawa chaplains were so occupied identifying the dead and holding burial services that they experienced difficulty getting beyond the gruesome and tedious work of graves registration. There was an urgency, of course, because bodies bloated and decomposed so rapidly that the stench became nearly unbearable. Also, because the Americans were determined to treat the remains of their fallen comrades with utmost dignity, they did everything feasible to identify the bodies and place them underground before swarms of flies and the voracious appetites of birds and other animals of prey wrought still more unspeakable desecration.

To be sure, many chaplains made their way up to the front lines—holding small services when possible and sprinting from squad to squad with words of encouragement and prayer. E. B. Sledge, who fought with the First Marine Division at Peleliu and Okinawa, recalled how often he uttered prayers to keep up his courage during the emotionally and physically debilitating terror of combat. His son, Henry, has his father's pocket-sized New Testament. This little book, always carried in his uniform, served as a source of comfort during harrowing experiences of war.[41] In Private First Class Sledge's brilliant memoir, *With the Old Breed at Peleliu and Okinawa*, there is a graphic account of a Protestant chaplain who did his best to minister to exhausted, beleaguered marines in the thick of combat. "Late in the afternoon, we halted temporarily along a muddy trail running along the treeless slope of a muddy ridge." Sledge noted that "Japanese shells whistled across the ridge and burst to the rear." In the midst of this rattle and roar of rifle and artillery, with "explosions booming and thundering," the regimental chaplain "set up a little altar made out of a box from which he was administering Holy Communion to a small group of dirty Marines."

> *I glanced at the face of a Marine opposite me as the file halted. He was filthy like all of us, but even through a thickly mud-caked dark beard I could see he had fine features. His eyes were bloodshot and weary. He slowly lowered his light machine gun from his shoulder, set the handle on his toe to keep it off the mud, and steadied the barrel with his hand. He watched the chaplain with an expression of skepticism that seemed to ask, "What's the use of all that? Is it gonna keep them guys from gettin' hit?" That face was so weary but so expressive that I knew he, like all of us, couldn't help but have doubts about his God in the presence of constant shock and suffering. Why did it go on and on? The machine gunner's buddy held the gun's tripod on his shoulder, glanced briefly at the muddy little communion service, and then stared blankly off toward a clump of pines to our rear—as though he hoped to see home back there somewhere.*
>
> *"Move out," came along their file.*
>
> *The machine gunner hoisted the heavy weapon onto his shoulder as they went slipping and sliding around a bend in the trail into the gathering dusk.*[42]

Doubts about God's existence and goodness certainly haunted Sledge and plenty of other men. But during times when they could speak, Christian chaplains reminded the men: "Faith is the sub-stance of things hoped for, the evidence of things not seen."[43] In any case Sledge immediately went from the pastoral interlude with Holy Communion to hastily scooping a foxhole. But they no sooner hunkered down in the foul mud and slime, than their buddy "Doc Caswell got hit." Sledge said, "I forgot about the shells and felt sick. I ran in the direction of the shout to look for Kent Caswell, praying with every step that he wasn't hurt badly." The wound turned out to be severe—but Caswell survived.[44]

IN THE FIRE, smoke, and deafening thunder of battle, men seldom had time to reflect on God's goodness, sovereignty, and the problem of evil. Instead, most men embroiled in battle instinctively reacted—at once to survive and simultaneously to reach out to help others in need. In the throes of this horror, men naturally drew upon the spiritual resources that had been deposited in the banks of their souls—at home and during those quieter times at camp chapel ser-vices and during the worship services on ships, before sailing or fly-ing into combat zones.

One of the most publicized examples of combatants reflexively and sacrificially drawing on their deeply imbedded spiritual resources took place just a few days before the army and marines invaded Okinawa. In the Pacific waters where offensive operations were focused on Okinawa and other islands of Japan, Father Joseph T. O'Callahan already had been spiritually preparing sailors and air-men on the USS *Franklin* for the struggle that lay ahead. There were two chaplains aboard the 27,000-ton carrier—O'Callahan the Catholic and Grimes W. Gatlin, a Methodist. Father O'Callahan, a Jesuit who was two months from his fortieth birthday, had been serving the navy as a chaplain since 1940. Having already attained the rank of lieutenant commander, this graduate of colleges and seminaries in New York and Massachusetts had recently been assigned duty on the *Franklin*, after serving in Florida, Hawaii, and on the USS *Ranger*. Chaplain Gatlin, known as "Gats" to the *Franklin* crew, held the rank of lieutenant J.G. (lieutenant junior grade). A native of Prescott, Arkansas, he had attended college in Oklahoma and seminary at Southern Methodist University in Texas. Chaplain Gatlin seemed like an old man to most of the young sailors aboard. But at age thirty-three, he was clearly junior to the experienced and "salty" priest from New York.[45]

"Gats" and the "Padre" got on well together. Each man had a sense of humor, as well as a keen sense of his calling as a doctor of souls. Both men had been on the *Franklin* only a few weeks, yet they had grown well acquainted with the thirty-three hundred members of the crew. The two chaplains, like most of the officers and men, were beginning to feel at home on the massive ship that seemed like an impregnable fortress—a little city of gray-painted solid steel.[46]

Early in the morning on March 19 a Japanese bomber managed to remain concealed in the clouds. Then like a bolt of lightning the plane dove down to about fifteen hundred yards in front of the ship and dropped two bombs on the carrier. The timing of the bombs was perfect for optimum effect. Airplanes, fully fueled and ready for takeoff, crowded the flight deck. The planes began exploding. And the ship's arsenals of bombs, artillery shells, and machine gun ammunition likewise began to explode with regularity. One formal report described the scene in retrospect: "From that time on for nearly 8 hours, the *Franklin* was simply a floating ammunition dump in the process of blowing up." Naval historian Clifford Merrill Drury described the inferno that twisted and tore up the heavy-gauge steel of the once pristine carrier this way:

The tremendous explosions of 2-ton bombs ripped great holes in the planked flight deck. Sixty 500-pound bombs exploded and twenty-two 250-pounders, in addition to an estimated 12,000 gallons of aviation gasoline which either exploded or burned. Detonated rockets roared down the blazing decks at waist-high level or soared into the sky. Ready ammunition lockers blew up. The fire spread below decks where other explosions took place. Hundreds of men were trapped in compartments, some of whom managed to escape. Others trapped by flames leaped into the sea to escape certain death. For a time the ship lay dead in the water.[47]

By mid-afternoon—some six or seven hours after the attack—firefighters stopped the blazes on the main hangar deck. But the *Franklin* drifted helplessly toward Japan. As soon as the enemy realized the *Franklin's* helpless condition, they launched forty-five planes to finish her off. But the U.S. Navy and Marine planes from other carriers rallied to protect their sister ship. Forty-one of the Japanese planes were shot down and the four surviving Japanese fighters turned back.[48]

The survivors on the *Franklin* were too busy fighting fires, pulling men out of the water, and tending the wounded and dying to realize they had drifted within thirty-eight miles of Japan. Heroic actions became commonplace aboard the crippled vessel that had taken her maiden voyage only seventeen months earlier. Without the total efforts of all the men—many themselves burned and bleeding—the casualties would have been even higher. But in the final count nearly one-third of the crew became casualties: 432 dead and more than 1,000 wounded.

The skipper of the USS *Pittsburgh* courageously put his ship in harm's way to tow the powerless *Franklin* out of close reach of Japanese kamikazes and bombers. He towed the wounded carrier until her engines restarted during the long, frightful night.

While heroic actions were performed all around on the *Franklin*, and while all the crew able to work put themselves in danger to stop fires and save trapped and wounded men—one man caught the attention of almost every officer, sailor, and cameraman—Father O'Callahan. Captain L. E. Gehres, commander of the *Franklin*, saw O'Callahan "manning a hose which sprayed water on bombs so they would not explode. That chaplain gave last rites of his church to the dying; he ministered to the wounded; he organized fire-fighting parties; and repeatedly at the risk of his own life helped to wet down ammunition or assisted in dumping shells overboard." In the last analysis, Captain Gehres declared: "O'Callahan is the bravest man I've ever seen in my life."[49]

For these actions and more—even after being wounded—Chaplain O'Callahan became the first chaplain of the armed forces to receive the Congressional Medal of Honor. But that Medal of Honor recipient always manifested the deepest humility despite his honors. From the day the *Franklin* slowly returned to Pearl Harbor, to the publication of his wartime memoir in 1956, he maintained that his fellow chaplain "Gats" had served equally gallantly. "Gats" received a Purple Heart and was awarded the Silver Star for performing incalculable courageous deeds of service to every man he could reach.[50]

THE JAPANESE SACRIFICED between seventy thousand and a hundred thousand military personnel in their fanatical determination to hold Okinawa at all costs. At the end of the senseless carnage—which caused tens of thousands of civilian casualties as well—the Japanese commanders in charge of the island's defense took their own lives rather than surrender to the Americans.

With American control of Okinawa secured by the end of June 1945, plus General MacArthur's terse announcement on July 5 that the battle for the liberation of the Philippines is "virtually closed," there remained one more objective. The homeland of the Japanese stood as the final obstacle to ending World War II.

In preparation for this climactic operation, the first group of Yanks from the German front arrived in the Philippines on July 22. Thousands more were lining up to join them as part of the final push into Japan. No one knew what this final battle, named Operation Downfall, would cost. Estimates ranged from 1 to 3 million U.S. casualties alone. The specter of death emerged as only one dimension of this descent into hell. The Okinawa campaign not only took more American lives than any previous battle, the psychological toll also proved to be more devastating, by far, than any previous campaign. Donald F. Crosby wrote that "a record number of the men who had participated in the campaign suffered breakdowns or combat-induced insanity. Even chaplains fell victim to the endless days of counterattacks, Kamikaze strikes, and clashes with the enemy's fearsome artillery." Crosby revealed that a priest from New York, "physically exhausted from the battle and totally spent emotionally, had to leave the service before the war ended because of his shattered nerves. Although he lived for twenty more years, his psychological problems tortured him to the end of his days. He and others like him were as much casualties of the Okinawa campaign as the men who perished there."[51]

THE BURDENSOME QUESTIONS weighing heavily on President Harry S. Truman and his top military advisors in summer 1945 were perhaps the most difficult of the war. Could America sustain the continual escalation of casualties required to defeat Japan through a land invasion? Could they afford not to do so? For fourteen months the U.S. had been filling the sky over Japan with B-29 bombers. More than 160,000 tons of firebombs had already been dropped, and the Japanese homeland suffered from an ever-tightening naval blockade. Nevertheless, Japan's determination to fight only grew more fanatical. Then on July 28 the Allies, in the Potsdam Ultimatum, warned the Japanese that they must surrender now or be subjected to a devastating assault that would not stop until Japan had no ability to make war.

Japanese leaders promptly rejected the ultimatum. Therefore President Truman authorized the use of a new weapon that he described as "a new explosive of almost unbelievable destructive power," hoping it would be effective enough to spare a new wave of American losses that could double the numbers already lost since 1941.[52]

AT 11 P.M. on August 5, 1945, Protestant Chaplain William B. Downey, a twenty-seven-year-old Lutheran minister who had been the Protestant chaplain to the 509th Composite Group since November 1944, held a brief prayer service for crew members who, as one crew member phrased it, were "religiously inclined."[53] The crews of several B-29s had been alerted a few hours before that they were being sent early the next morning on the top secret "special" bombing mission that had been long in the making.

Chaplain Downey, a lean 150-pound man with piercing eyes and a winsome smile, always enjoyed the camaraderie of the men of the 509th. Known as a man's man "who would have the occasional glass of whiskey with the officers," he had become famous at their air training base in Wendover, Utah, for playing great hymns of the church over the loudspeakers of the base chapel early on Sunday morning, with blasts pointed toward the officers' sleeping quarters. Because he was so well liked, no one got angry. Instead they gave up on sleeping in and trudged over to the chapel to hear Downey's excellent sermons.[54]

Downey, who always recognized the blessing in brevity, kept the prayer brief:

We pray Thee that the end of war may come soon, and that once more we may know peace on earth. May the men who fly this night be kept safe in Thy care, and may they be returned safely to us. We shall go forward trusting in Thee, knowing that we are in Thy care now and forever. In the Name of Jesus Christ, Amen.[55]

At 2:45 A.M. August 6, several B-29s took off for a thirteen-hour bomb raid. One plane, the *Enola Gay*, piloted by Paul W. Tibbets, who had organized and overseen the training of the 509th, carried the first atomic bomb dropped in World War II. They successfully hit their target, Hiroshima, at 8:15 local time.[56]

Despite the explosion and firestorm of unprecedented proportions, Japan still refused to surrender. A second atomic bomb was dropped on Nagasaki August 9. The next day, Japan offered to surrender if they could keep their emperor.

E. B. SLEDGE expressed sentiments shared by combat veterans all over the Pacific—especially those who had survived the carnage of Okinawa. He said "rumors circulated that we would hit Japan next, with an expected casualty figure of one million Americans. No one wanted to talk about it." Then after word went out about the dropping of the first atomic bomb, rumors spread "about a possible surrender. Then on 15 August 1945 the war ended." The marines in Sledge's unit "received the news with quiet disbelief coupled with an indescribable sense of relief. We thought the Japanese would never surrender. Many refused to believe it. Sitting in stunned silence, we remembered our dead. So many dead. So many maimed. So many bright futures consigned to the ashes of the past. So many dreams lost in the madness that had engulfed us." There were only a few shouts of joy because "the survivors of the abyss sat hollow-eyed and silent, trying to comprehend a world without war."[57]

A similar mood of quiet settled over ships that had been in the thick of the final stages of the bloody climb up the ladder to Japan. Chief Petty Officer Albert G. "Bert" Hayes, chief storekeeper on the USS *Denver*, wrote home to his wife, Mary, in St. Louis on August 11 that the "scuttlebutt" was that Japan was going to surrender. There were no cheers—only men huddling in small groups to ponder among themselves if this had really happened. On August 15 they finally got the word aboard the *Denver*, a ship that had lost twenty-one men when they were torpedoed in the Solomons, and had gone back to shell islands and battle kamikaze planes off Iwo Jima and the Philippines. "Well, this is indeed our 'Red Letter Day.' . . . Finally this mess is all over, a dream of almost four years has finally come true, no more worries about the future." Chief Bert Hayes and his fellow sailors took the news in reflective silence: "I celebrated by going to Mass and Communion this morning and I certainly didn't want to miss being able to thank God for taking such care of me so many times."[58]

On the home front, many people celebrated loudly, wildly—even irresponsibly. In San Francisco the celebrations were so recklessly jubilant that news of the displays reached navy and marine personnel on Saipan. Although the battle-weary men were in a secure area at the time of surrender, these veterans of Guadalcanal, Saipan, and Tinian, according to navy chaplain George W. Wickersham, found the news of the Northern California city's behavior to be "utter foolishness." To be sure there were some cheers, but for the most part, the men were quiet and reflective. And at the end of the day they "sought out the house of God," where Wickersham led a low-key service of worship. In his brief message, he told several hundred men who listened carefully:

> Our choir has just sung "Be still my soul: the Lord is on thy side." . . . Is there anyone here who can so much as doubt whether the Lord has been on our side? My countrymen, he not only has been on our side, but he also will remain on our side, provided we remain on his.[59]

At a Japanese prisoner of war camp in Manchuria, a group of Russian soldiers marched in and declared the Japanese surrender and pronounced the several hundred American and Australian prisoners free. Within a few hours American Protestant chaplain Robert Preston Taylor, along with the Catholic chaplain Father Duffy, conducted a brief worship service. Taylor said:

> For three and one-half years we've prayed for liberation. Now our prayers are answered. To God be the glory! Not only are we happy, but we are humbled, and in that humility must commit ourselves to rebuilding a world where such a war can never occur again. We're going back to our families soon. Let's go back with love in our hearts and his work in our hands. Let's tell the world what God did in Cabanatuan, Bilibid, O'Donnell, Fukuoka 22, and Hoten. This is not the end but the beginning. Let's turn the world right side up—for God and for our country.

Father Duffy closed by leading men with tear-filled eyes in the Lord's Prayer.[60]

* * *

ON AUGUST 16, 1945, the day after Japan's surrender, Catholic, Jewish, and Protestant worship services were held throughout Europe. One of those solemn services was held in the heartland of Germany, at Michelstadt, approximately forty miles southeast of Frankfurt. Protestant Chaplain Howard W. Morgan gathered the 572nd AAA Battalion to a V-J Day Worship service. Grateful men with bare heads and sober faces sang the Doxology, read together "Washington's Prayer for the Nation," and sang "America the Beautiful" and "America" from copies of the ubiquitous maroon *Army and Navy Song and Service Book* distributed and shared among the troops by the chaplain's assistant. Everyone then enjoyed a few minutes of personal prayer and meditation. They read Psalm 67 responsively and listened to the chaplain read Philippians 2:1–16 and briefly comment on the text. The chaplain thanked Almighty God for His blessings and pronounced a Benediction.[61]

For tech corporal Jack Dorsett this V-J Day Worship service brought his experience with the U.S. Army chaplains full circle. Back in early 1943, two and a half years earlier, he had arrived at Fort Leavenworth, Kansas, for basic training. Soon after arrival he attended a chapel service, where he found an anchor of strength and familiarity in the swirl of homesickness caused by separation from his wife, extended family, and the city of his birth, where he had lived for all his thirty-one years. Now, in August 1945, his world began to shift once again. With the war's end, army life about to end, and closure coming to more than two years away from home, the chaplain led him to the Bible and the presence of God.

CHAPTER TEN

HOMEWARD BOUND

The Chaplains Corps' greatest achievement, I believe, was in making the soldier believe that the army did care about him as an individual. . . .We gave him a sense of his own importance. Together with the Medical Corps, we were the soul of the army.

CHAPLAIN MORRIS N. KERTZER[1]

B ING Crosby, one of America's most beloved singers, echoed the sentiments of millions of America's men and women in uniform late in 1943 when he sang "I'll Be Home for Christmas." That year, like every Christmas during the war, found troops scattered around the globe experiencing the bittersweetness of the beloved crooner's words at the end of the song: "I'll be home for Christmas, if only in my dreams."

When the Japanese surrendered in August 1945, many homesick GIs could finally do more than dream. Finally they could count those precious points that determined who would go home first—points based on such factors as time on active duty, combat engagements, and numbers of dependents at home.

In the wake of victory, war-weary troops and their leaders not only totaled points and looked longingly toward home, they also took time to assess their role in the war and the factors that had enabled them to win. They now had leisure to examine themselves and contemplate how they were going to fit into the families, occupations, and communities they'd left behind.

An army chaplain in Europe remembered an incident that captured the conflicted thoughts and emotions of many men. A sergeant pulled open the sky pilot's tent flap, looked in, and happily accepted the invitation to come in and chat. "Well, it's good-bye now, Chaplain. I've got all the points I need and a few extra to kick around. I'm going home and I wanted to be sure to see you before I left." It had been nearly three years since he'd said good-bye to his sweetheart and mother at the railway station in a Midwestern town. He admitted it had been sad to say his farewells to home folks, but now he confessed difficulty at saying good-bye to his wartime pastor. The battle-seasoned noncommissioned officer said, "It's funny, Chaplain, my being so keen on seeing you before I left." Then pointing to a piece of brown wood with hand-carved words—DON'T FORGET YOUR TESTAMENT—the same sign he had seen outside the chaplain's hut before each assignment into combat. The twenty-two-year-old soldier pulled out a worn Testament from his pocket. "Seriously, I'm not going to forget that sign. You know, it's because of you that I'm going home. I'd a never had the guts to get through those three years alone, without you." The chaplain thanked the lad for his encouragement but immediately diverted attention from himself. "It wasn't me, son. It was your Faith that saw you through."[2]

These words were not from the mouth of a falsely humble man. The sage chaplain knew that his efforts to keep men's morale strong yielded the most fruit when a soldier or sailor came into the war with a strong threefold background. As one chaplain put it, character is shaped by home training, secular education, and religious instruction. "One can tell much about an individual's background by the way he acquits himself in action. He is either a credit or a discredit to his parents, teachers, and those who helped shape his character."[3]

It was true that seeds planted by homes, schools, and churches proved invaluable, but the young seedlings required nurture along the way. The influence of chaplains cannot be quantified, but reflective observers noticed that before battles and invasions, and even during lulls in fighting, soldiers had time to think and read. It became commonplace to see a marine or a soldier hunkered down reading a "prayer book, or religious tract, a Protestant Testament, or a Jewish Old Testament, sent to him from home or given to him by his chaplain." This observer wrote that he had seen men reading these, "their only companions," during a lull in front line foxholes or shelters.[4]

MEN PREPARING TO return to the States expressed more than excitement about seeing their loved ones and gratitude that they had survived. Many veterans acknowledged fears about returning home. "I'm afraid of going home," one man told his chaplain. "It's not that I'm not anxious to get home. It's just that I'm leery of getting home, what I'm going to do when I put on civies." The army had made him a soldier, and now "I'm wondering who's going to help make a civilian out of me again?"[5]

How did a person who had seen and experienced so much go back to business as usual? As historian Deborah Dash Moore put it, "They had crammed a lifetime of experiences into a couple of years. Now they were returning to start a new life even as they resumed their old activities."[6] One soldier described his apprehensions this way: "I felt that I had spent a lifetime away."[7]

These veterans had encountered life that the folks at home only met in books and movies. They had crossed oceans in ships; some had even flown overseas on planes. They had met people of other cultures who spoke strange languages. In their years abroad, they'd witnessed sacrificial love where both combatants and civilians risked or gave their lives to aid another person. They'd observed, too, depths of human degradation that destroyed forever their home-grown idealism about the basic goodness of human beings.

Twenty-first-century readers might find it difficult to under-stand the folkways and moral constraints of the early twentieth cen-tury. Nevertheless, World War II–era men were apt to carry guilt that later generations cannot understand. If most married men had remained faithful to their wives during the war, some had suc-cumbed to one-night-stand temptations while on leave; or they had engaged in a tawdry tryst with a prostitute during a drinking spree. These encounters could be debilitating, leaving some men burdened with shame and feeling tentative about going home. But men who had the courage to confess to a chaplain frequently learned from a pastoral counselor that God offers forgiveness, and through such counsel they found freedom from the weight of guilt.

Some men, however, had more than mental and emotional scars from their indiscretions—some had committed infidelities that haunted them for life. Novelist Sloan Wilson probably captured one kind of guilt as well as anyone in *The Man in the Gray Flannel Suit*. The protagonist, Tom Rath, experienced the ravages of heavy com-bat in Europe. Despite the fact that he was married, during an extended period of R & R in Italy he met a young Italian woman, had an affair that lasted several weeks, and then left her to rejoin his regiment for the duration of the war. Years later he discovered that he had left his Italian lover pregnant. She never married, and she kept the child and raised him in the midst of her poverty and shame. When this affair came to light several years later, it nearly shattered Rath's marriage and career.[8] *The Man in the Gray Flannel*

Suit became a best seller in 1955, at least in part because it reso-
nated with the World War II generation.

Plenty of combat veterans went home haunted by their memories
of those they had killed. At a gathering of historians one night in the
early 1970s in Rapid City, South Dakota, Senator George McGovern
said in his speech that the only reason he had not suffered horrid guilt
from killing Germans was that he did it from the air in his Eighth Air
Force B-24 bomber. He never had to look his victims in the eye, and
he felt sorry for the ground troops, who had to see the devastation.

Chaplains who helped troops get psychologically prepared for
home had to help them get past more than guilt caused by personal
indiscretions and taking other men's lives; those who'd served in
fighting units with heavy casualties frequently suffered survivor's
guilt. Men who lived through battles that claimed the lives of many
of their comrades needed sensitive counsel and plenty of time to
process why they had been spared when so many others were not.

THOUSANDS OF COMBAT veterans lived with shame because
they suffered nervous breakdowns in the midst of extended periods
of combat. A man who had to be carried off a battlefield because he
shook too violently to walk, or who panicked and ran from his battle station, carried a load of self-reproach, and he desperately needed
help before he could go home and resume life as usual. To the credit
of the U.S. Armed Forces, transition camps were opened in fall
1945 in France. These embarkation camps—each with a cigarette
brand name—served as processing centers where troops were
assisted in their preparations to sail home. Camps with names like
Lucky Strike, Camel, Chesterfield, Philip Morris, and Old Gold
processed hundreds of thousands of men and women as they began
their journeys.

Chaplains who had served alongside men in combat now helped them fill out paperwork, acquire new clothing, and find medical and dental care during the weeks and even months of "hurry up and wait" before shipping out. Chaplains organized recreation programs to stave off boredom. Football, baseball, and softball teams were formed, as well as track meets and wrestling and boxing matches. Tent and Quonset hut libraries were hastily assembled. And little theater companies and movies provided much-needed entertainment. Likewise, chappies offered a wide range of Jewish, Protestant, and Catholic worship services, as well as religious education classes.

The clergy not only led worship and taught Bible studies and religious classes, they devoted long hours to one-on-one counseling. Stories are legion from veterans who remembered how chaplains and chaplain assistants, and deeply devout fellow GIs, listened to their stories and helped them overcome fears about returning to the States. Many veterans found inner peace when chaplains listened to their concerns and imparted wise counsel on everything from how to behave with a family they had not seen for two or three years, to forgiving a wife who'd had an affair, or simply figuring out how to file paperwork to receive back pay and a variety of GI benefits.

Typical of chaplains who served at ports of embarkation in the Pacific or in Europe, was Bernard S. King, who served at the staging area in La Havre, France. With the Eighty-Ninth Infantry Division at Camp Philip Morris, King's monthly reports revealed that he counseled army couples, performed weddings, made hospital visits, and distributed hundreds of Bibles, New Testaments, and various kinds of religious literature. He helped soldiers write letters home, oversaw a project to construct a chapel that seated 490 people, and conducted innumerable one-to-one counseling sessions. King reported that during the last four months of 1945 his primary objective could be most succinctly described as "preparing men and women to be spiritually prepared to return to civilian life." A man who had been on the front with the men of his battalion throughout the last months of heavy combat in central Europe, this thirty-two-year-old Protestant, who had left a wife and young daughter behind in Minnesota, easily related to combat soldiers. He had shared many of their experiences, hopes, and fears. Evaluations by his superior officers reveal that he ably helped veterans adjust as they awaited their cruise home.[9]

MILITARY CHAPLAINS, LIKE everyone else who served, felt a need to assess their own overall contribution to the war effort. After all, they, too, had given up some of the best years of their lives, and they were coming home with mental and physical scars, as well as the deep-seated grief that came from praying with the wounded and dying, and overseeing the interment of countless valiant men. Chaplain Ben L. Rose, a Presbyterian pastor from North Carolina who'd volunteered for the Army Chaplain Corps seven months before the Pearl Harbor attack, looked back on his service time when the Historical Office of the U.S. Army Chaplain Center and School asked him to give an account of his "most significant contribution(s) to the US Army Chaplaincy." He wrote from his Protestant point of view:

> That for four and a half years during World War II I preached the Gospel of Jesus Christ to the men of the Armed Forces of my country, and thereby offered them spiritual strength which they needed for living and dying and the courage to do their duty without shirking. I asked only for the opportunity to share my knowledge of Christ with them. I was given that opportunity. That was my most significant contribution.[10]

A Kansas Baptist pastor who became a navy chaplain, L. C. Lemons, expressed the chaplaincy's contribution this way:

The Chaplain reaches men who would never darken the door of a church back home but who, in the world of conflict, have suddenly become conscious of needing God. He is with them in their hours of supreme need. To me it is most interesting to see young men wading great distances through mud to attend services; it is interesting to see them sitting there before you, feet planted in the mud, using their helmets for seats, singing with all their hearts, and listening attentively to the message. And then to have them come up afterwards and say, "Chaplain, we have a unit about two miles from here. Won't you come over and hold a service for us so all our men can attend?" I couldn't help thinking of the times back home I had met our young on the street or in their homes, invited them to attend services, and received the usual evasive answers. War does things to young men, and it is a pastor's greatest opportunity to win them, and I might add, to indirectly win the hearts of their parents and loved ones at home.[11]

Morris N. Kertzer, a Conservative rabbi with keen insight and charitable spirit, wrote that "somewhere in the history of the Jewish military Chaplaincy there should be recorded the simple fact that our ministration to the half-million or more men entrusted to us would never have been possible if it were not for the active help and blessing of our Christian colleagues."[12]

Rabbi Kertzer amplified the ecumenism that the Chaplain Corps encouraged, and he showed how this produced a wide-ranging effect that would bless Americans for years to come. The credit went to conditions of military life in general, but in the final analysis it had a "tremendous effect on most chaplains." To illustrate, Kertzer wrote:

A Southern Methodist preacher, who had never seen a Jew out on the Texas range, who had first heard of Catholics when his mother spoke of the bogeyman, shared a tent or a foxhole with a rabbi and a priest. A rabbi leaving his Orthodox synagogue in Flatbush, whose life had been confined within the four walls of Brooklyn Jewry, visited the bedsides of Catholic and Protestant boys. A Benedictine priest, fresh from the cloistered life of a parochial boys' school, shared a room with a Jewish medical officer and became his constant companion. These were experiences that leave permanent marks on our thinking, and what is more important, on our preaching. It is easy to denounce another faith, if one does not have a precious friend who adheres to it.[13]

Many Christian chaplains shared Kertzer's conclusion that their experiences fostered a healthy ecumenical spirit. Clergy who had lived in ignorance of one another's traditions came to recognize that the firstborn child of ignorance is bigotry. And while the war and the chaplaincy did not cause honest and devout clergymen to surrender their own beliefs, they could now respect and admire the traditions of their brothers of other faiths. Indeed, Captain Dave Chambers, who stayed in the service and became a career navy chaplain, spoke at the National Conference on Ministry to the Army Forces on the fiftieth anniversary of the Pearl Harbor attack. In his assessment of the war, he maintained that the religious community of America was changed in World War II chapels:

Many will say that the ecumenical movement was born in the chapels where people of all faiths sat down next to each other. They had never done this before—sang hymns, and prayed and listened to a chaplain whose faith they didn't know, but yet, they were spiritually

*enriched. Three chaplains working together—pluralistic coopera-
tion. That had so seldom happened before.*[14]

IF THE WAR caused Catholic, Jewish, and Protestant ministers to
work together, it also brought whites and African-Americans
together in ways that had been extremely rare before 1941. World
War II at once heightened racial tensions and began to bring those
barriers down. Inside the black communities, as well as among
whites, sharp divisions existed about the wisdom of desegregation
and what the impact of integration would be on troop morale and
race relations in general. Some influential African-Americans
stressed that as long as segregation was the cultural norm, it would
be disastrous to bring down those walls in military installations.
Most whites agreed. On the other hand, vocal and influential members of each race urged desegregation, arguing that forced segregation manifested the undemocratic ideas espoused and employed by
the Axis nations, and as such stood in contradistinction to the ideals
Americans claimed to be fighting to preserve.[15]

Although there were gradual examples of desegregation in small
pockets of the U.S. Armed Forces, no one took a more purposive
stand than the Army Chaplain Corps. As early as April 1942 there
were at least nine African-American army officers integrated into
the chaplain school at Fort Benjamin Harrison in Indiana. They sat
in classes together, marched together, and practiced first aid on one
another. The clergy integrated well and became pioneers in the
integration of the U.S. Armed Forces before President Harry S. Truman's Executive Order 9981 of July 1948.[16]

The Navy Department proved to be much slower than the army
in providing opportunities for African-Americans. Although
African-American enlisted personnel gradually found their way into

the navy and the marines, the first black officer to enter the navy chaplain school, James Russell Brown, did not begin training at the Williamsburg Training School until April 1944—two years after the army opened its doors. Chaplain Brown, a native of Guthrie, Oklahoma, and a graduate of Friends University in Kansas, where he earned a B.A., went on to Howard University in Washington, D.C., where he received a master of Divinity degree in 1935. Ordained in the African Methodist Episcopal Church, Reverend Brown was nearly thirty-four years old when he broke the wall of segregation at the navy chaplain school. He did not always find it easy there. He recalled that even though he took classes, "I was always by myself so far as being among officers and chaplains is concerned."[17]

The confusing status of being the first African-American chaplain in the navy, yet still serving in a segregated environment, caused Brown to suffer an unforgettably painful experience. Walking down a street one day in Williamsburg—still a segregated Virginia city— the black officer did his utmost not to draw attention to himself. But a young white soldier approached, and Lieutenant (Junior Grade) Brown was so accustomed to being ignored that when "the white enlisted man rendered a tremendous salute," Brown "was so startled he couldn't respond, but simply walked by. The experience never left him."[18] He recalled: "How I regretted the incident! I've prayed about that a million times since, because I felt so sorry for the fellow who didn't receive a response from me. I've used it as an illustration in sermons many times, to point out how we can condition ourselves negatively."[19]

In the wake of this wrenching incident, Chaplain Brown went on to help topple racial barriers at Great Lakes Naval Training Center in Illinois and at a base on Guam. And it was his positive and cooperative attitude with white chaplains and officers, as well as African-American servicemen, that enabled him to become an influential warrior in the twin battles to defeat the Axis powers and liberate Americans in the bondage of racism.[20]

IN THE FINAL analysis, professional military historians and high-ranking career military officers have the last word on evaluating the role chaplains played in America's involvement in World War II. U.S. Marine Corps historians Benis M. Frank and Henry I. Shaw, Jr., have drawn this conclusion:

> *The most important thing that can be said about Chaplains, doctors, and corpsmen in any war is that they were "there," and that they were there with the troops when they were needed. The services performed by these Naval personnel . . . have been praised by generals and privates alike. [They] ministered to the spiritual and physical needs of all ranks and religions under all conditions. Although unarmed, they were subjected to the same rigors and discomforts in combat as Marine assault troops.*[21]

Rabbi Morris N. Kertzer offered a similar assessment of the army chaplains' work:

> *The Chaplains Corps' greatest achievement, I believe, was in making the soldier believe that the Army did care about him as an individual. We were a symbol to him, a guarantee that the Army, recognizing its fallibility in dealing with large masses of men, was sufficiently concerned for his welfare to set aside seven thousand trouble-shooters in the Chaplains Corps to short-circuit red tape, to right wrongs, to deal with injustices. We talked and we talked with G.I. Joe. We made him laugh when his heart was heavy. We passed his bed of pain with a pleasantry. We gave him a sense of his own*

importance. Together with the Medical Corps, we were the soul of the army.[22]

Speaking to the Washington, D.C., chapter of the Army and Navy Chaplains Association on October 23, 1945, General A. A. Vandegrift, commandant of the U.S. Marine Corps, said this:

The ministrations you have carried to our fighting men have been an epic of spiritual heroism. Never at any time, to my knowledge, have our men lacked for religious care and guidance.

You have gone wherever they have gone. To millions of American boys, you have been 'A friend that sticketh closer than a brother.'

In this war, they turned to you constantly. You were more than conductors of devotional services. You were helpers, advisors, listeners and comforters. You prayed with them, toiled with them, laughed with them. I recall a sign on one chaplain's tent which made it easier for many a man to talk to him. It read: 'See me at your earliest inconvenience.'

Like the teachers of old, you did not wait for men to come to you. You went out to the men. You made any sacrifice to carry on the task of bringing God to men—and men to God. Your life in the field was rigorous and perilous. Once when a chaplain came in weary and dirty from a day in the lines, I remember hearing a young marine say, with awe in his voice: 'That man sure is doing God a lot of good out here.'

Samuel Johnson once wrote: 'Religion . . . which is animated only by faith and hope, will glide by degrees out of the mind, unless it be invigorated and re-impressed by external ordinances, by stated calls to worship, and the salutary influence of example.'

America's young men travelled far from home, but they did not go one step away from their churches. Their faith could not, and did

not, fade. Stated calls to worship, and the salutary influence of
example, went with them even into the thick of battle.

Men from your ranks marched at their side into the valley of the
shadow of death. I frequently noted in the field, how chaplains—to
a man—sought out front-line action. And I assume that that was
because, as one put it, at the time: 'That is where the fighting man
needs God most—and that's where some of them know him for the
first time.'[23]

THE STORY OF World War II chaplains would be incomplete without mentioning the fact that they, like combat doctors, nurses, medics, and corpsmen, comprised a group of military personnel who
had a difficult time finding people to provide them with the services they provided others. Because medical and soul physicians
were expected to stay strong and always be available to serve others,
their own emotional and spiritual needs were seldom met. To be
sure, chaplains theoretically could have ministered to one another.
And occasionally they found time to do so. But considering the
perennial problem of combat chaplain shortages in all branches of
the armed forces, it is understandable that chaplains seldom found
others who could minister to them.

Neither medical nor soul physicians were immune to what we
would call PTSD—post-traumatic stress disorder. And, like many
men who had endured the horrors of war, they came home with emotional problems that were seldom discussed or diagnosed except in
the most severe cases. The truth is that many American families were
broken and devastated by the psychological wounds of war, while
others merely survived, like broken-down jalopies held together by
bailing wire and mismatched nuts and bolts. Thomas Childers, a historian and the author of several books on World War II, wrote *Soldiers*

from the War Returning, in which he brings into sharp relief what he describes as "the last great battle of the war. That battle," he argued, "was not fought on the fields of Europe or the jungle islands and coral atolls of the South Pacific." That battle was fought in hospitals and divorce courts, "but more often in parlors, kitchens, and bedrooms, buried in the deepest privacy."[24] Childers rightly maintains that the troubled relationships poignantly displayed in the 1946 Oscar-winning film *The Best Years of Our Lives* realistically represented some of the dreadful pain interjected into American families at that time—a malady that, alas, was seldom admitted.[25]

The extent to which chaplains were affected by PTSD has never been studied. Nevertheless, the story of navy chaplain Harold L. Fickett, Jr., is certainly far from unique. Chaplain Fickett was born in Tuscon, Arizona, in 1918. A devout Baptist, Fickett attended Baylor University, where he earned a B.A. in 1938, and then went to Southern Baptist Theological Seminary, receiving a Th.M. in 1941. While in seminary Harold Fickett married. Then he volunteered as a navy chaplain two months before his twenty-fifth birthday. Immediately upon completion of chaplain school in May 1943, this married man with no children received his first assignment, to a naval hospital in San Diego, California. A year later in May 1944, with a year's experience in ministering to men who had been seriously wounded in the Pacific, Fickett found himself reassigned to the USS *Darke*, an attack troop transport ship.

After the war Chaplain Fickett told his son that a year's service among hospitalized men who had been dreadfully wounded and maimed turned out to be important training for serving men on the USS *Darke*. He needed to be prepared because after delivering marines to invade Iwo Jima and Okinawa, the *Darke* lay anchored offshore from these islands of carnage, where attack transports were hastily converted into floating emergency hospitals in which wounded men were patched and stabilized enough to be transferred to proper hospital ships.

Chaplain Fickett recalled that for extended periods—sometimes days on end—he comforted and prayed with men—many of whom never lived long enough to get off the *Darke*. He remembered bending down and cradling one fatally wounded man. The Christian marine asked the Protestant minister: "Will I live?" Fickett responded to the young dying lad that given his faith, he would indeed live. Although Fickett never talked much about his experiences, he did express gratitude that he could comfort many wounded and dying men. On the other hand, he carried ghastly memories of the hours he devoted to assisting busy surgeons by gathering amputated body parts and discarding them so that the doctors could stay on task in a relatively debris-free area.

These experiences haunted Harold Fickett for several years after he returned home and resumed his pastoral duties in Texas. Indeed, during his first year after coming home, the demons of war stalked the courageous pastor so relentlessly that one Sunday morning while speaking from the pulpit, he suffered an anxiety attack and collapsed weeping. Medication and rest soon stabilized the war-weary chaplain, but the emotional scars never completely disappeared.[26]

CHAPLAINS, LIKE THE other 12 million men and women who wore the uniform of the United States during World War II, began their homeward journeys in late 1945 and early 1946. After the fashion of all veterans who, at a minimum, sacrificed some of the best years of their lives, they carried the satisfaction that they had been involved in a worthy enterprise. They were under none of the illusions veterans of World War I carried home—that they had "saved the world for democracy." They could already see the specter of future problems among liberated peoples and those nations who freed them. Nevertheless, they knew their efforts had protected America and freed many nations and ethnic groups from the ravages of Nazi and Japanese aggression and occupation.

Both the U.S. Navy and Army urged chaplains to remain on active duty or at least serve as reservists after the war. America's occupation forces were all over the globe, and these troops also needed spiritual care. A few chaplains answered the call and stayed on. But most longed to return to civilian life. Chaplains like Rabbi Morris N. Kertzer wanted to get back to family, to get home and garner American support for the aid of Jewish refugees seeking to build a homeland in Palestine. Father William J. Leonard yearned to return to his students—many of them war veterans—at Boston College. And while Carol Lemons admitted he loved the navy and "I had been in the right place at the right time . . . that was past; now my place was with my family," who had already been deprived of a husband and father for a long time.[27]

Thus they returned, picked up the pieces as best as possible, and most spent their remaining days at home doing what they did while in the war—ministering to the broken, hurting, guilt-ridden, and grieving. "Serving God and Country" was no mere slogan, but the underpinning of what drove these valiant men to serve regardless of location. As much as those who carried weapons, these spiritual warriors are heroes in the epic battle of World War II.

ACKNOWLEDGMENTS

For more than a decade and a half, I have been collecting primary sources and memorabilia related to American military chaplains in World War II. The person who unquestionably has contributed most to this book is Mary Hayes Dorsett. My faithful wife and closest friend, Mary has always been an able coworker in the search for living and deceased chaplains and their long-overlooked stories. Together we have panned the sands of military archives, libraries, secondhand bookstores, antique shops, flea markets, and eBay listings and sifted gems that are best described as priceless treasures comprising part of our rich national heritage. But Mary has been more than a boon companion on exciting journeys; she encouraged me to write the book, typed every chapter, and served as my best critic. She also helped me collect and identify hundreds of photographs and eventually select and label the ones to be published. And finally, she suggested the title that surpassed all those I put forward.

I am indebted to many other generous people. Good friends Dale Hoskinson, Chaplain Robert Nay, and Bill Search—all fellow collectors of chaplain memorabilia—shared their considerable knowledge of my subject and offered enthusiastic support. Richard Kepner, longtime friend and fellow traveler to a number of historic sites, devoted many days of his limited vacation time to helping me dig through *scores* of the nine thousand files of chaplains' reports in the National Archives.

My friend and fellow historian Stanley Lemons donated numerous items that belonged to his father, Chaplain Leland Carol Lemons, including uniforms, copies of photos, and his unpublished autobiography. Likewise, Janet Kuhns Howard provided pictures, documents, a diary, and other personal items that belonged to her father, Chaplain Bernard King. Both Bernard Ciolek and Don Green contributed a photograph and personal information on Father Venanty Szymanski and his jeep driver Sergeant Earl Conklin. Dan Olson generously gave me a copy of his grandfather's autobiography, *Give Me This Mountain* by Arnold T. Olson, a chaplain who served during the war.

My Ph.D. mentor in the discipline of history, Professor Richard S. Kirkendall, encouraged me in the pursuit of the World War II chaplaincy. He also pointed me to sources at the Harry S. Truman Library. My good friend John Bishop, a retired career Marine Corps officer, managed to open some government doors, and he introduced me to an invaluable living primary source—Richard T. Spooner—a career marine who fought in World War II and had some vivid and fascinating memories of two chaplains who served with him.

Richard Spooner also personally escorted me to meet Dr. Jim Ginther, who ably oversees the Archives and Special Collections Branch, Library of the Marine Corps, Marine Corps University, Quantico, Virginia.

Dr. Ginther is only one of many acrchivists who helped me find material. William E. Taylor, head of the Chaplain Corps Archives,

Fleet Ministry Center, U.S. Naval Station, Norfolk, Virginia, located sources, and he donated some items from his personal collection. The staff at the National Archives Annex, College Park, Maryland, served me for many weeks over several summers. The U.S. Army Chaplain Museum staff at Fort Jackson, South Carolina, proved to be unusually generous and efficient. Particularly helpful were Chaplain (Lieutenant Colonel) Kenneth Lawson, Charlene Brandt, and Donna Dellinger. And museum technician Tim Taylor helped Mary and me in so many kind and thoughtful ways. We are in his debt.

I am grateful to Taffey Hall at the Southern Baptist Historical Library and Archives, Nashville, Tennessee, for locating and making copies of the Eddie Martin papers relating to his service to troops in World War II. David Clark, archivist, Harry S. Truman Museum Library, Independence, Missouri, and his staff, including Randy Sowell and Pauline Testerman, offered able assistance with the L. Curtis Tiernan papers. Also the Minnesota Historical Society generously allowed me to quote from their oral history interview with Chaplain Delbert Kuehl.

I am indebted to Dean Timothy George and Professor Paul House at Beeson Divinity School, Samford University. They approved funds to cover travel expenses and the purchase of books, photographs, and documents. They also provided funding for student assistants: Carol Ford Griggs, Scott Laslo, Matt Rush, and Tim Shepherd. A member of the staff at Beeson Divinity School, Valerie Merrill, did some online sleuthing, introduced me to the son of a World War II chaplain, Harold L. Fickett III, and typed the bibliography.

I owe a special thanks to Rabbi Bernard Honan. Because I am a Christian scholar and pastor, I needed the watchful eye of a Jewish chaplain and rabbi to protect me from misinterpreting information related to the Jewish faith tradition. Rabbi Honan carefully read the entire manuscript.

With much gratitude I thank my friend and fellow writer and historian Denise George, for urging me to meet her literary agent, Greg Johnson. Thank you, Greg, for taking on this book and placing it with the delightful people at the Penguin Group, especially the folks with the Berkley Group: editor Natalee Rosenstein and her assistants, Michelle Vega and Robin Barletta.

Finally, I thank the people who shared their wartime stories, enabling me to tie in the chaplains' contribution to the war effort in personal ways. I am grateful to these veterans and the wife of one chaplain for granting interviews:

Wilmar Bernthal	Thurman I. Miller
Bert Biddulph	Jim "Pee Wee" Morton
Raymond P. "Speedy" Biel	Sid Phillips
R.V. Burgin	William Nesbitt
Henry Cobb	Eugene Richardson
Emmett Dendy	Robert H. Rivers
Ernest Denk	Chester "Chet" Root
Mrs. William B. Downey	Hal Sessions
Dean Dudgeon	John Robert Slaughter
Robert Evans	Robert Spivey
Bradford Freeman	Richard T. Spooner
Ray "Hap" Halloran	Lee Watson
Delbert Keuhl	Red Wells
John Lyes	Hugh Wendorf
Harold MacKenzie	Robert L. Williams
Earl McClung	Tommy Wilson
C. Winsor Miller	Theodore J. "Dutch" VanKirk

May God bless you all for your service to God and Country and your generosity to me.

A NOTE ON SOURCES

Most of this book is based on previously untapped primary sources, in particular more than thirty oral history interviews that I personally conducted with World War II veterans. I have also drawn extensively on my own World War II Chaplain Collection, consisting of a rich archive of unpublished letters, photographs, service records, worship service bulletins, diaries, journals, books, and sundry documents, artifacts, and memorabilia. My collection also consists of scores of chaplains' autobiographies. Many of these are rare, self-published or in manuscript form.

Besides the interviews and the Dorsett Collection, this book is based on extensive research in the National Archives Annex, College Park, Maryland, especially Record Group 247, consisting of monthly reports submitted by nine thousand U.S. army chaplains to their commanders. Also, the U.S. Army Chaplain Museum at Fort Jackson, South Carolina, has a rich library and archive of photographs and various sources.

Naval records are located in the Chaplain Corps Archives, Fleet Ministry Center, U.S. Naval Station, Norfolk, Virginia. And the

Library of the Marine Corps, Marine Corps University, Quantico, Virginia, also houses some important primary source materials.

The papers of Chaplain L. Curtis Tiernan are housed in the Harry S. Truman Library, Independence, Missouri. The evangelist Eddie Martin's papers are in the Southern Baptist Historical Library and Archives, Nashville, Tennessee. And the Delbert Kuehl oral history interview, conducted by Thomas Saylor, is in the Minnesota Historical Society collection.

An invaluable resource is the wartime file of *The Army and Navy Chaplain: A Professional Journal for Chaplains and Religious Workers, 1941-1946*, which is located in the Army Chaplain Museum in Fort Jackson, South Carolina.

NOTES

CHAPTER ONE

1 Quoted in the "Introduction to Office of the Chief of Chaplains, the Chaplain Serves: Chaplain Activities," 1943 (Washington, D.C.: 1944).

2 Author's interview of Sergeant Robert Slaughter, Louisville, Kentucky, March 6, 2009. Slaughter served in Company D, 116th Regiment, 29th Infantry Division. See also his memoir, *Omaha Beach and Beyond* (Minneapolis: Lenith Press, 2007), pp. 131–32. The details of what he told me and what appear in the book are slightly different, but the valor of the chaplain is identical.

3 Author's interview of Lieutenant Henry Cobb, Birmingham, Alabama, December 15, 2007. Cobb was an infantry platoon leader with the Fourth Infantry Division.

4 I. Kaufman, *American Jews in World War II* (New York: Dial Press, 1947), pp. 313–14.

5 *Army and Navy Chaplain*, January-February 1946, p. 4.

6 Donald F. Crosby, *Battlefield Chaplains: Catholic Priests in WWII* (Lawrence, KS: University of Kansas, 1994), p. xxiii.

7 Statistics on the numbers of chaplains who served are in Clifford M. Drury, *The History of the Chaplains Corps, United States Navy*, Vol. 2 (Washington, D.C.: U.S. Gov't Printing Office, n.d.), and Rodger R. Venzke, *Confidence in Battle, Inspiration in Peace: The United States Army Chaplaincy, 1945–1975* (Washington, D.C.: Department of the Army, 1977).

8 The sermon quoted here is in Catherine Marshall, *Mr. Jones, Meet the Master* (New York: Revell, 1950) pp. 21–32. For a biography of Peter Marshall see Catherine Mar-

shall, *A Man Called Peter: The Story of Peter Marshall* (New York: McGraw-Hill, 1951).

CHAPTER TWO

1 Andy Rooney, *My War* (New York: Random House, 1995), p. 259.

2 Carol Lemons, typescript of unpublished autobiography in the author's World War II chaplain memorabilia collection, p. 180.

3 Ibid.

4 Ibid., pp.180–82.

5 James MacGregor Burns, Roosevelt: *The Soldier of Freedom* (New York: Harcourt Brace Jovanovich, 1970), pp. 164–67.

6 Ibid.

7 Ibid.

8 Quoted in James MacGregor Burns, *Roosevelt: The Soldier of Freedom* (New York: Harcourt, Brace, amd Jovanovich, 1970), p. 166, 167.

9 The Gospel of Matthew 22:37–40 (KJV).

10 William Manchester, *Goodbye, Darkness: A Memoir of the Pacific War* (Boston: Little Brown, 1980), pp. 393–95.

11 Frank Luther Mott, *Golden Multitudes: The Story of Best Sellers in the United States* (New York: Macmillan, 1947), p. 331.

12 Gerald L. Sittser, *A Cautious Patriotism: The American Churches and the Second World War* (Chapel Hill: University of North Carolina Press, 1997), pp. 24–25.

13 Rooney, *My War*, pp. 11–12.

14 John J. Morrett, *Soldier-Priest: An Adventure in Faith* (West Conshohocken, PA: Infinity Publishing, 2003), pp. 1–8.

15 See evidence presented by Robert L. Gushwa, *The Best and Worst of Times: The U.S. Army Chaplaincy, 1920–1945*, Vol. IV (Washington, D.C: Chief of Chaplains Office, 1977), and Clifford M. Drury, *The History of the Chaplain Corps, U.S. Navy*, Vol. II, 1939–1949 (Washington, D.C.: U.S. Government Printing Office, n.d.). The direct quotation from the Presbyterian Church is in Gushwa, *Best and Worst of Times*, p. 79.

16 Ibid., see Chapter 2 and p. 79.

17 As late as October 1940, David Max Eichhorn realized that many American Jews were espousing "a policy of appeasement," but he would not. See Greg Palmer and Mark S. Zaid, eds., *The G.I. Rabbi: World War II Letters of David Max Eichhorn* (Lawrence, KS: University of Kansas Press, 2004), p. 34.

18   Oral History Transcript, Chaplain John Harold Craven, 1980, U.S. Navy Chaplain Corps Oral History Program, U.S. Marine Corps University, Quantico, VA, p. 4.

19   See Warren Kozak, *The Life and Wars of General Curtis LeMay* (Washington, D.C.: Regnery, 2009), and his article in the *Wall Street Journal*, May 15, 2009, p. A13.

CHAPTER THREE

1   Quoted in Ellwood C. Nance, *Faith of Our Fighters* (St. Louis: Bethany Press, 1944), p. 106.

2   Clifford M. Drury, *The History of the Chaplain Corps, United States Navy*, Vol. II (Washington, D.C.: U.S. Government Printing Office, n.d.); Chapter 3 contains Navy statistics. Craven's experience is from Oral History Transcript, Chaplain John Harold Craven, 1980, U.S. Navy Chaplain Corps Oral History Program, U.S. Marine Corps University, Quantico, VA, pp. 5–6.

3   Drury, *History of the Chaplain Corps*, p. 41.

4   I did a random sampling of individual files at the National Archives. RG 247 contains approximately nine thousand files—one for each chaplain who served in the army.

5   The Johnstone story is in file 201, RG. 247, National Archives. Also, the author has Johnstone items in his personal World War II chaplain memorabilia collection.

6   Isaac Klein, *The Anguish and the Ecstasy of a Jewish Chaplain* (New York: Vantage Press, 1974), pp. 10–11.

7   Steve O'Brien, *Blackrobes in Blue: The Naval Chaplaincy of John P. Foley, S.J., 1942–1946* (New York: Writers Club Press, 2002), pp. 40–43.

8   Ibid.

9   See, for example, Drury, *History of the Chaplains Corps*, pp. 44–49; Robert L. Gushwa, *The Best and Worst of Times: The U.S. Army Chaplaincy, 1920–1945*, Vol. IV, especially Appendix C (Washington, D.C: Chief of Chaplains Office, 1977). Also Roy J. Honeywell, *Chaplains of the U.S. Army* (Washington, D.C.: Government Printing Office, 1958), Chapters 13, 14, and 15.

10   Gushwa, *Best and Worst of Times*, pp. 208–9.

11   Statistics are in Drury, *History of the Chaplain Corps*, pp. 310–11, and Ray J. Honeywell, *Chaplains of the U.S. Army*, pp. 214–17.

12   Gushwa, *Best and Worst of Times*, pp. 108-9.

13   Drury, *History of the Chaplain Corps*, Chapter 4 and pps. 80–81.

14   Ibid., Chapter 4.

15   Lemons, unpublished autobiography, in the author's personal World War II chaplain memorabilia collection, hereafter cited as Dorsett Collection.

16   See RG 247, National Archives.

17   Wiliam J. Leonard, S.J., *The Letter Carrier: The Autobiography of William J. Leonard* (Kansas City, MO: Sheed and Ward, 1993), p. 102.

18   Klein, *The Anguish and the Ecstasy*, p.20.

19   Ibid., page 22.

20   *Army Chaplain Technical Manual* TM 16-205 (April 21, 1941), paragraph 37, p. 19.

21   Edward K. Rogers file, RG 247, National Archives. His autobiography, *Doughboy Chaplain* (Boston: Meador Publishing Co., 1946) is also useful.

22   Klein, *The Anguish and the Ecstasy*, p.22.

23   The Carlson material in this paragraph and below is taken from the Alvin O. Carlson file, RG 247, National Archives.

24   Ibid.

25   Ibid.

26   Jean P. Cossette file, RG 247, National Archives.

27   A copy of this memorandum, dated October 6, 1943, is in the Dorsett Collection.

28   Ibid.

29   Ibid.

30   J. H. Cosby file, RG 247, National Archives.

31   Such signs as these can be found in various denominational histories of the war, such as *Chaplains of the Methodist Church in World War II* (Washington: Methodist Commission on Chaplains, 1948) and *The Priest Goes to War* (New York: Society for the Propagation of the Faith, 1945), and in the photo files at the Chaplain School Archives, Fort Jackson, South Carolina, the Navy Archives at Norfolk, Virginia, and the National Archives in Washington, D.C. The author has unpublished photos in the Dorsett Collection.

32   *Army and Navy Chaplain*, April–May 1944, pp. 28–30. See also *Army Chaplain Technical Manual* , p. 56. The "temple of God" quotation comes from the Catholic office of the chaplains. Langley Field, Weekly Letter, November 29, 1942, in Dorsett Collection.

33   Letter from Wilmar Bernthal to Lyle Dorsett, January 9, 2009; Jack Sacco, *The True Story of the 92nd Signal Battalion and the Liberation of Dachau* (New York: Harper Collins, 2003), p. 90.

34   Records of the 142nd AAA Mobile Gun Battalion, 270 Branch, Box 16974.

35 James A. Bryant, "To Whom It May Concern," March 30, 1943, in the Eddie Martin Papers, (1941–1946), Southern Baptist History Archive, Nashville, Tennessee.

36 Charles Albright to "Dear Sirs," September 1943, Martin Papers.

37 See Mrs. Ernestine Mabry, "To Whom It May Concern," November 11, 1943, as well as dozens of other letters in the Martin Papers.

38 See Captain Herbert H. Hunsberger, Hunter Field, Georgia, to "Sir," June 1, 1944, Martin Papers; an activity listing dates from December 7–30, 1944, Camp Bowie, Texas.

39 Postcard from Chaplain Draffin to Mrs. Dorsett dated September 1943 and the letter to Mrs. Leske from Chaplain Holland dated January 19, 1944, are in the Dorsett Collection.

40 These orders of worship are part of the Dorsett Collection.

CHAPTER FOUR

1 "White Letter," Box 30, "Combat Ministry" Folder, Marine Corps Library, Marine Corps University, Quantico.

2 George W. Wickersham, *Marine Chaplain, 1943–1946*, fourth edition (Bennington, VT: Merriam Press, 1997), p. 11.

3 Ibid., 12.

4 Author's interview with Chester (Chet) Root, Wheaton, Illinois, September 8, 2001.

5 Box 30, "Combat Ministry" Folder, Library of the Marine Corps, p. 2.

6 Robert L. Gushwa, *The Best and Worst of Times: The U.S. Army Chaplaincy, 1920–1945 Vol.IV* (Washington, D.C.: Chief of Chaplains Office, 1977), pp. 215–16, and Clifford M. Drury, *The History of the Chaplain Corps, U.S. Navy*, Vol. II (Washington, D.C.: U.S. Government Printing Office, n.d.), 155–59.

7 Christopher Cross, *Soldiers of God* (New York: E. P. Dutton, 1945) pp. 23–25, and Elwood C. Nance, *Faith of Our Fighters* (St. Louis: Bethany Press, 1944), p. 64.

8 Ibid., 26–43.

9 William A. Maguire, *Rig for a Church* (New York: Macmillan, 1942).

10 Cross, *Soldiers of God*, Part One, pp. 21–43.

11 "History of Chaplains' Activities in the Pacific" (unpublished manuscript, compiled GHQ, AFPAC, 1946). See, for example, pp. 183–88.

12 Ibid.

13 These pictures are in the Dorsett Collection.

14   *Yank*, January 20, 1943, quoted in "History of Chaplains' Activities," pp. 317, 448, and 449.

15   Author's interview with Chet Root, September 8, 2001, Wheaton, Illinois.

16   See, for example, Arthur F. Glasser, *And Some Believed: A Chaplain's Experience with the Marines in the South Pacific* (Chicago: Moody Press, 1946), Chapter 3, and William C. Taggart, *My Fighting Congregation* (New York: Doubleday, 1943), Chapter 10.

CHAPTER FIVE

1   Author's interview with Richard T. Spooner, Quantico, Virginia, July 17, 2008.

2   *Army and Navy Chaplain*, October-November 1943, p. 35.

3   See George W. Wickersham, *Marine Chaplain, 1943-1946* (Bennington, Vermont, Merriam Press, 1997), p.11.

4   Evidence of this improvisation is in a photo in the Dorsett Collection, the caption on which reads: "Sky Pilots Jump too."

5   "History of Chaplains' Activities in the Pacific" (unpublished manuscript, compiled GHQ, AFPAC, 1946), p. 400, on lay preachers. For information on Bowman, see Donald F. Crosby, *Battlefield Chaplains: Catholic Priests in WWII* (Lawrence, KS: University of Kansas, 1994), pp. 61–63.

6   "History of Chaplains' Activities," p. 401.

7   Ibid., pp. 398–99.

8   The photograph and clipping from the *Times* are in the Dorsett Collection.

9   "History of Chaplains' Activities," p. 316.

10   J. Edwin Orr file, RG 247, National Archives.

11   Ibid.

12   See his autobiography of his service in the war: J. Edwin Orr, *I Saw No Tears* (London: Marshall, Morgan and Scott, 1948) and his records in RG 247, National Archives.

13   Orr, *I Saw No Tears*, p. 69.

14   Ibid., pp. 35 and 36.

15   A. A. Vandegrift, *Once a Marine: The Memoirs of General A. A. Vandegrift, U.S.M.C.* (New York: Norton, 1964), pp. 101–05.

16   Richard Tregaskis, *Guadalcanal Diary* (New York: Random House, 1943), p. 3.

17   Ibid., pp. 21 and 22.

18   Ibid.

19   Clifford M. Drury, *U.S. Navy Chaplains 1778–1945* (Washington, D.C.: U.S. Government Printing Office, 1948), p. 229. See also Crosby, *Battlefield Chaplains*, pp. 36–44.

20   Crosby, *Battlefield Chaplains*, p. 40.

21   Ibid., pp. 40 and 44.

22   Ibid., p. 40.

23   Dorothy Freemont Gray, *War Is My Parish* (Milwaukee: Bruce Publishing Co., 1944), p. 73.

24   Drury, *Navy Chaplains*, pp. 145 and 146.

25   Crosby, *Battlefield Chaplains*, p. 48.

26   Ibid.

27   Ibid.

28   W. Wyeth Willard, *The Leathernecks Come Through* (New York: Revell, 1944), p. 139.

29   Lemons, unpublished autobiography, Dorsett Collection, p. 179.

30   Glyn Jones, "Combat Chaplain," *Army and Navy Chaplain*, June 1944, p. 28.

31   Ibid.

32   The glass communion cups are in the MacKorell Grouping in the Dorsett Collection. Details on MacKorrell services are from the Jacob S. MacKorrell, Jr., file, RG 247, National Archives.

33   RG 247, National Archives.

CHAPTER SIX

1   D. D. Nicholson, *Marine Corps Gazette*, December 1953.

2   Allan R. Millett, *Semper Fidelis: The History of the U.S. Marine Corps* (New York: Macmillan, 1980), p. 370.

3   W. Wyeth Willard, *The Leathernecks Come Through* (New York: Revell, 1944), p. 184.

4   Author's interview with Robert H. Rivers, Birmingham, Alabama, March 6, 2006.

5   Arthur F. Glasser, *And Some Believed* (Chicago: Moody Press, 1946), Chapter IV.

6   Willard, *Leathernecks Come Through*, Chapter XX.

7   Ibid., pp. 202 and 203.

8   Ibid., pp. 199 and 200.

9   Both Glasser, *And Some Believed*, and Willard, *Leathernecks Come Through*, provide material on these topics.

10   A copy of this item is in the Dorsett Collection.

11   Williard, *Leathernecks Come Through*, p. 206.

12   Donald F. Crosby, *Battlefield Chaplains: Catholic Priests in WWII* (Lawrence, KS: University of Kansas, 1994), p. 59.

13   Ibid.

14   This paragraph and the following section on Father Paul Redmond come from O'Briend, "Raiders' Priest of Three Faiths," *Marine Corps Gazette*, November 1979; R. D. Workman, *Marine Corps Gazette*, October 1943; Anonymous Author, *Leatherneck*, April, 1944; and Clifford M. Drury, *U.S. Navy Chaplains 1778–1945* (Washington, D.C.: 1948), p. 230.

15   *Leatherneck*, April, 1944.

16   O'Briend, "Raiders' Priest."

17   Deborah Dash Moore, *GI Jews: How World War II Changed a Generation* (Cambridge, MA: Harvard, 2004), p. 142.

18   John Monks and John Falter, *A Ribbon and a Star: The Third Marines at Bougainville* (New York: Holt, 1945), p. 36.

19   Ibid.

20   Ibid., pp. 36–38.

21   A sketch on Kempker is in Drury, *Navy Chaplains*, 146. See also Monks and Falter, *A Ribbon and a Star*, p. 211.

22   Monks, *A Ribbon and a Star*, p. 236.

23   D.D. Nicolson, *Marine Corps Gazette*, Dec. 1953.

24   Clipping in the Dorsett Collection.

25   Crosby, *Battlefield Chaplains*, p. 68.

26   Photos like the scenes described here are in volumes such as *The Priest Goes to War* (New York: Society for the Propagation of Faith, 1945), unit histories of marine and army divisions, and in the Dorsett Collection.

27   S. G. Silcox, *A Hillbilly Marine* (privately published, 1977).

28   Ibid., pp. 88, 90, and 115, argues that every dead marine was carefully located and accounted for, but chaplains and other observers knew better what sometimes happened.

29   See Chapter 4 in Crosby, *Battlefield Chaplains*.

30   Drury, *U.S. Navy Chaplains*, p. 212.

31   Crosby, *Battlefield Chaplains*, p. 74.

32   Ibid.

33   Ibid., p. 76.

34   Grime's bracelet and some of the correspondence is in the Dorsett Collection.

35   Author's interview with Robert Spivey, April 29, 2009, Birmingham, Alabama.

36   Jack Kinkopf, *The Chalice and the Heavy Coat* (privately published, 2002), p. 82.

37   Author's interview with Spivey.

38   Moore, *GI Jews*, pp. 90–98.

39   RG247 files in the National Archives show that in the army, for instance, battalion commanders wanted monthly statistics on numbers of worship services, baptisms, catechism classes, etc.

40   Henry Shaw, Bernard C. Nalty, and Edwin Turnbach, *History of U.S. Marine Corps Operations in World War II*, Vol. III, *Central Pacific Drive* (Nashville: Battery Press, 1994), p. 346.

41   Ibid., p. 422.

42   Ibid., p. 568.

43   Ibid.

44   Crosby, *Battlefield Chaplains*, pp. 176 and 177.

45   Quoted in Allen G. Mainard, "Since November 28, 1775," *Leatherneck*, November 1955. A sketch on Michaels is in Drury, *U.S. Navy Chaplains*, p. 190.

46   Oral History Transcript, Chaplain John Harold Craven, 1980, U.S. Navy Chaplain Corps Oral History Program, U.S. Marine Corps University, Quantico, Virginia, p.18.

47   Ibid.

48   Ibid.

49   Max Vorspan file, RGA247, National Archives.

50   Ibid.

51   A sketch of Whalen is in Drury, *U.S. Navy Chaplains*, p. 292. Whalen's story is in Crosby, *Battlefield Chaplains*, pp. 117 and 177.

52   A sketch of Gallagher is in Drury, *U.S. Navy Chaplains*, p. 100, and Gallagher's reminiscences are in Crosby, *Battlefield Chaplains*, Chapter 10.

53   Ibid., 181.

54   Author's interview with Rick Spooner, July 17, 2008, Quantico, Virginia.

55   Craven Oral History Interview, 20.

56   Author's interview with Tommy Wilson, September 1, 2009, Birmingham, Alabama.

57   Harold Helfer, "Diversity in Dungarees," *Leatherneck*, August 1945.

58 Rick Spooner, *The Spirit of Semper Fidelis* (Williamstown, N.J.: Phillips Publications, 2005), Chapter 3; author's interview with Spooner, July 13, 2008.

59 Craven Oral History Interview, p. 23.

60 Ibid., p. 24.

61 *Western Pacific Operations*, Vol. IV., pp. 475 and 476.

62 Crosby, *Battlefield Chaplains*, pp. 212 and 213; Craven Oral History Interview, p. 28.

63 Louis Barish, ed., *Rabbis in Uniform: The Story of the American Jewish Chaplain* (New York: Jonathan David, 1962), Appendix 8; Craven Oral History Interview, pp. 27 and 28; and Crosby, *Battlefield Chaplains*, Chapter 12.

64 Craven Oral History Interview, p. 27.

65 George W. Garand and Truman R. Strobridge, *Western Pacific Operations, History of U.S. Marine Corps Operations in WW II* (Nashville, Tennessee: 1994),Vol. IV, Appendix H.

66 Ibid., p. 527.

67 A sketch of Hotaling is in Drury, *U.S. Navy Chaplains*, p. 130, and his remarks appear in Vernon Langille and Stanley Linn, *Leatherneck*, April 1948.

68 Crosby, *Battlefield Chaplains*, 221, 222. See photo on 222.

69 For a sketch of Martin, see, *U.S. Navy Chaplains*, 175; Crosby, Battlefield Chaplains, 222.

70 A. A. Vandegrift, *Once a Marine: The Memoirs of General A. A. Vandegrift, U.S.M.C.* (New York: Norton, 1964), p. 276.

71 *Western Pacific Operations*, Vol. IV, pp. 727 and 728.

72 D. D. Nicholson, *Marine Corps Gazette*, December 1953.

73 A copy of this address is in the Archives and Library of the Marine Corps University, Quantico, Virginia. A sketch of Gittelsohn is in Drury, *U.S. Navy Chaplains*, p. 105.

CHAPTER SEVEN

1 Jack Alexander, "He's Our Guy," *Saturday Evening Post*, April 26, 1945.

2 Published autobiographies of chaplains frequently contain evidence of these last-minute problems they were called upon to solve. And examples of "checklists" are in the Glen Trent and Jack Dorsett files in the Dorsett Collection.

3 B. L. Bowman, *Transport Chaplain* (Sarasota, FL: Star Printing, 1947), pp. 16 and 17.

4 Ibid., p. 17.

5   Arnold T. Olson, *Give Me this Mountain: An Autobiography* (privately published, 1987), p. 101.

6   Clyde E. Kimball, *A Diary of My Work Overseas* (Nashua, N.H.: privately published, 1947), p. 123.

7   Bowman, *Transport Chaplain*, pp. 51–53.

8   Ibid., p. 87.

9   Robert L. Gushwa, *The Best and the Worst of Times: The U.S. Army Chaplaincy, 1920–1945*, Vol. IV (Washington, D.C.: Chief of Chaplains Office, 1977), pp. 127 and 128.

10 Dan Kurzman, *No Greater Glory: The Four Immortal Chaplains and the Sinking of the Dorchester in World War II*, (New York: Random House, 2004), p. 114.

11 Ibid.

12 Gushwa, *Best and Worst of Times*, p. 128.

13 Ibid., pp. 128 and 129. These stories are by Kurzman, *No Greater Glory*, and Francis B. Thornton, *Sea of Glory: The Magnificent Story of the Four Chaplains* (New York: Prentice Hall, 1953).

14 Gushwa, *Best and Worst of Times*, p. 128.

15 Ibid., p. 140.

16 A glimpse of the work of an army chaplain's assistant can be seen in a little volume titled *Chaplain's Assistant* (Seattle: Crafstman Press, 1945). This book is based on letters written home by Corporal Kenneth A. Connelly, Jr., who served as an assistant with the 333rd Regiment of the Eighty-Fourth Infantry Division.

17 Kimball, *Diary of My Work*. Page 1 has his Silver Star Citation. Pages 125–60 are excellent descriptions of his duties in England between combat missions.

18 Ibid., p. 129.

19 Ibid., p. 130.

20 Ibid.

21 Ibid.

22 Ibid., pp. 110 and 136.

23 Ibid., p. 125.

24 RG 247, National Archives, which contains monthly Army Chaplains Reports, is replete with examples of kindnesses performed by Americans under the direction of their chaplains. See, for example, the files of A. D. Votaw, E. A. Autrey, and N. G. Crosby. For material on L. Curtis Tiernan, including a photo of him on his bicycle, see Tiernan Papers, Harry S. Truman Library, Independence, Missiouri.

25 Newton Gordon Cosby file, RG 247, National Archives.

26   Evidence of this can be found in Cosby's book, *By Grace Transformed* (New York: Crossroad Publishing Co., 1999) as well as in his file in RG 247, National Archives.

27   Cosby and E. A. Autrey files, RG 247, National Archives.

28   Cosby, *By Grace Transformed*, p. 3.

29   The *Army Chaplain Technical Manual* (TM 16-205) was issued April 21, 1941. A revised and expanded version of TM 16-205 was published July 5, 1944. The navy chaplain's manual is NAVPERS 15664-A.

30   Jack Alexander, "He's Our Guy," *Saturday Evening Post*, April 26, 1945.

31   Ibid.

32   Ibid.

33   Mac Davis, *Jews Fight, Too!* (New York: Hebrew Publishing Co., 1945), 78.

34   Ibid., p. 79.

35   Albert Isaach Slomovitz, *The Fighting Rabbis: Jewish Military Chaplains and American History* (New York: New York University Press, 1999), p. 87.

36   Ibid., pp. 87 and 88.

37   Philip H. Oxnam, "I Know They Believe," in Ellwood C. Nance, ed., *Faith of Our Fighters* (St. Louis: Bethany Press, 1944), pp. 23–27.

38   Ibid., p. 25.

39   Ibid., p. 26.

40   Ernie Pyle, *Here Is Your War,* (Chicago: Consolidated Book Publishers, 1944), pp. 131-132.

41   R. A. Gabriel, ed., *Military Psychiatry: A Comparative Perspective* (Westport, CN: Greenwood Press, 1986). See Chapter 2, Lawrence Ingraham and Frederick Manning, "American Military Psychiatry," pp. 35–37, 38–46.

42   Ibid., p. 38.

43   Ibid., p. 45.

44   I heard this from scores of World War II combat veterans whom I have interviewed. Also, diaries and memoirs of chaplains, as well as of ordinary soldiers, reveal the assurance that is felt when a chaplain is present during combat. See Chapter 1 of this book for references to Slaughter, *Omaha Beach and Beyond*, pp. 131–132; Kaufman, *American Jews in World War II* , pp. 313–314; my interview with Henry Cobb; and see H. Dean, personal diary of Private H. Dean, First Pursuit Group, Seventy-First Pursuit Squad (unpublished memoir in Dorsett Collection), p. 55.

45   Ingraham and Manning, "American Military Psychiatry," p. 46.

46   Frederick C. Proehl, ed., *Marching Side by Side: Stories from Lutheran Chaplains on the Far-flung Battlefronts* (St. Louis: Concordia, 1945) pp. 52 and 53.

47 Ibid., pp. 53 and 54.

48 Louis Barish, ed., *Rabbis in Uniform: The Story of the American Jewish Military Chaplain* (New York: Jonathan David, 1953), Part II, Judah Nadich, "Rabbis to the Rescue," p. 36.

49 Ibid., p. 36.

50 Donald F. Crosby, *Battlefield Chaplains: Catholic Priests in WWII* (Lawrence, KS: University of Kansas, 1994), p. 98.

51 Ibid., p. 121.

52 H. R. Knickerbocker, "Chaplains at the Front," in Ellwood C. Nance, ed., *Faith of Our Fighters* (St. Louis: Bethany Press, 1944).

53 Oral History interview conducted by Thomas Saylor with Chaplain Delbert Kuehl, April 5, 2003, Alexandria, Minnesota. Transcription online courtesy of the Minnesota Historical Society Web site.

54 Israel A. S. Yost, *Combat Chaplains* (Honolulu: University of Hawaii Press, 2006), p. XV.

55 Yost, *Combat Chaplains*, p. 1.

56 Ibid., Chapters 5–9, pp. 47–179.

57 *Chaplains of the Fifth Army* (Milan, Italy: Pizzi and Pizzi Printers, 1945), no author or edition listed, passed by the Military Censor for the Fifth Army, pp. 17 and 18.

58 Ibid., p. 39.

59 Yost, *Combat Chaplains*, p. 226.

60 Ibid., p. 227.

61 *Chaplains of the Fifth Army*, p. 18.

62 Crosby, *Battlefield Chaplains*, pp. 104–106.

63 Ibid., p. 106.

64 Cleo W. Buxton, with assistance of David A. Church and Betsy Buxton, "For Me to Live Is Christ," unpublished manuscript in the Dorsett Collection, p. 52.

65 Ibid., pp. 52 and 53.

66 Ibid. and author's interview with Harold MacKenzie, June 27, 2007, Wheaton, Illinois.

67 RG 247 National Archive files contain substantial evidence that sexual promiscuity brought disease, personal problems, and emotional pain. And some chaplains were furious with other chaplains who refused to speak out against sexual activity outside of marriage.

68 Buxton, "For Me to Live," p. 53.

69 Besides Buxton's memoir, several veterans I knew well personally recalled observing brothel lines and chaplains urging men to fall out.

70 Buxton, "For Me to Live," pp. 53–55.

71 Francis L. Sampson, *Look Our Below!: A Story of the Airborne by a Paratrooper Padre* (Sweetwater, TN: 101st Airborne Association, 1989), p. 75. See also Crosby, *Battlefield Chaplains*, pp. 126–126 and 133.

72 Edward K. Rogers, *Doughboy Chaplain* (Boston: Meador Press, 1946), pp. 228 and 229.

73 *Chaplains of the Fifth Army*, p. 41.

74 Ibid., pp. 41 and 42.

75 Ibid., p. 42.

76 Psalm 139:8.

CHAPTER EIGHT

1 H. R. Knickerbocker, "Chaplains of the Front," in Ellwood C. Nance, ed., *Faith of Our Fighters* (St. Louis: Bethany Press, 1944), p. 156.

2 Stephen E. Ambrose, *Citizen Soldiers* (New York: Simon & Schuster, 1997), p. 299.

3 Ibid.

4 Ibid., p. 293.

5 Author's interview with Lee Watson, January 14, 2008, via telephone from Birmingham Alabama.

6 Janelle T. Frese, with George Russell Barber, *Oh Chaplain! My Chaplain!: Man of Service* (Victoria, Canada: Trafford, 2005) p. 12.

7 Ibid.

8 Ibid., p. 13.

9 Ibid. p. 14.

10 Letter to Lyle and Mary Dorsett from William Nesbitt, M.D., February 6, 2006.

11 Quoted in Steve Rabey, *Faith Under Fire* (Nashville: Thomas Nelson, 2002), p. 95.

12 Christopher Anderson, "Ralph Haga's Call to Duty," *World War II*, June 2005, p. 58.

13 *Stars and Stripes*, July 4, 1944, p. 2.

14 Stephen E. Ambrose, *D-Day, June 6th 1944: The Climatic Battle of World War II* (New York: Simon and Schuster, 1994), p. 576.

15 Richard B. Morris, ed., *Encyclopedia of American History* (New York: Harper and Row, 1965), p. 378.

16   Author's interview with Ernest Denk, July 3, 2007, via telephone from Chicago, Illinois.

17   Author's interview with Burt Biddulph, May 28, 2009, via telephone from Florida.

18   Ibid.

19   The diary and official papers of Chaplain Bernard S. King, as well as photographs that illumine some of his ministry environment, are in the Dorsett Collection.

20   A copy of this roster is in the Dorsett Collection.

21   A copy of the Marinos "Individual Deceased Personal File" is in the Dorsett Collection.

22   Francis L. Sampson, *Look Out Below: A Story of the Airborne by a Paratrooper Padre* (Sweetwater, TN, 1989), p. 56.

23   Ibid., p. 59.

24   Ibid., p. 60.

25   Ibid.

26   Ibid.

27   Ibid., pp. 63 and 64.

28   Ibid., p. 67.

29   Ibid., pp. 67 and 68.

30   Ibid., p. 68.

31   Chaplain Cornelius Van Schouwen, *My Diary (1943–1946)* (privately published), p. 70.

32   Ibid., p. 81.

33   Ibid.

34   Morris N. Kertzer, *With an H on My Dog Tag,* (New York: Behrman House, 1947) pp. 22 and 23.

35   Van Schouwen, *My Diary*, pp. 82 and 83.

36   Ibid., pp. 89 and 93.

37   Jean Cossette file, RG 247, National Archives.

38   Ibid.

39   Jean Cossette file, RG 247, National Archives, see especially the December 1944 report. See also General Order Number 215, Headquarters Eighty-Third Infantry Division, October, 18, 1945.

40   Oscar W. Schoech file, RG 247 National Archives.

41 Ibid., see file dated May 1, 1945.

42 Ambrose, *Citizen Soldiers*, Chapter 7, "The Ardennes, December 16–19, 1944."

43 Quoted in Ambrose, *Citizen Soldiers*, p. 191.

44 Clyde E. Kimball, *A Diary of My Work Overseas* (Nashua, NH: Granite States Press, 1947), December 6 entry, p. 188.

45 Ibid., December 8, 1944, pp. 188 and 189.

46 Ibid., p. 1.

47 Ambrose, *Citizen Soldiers*, p. 357.

48 On the Battle of the Bulge and for material on Malmédy, see Charles B. MacDonald, *A Time for Trumpets: The Untold Story of the Battle of the Bulge* (New York: William Morrow, 1984); Ambrose, *Citizen Soldiers*, Parts II and III; and Donald F. Crosby, *Battlefield Chaplains: Catholic Priests in WWII* (Lawrence, KS: University of Kansas, 1994), Chapter 8.

49 Crosby, *Battlefield Chaplains*, p. 150.

50 Ibid.

51 These observations come from the Jesse Marlow Williamson material in the Dorsett Collection.

52 William Turner Papers, Dorsett Collection.

53 Ibid.

54 Ibid.

55 Author's interview with Burt Biddulph, May 28, 2009, via telephone from Florida.

56 Files related to PW Camps at Bad Orb and Hammelburg, OFLAG 13B, National Archives. See also Robert L. Gushwa, *The Best and Worst of Times: The U.S. Army Chaplaincy, 1920–1945*, Vol. IV (Washington, D.C.: Chief of Chaplains Office, 1977), 184.

57 File on Weiden, OFLAG 13B, National Archives.

58 Sampson, *Look Out Below*, p. 142; see also Crosby, *Battlefield Chaplains*, Chapter 9.

59 Sampson, *Look Out Below*, p. 150.

60 Ibid., p. 149.

61 Ibid., pp. 153 and 154.

62 Information on Eichhorn's upbringing is scattered throughout the pages of Greg Palmer and Mark S. Zaid, eds., *The GI's Rabbi: World War II Letters of David Max Eichhorn* (Lawrence, KS: University Press of Kansas, 2004).

63 Ibid., p. 149. Doris Bergman's introduction is rich in details of Eichhorn's prewar life.

64 Ibid. See the photos between pages 222 and 224.

65 Ibid., p. 5.

66 Ibid., pp. 82 and 83.

67 Kertzer, *With an H on My Dog Tag*, p. 134.

68 Ibid., p. 137.

69 Palmer and Zaid, *The GI's Rabbi*, p. 156.

70 Ibid., pp. 130 and 131.

71 Ibid., p. 102.

72 Elie Weisel, *Night* (New York: Bantam, 1982), p. 5.

73 Robert H. Abzug, *Inside the Vicious Heart: Americans and the Liberation of Nazi Concentration Camps* (New York: Oxford University Press, 1985), p. 19.

74 Ibid., pp. 21–26.

75 Ibid., Chapter 3.

76 Author's interview with Harold MacKenzie, Wheaton, Illinois, June 27, 2007.

77 Ibid.

78 Palmer and Zaid, *The GI's Rabbi*, p. 178.

79 Ibid., p. 164.

80 Ibid., p. 178.

81 Ibid., p. 178.

82 Ibid., p. 179.

83 Ibid.

84 Albert Isaac Slomovitz, *The Fighting Rabbis: Jewish Chaplains in American History* (New York: New York University Press, 1999), pp. 101 and 102.

85 Ibid., p. 103.

86 Ibid.

87 Alex Grobman, *Rekindling the Flame: American Jewish Chaplains and the Survivors of European Jewry, 1944–1948* (Detroit, MI: Wayne State University Press, 1993), p. 48.

88 Ibid.

89 Crosby, *Battlefield Chaplains*, p. 174.

90 Gushwa, *Best and Worst of Times*, p. 184.

CHAPTER NINE

1   Father Joseph T. O'Callahan, S.J., *I Was Chaplain on the Franklin* (New York: Macmillan, 1956), p. 86.

2   William Manchester, *American Caesar: Douglas MacArthur 1880–1964* (New York: Dell, 1978), p. 452.

3   Don McCombs and Fred L. Worth, *World War II: Strange Facts and Fascinating Figures* (New York: Crown, 1983) pp. 42 and 43. See also, Donald F. Crosby, *Battlefield Chaplains: Catholic Priests in WWII* (Lawrence, KS: University of Kansas, 1994), pp. 28–32.

4   Crosby, *Battlefield Chaplains*, pp. 30 and 31.

5   Hampton Sides, *Ghost Soldiers* (New York: Doubleday, 2001), p. 23.

6   Ibid., pp. 8–24.

7   On atrocities, see "Japanese Atrocities to Prisoners of War," 2nd Session, 78th Congress, House Document #393, 1944. See also Billy Keith, *Days of Anguish, Days of Hope* (Fort Worth, Texas: Scripta Publishing Co., 1944). Also see unpublished summary of the World War II service of Chaplain Robert P. Taylor in the Archives, Chaplain School, Fort Jackson, South Carolina.

8   Richard S. Roper, *Brothers of Paul: Activities of Prisoner of War Chaplains in the Philippines During WWII* (Odenton, MD: Revere Printing, 2003), p. 19.

9   Ibid., p. 20.

10 "Japanese Atrocities," House Document #393, p. 7.

11 Alfred C. Oliver, Jr., "But I Didn't Lose God," *Army and Navy Chaplain*, July-August 1945, p. 6.

12 Ibid., pp. 4–7; *Time*, November 12, 1946, p. 9; John K. Boenerman, "From Bataan Through Cabanatuan," *Army and Navy Chaplain*, April-May, 1946, pp. 23–27.

13 *Army and Navy Chaplain*, July-August 1945, p. 6.

14 Ibid.

15 James E. Davis, "Religion in a Prisoner of War Camp in Japan," *Army and Navy Chaplain*, April-May 1946, p. 6.

16 Ibid.

17 Ibid.

18 Ibid. and Clifford M. Drury, *U.S. Navy Chaplains 1778–1945* (Washington, D.C.: 1948), p. 70.

19 Details of Chaplain Taylor's life and World War II service are taken from Keith, *Days of Anguish*, and a brief biography from the U.S. Air Force military Web site: www.af.mil/information/bios.

20   See Chapter 10 of Keith, *Days of Anguish*.

21   Keith, *Days of Anguish*, Chapter 11, "The Miracle," and Robert Taylor, "Chaplains in POW Hospitals," *Army and Navy Chaplain*, July-August 1946, pp. 1–3.

22   Keith, *Days of Anguish*, p. 6 and Chapters 11 and 12.

23   Crosby, *Battlefield Chaplains*, p. 201.

24   Ibid., pp. 20 and 21.

25   Ibid., p. 201.

26   Quoted in Ibid., p. 202.

27   Ibid.

28   The quotation comes from Oliver, "But I Didn't Lose God," pp. 4–7; the liberation of the camp is covered in Sides, *Ghost Soldiers*; see also Chaplain John K. Borneman, "From Bataan Through Cabanatuan," *Army and Navy Chaplain*, April-May 1946, pp. 23–27.

29   I have heard this from scores of veterans I have interviewed and my findings are supported by such books as John. J. Morrett, *Soldier-Priest: An Adventure in Faith* (West Conshohocken, PA: Infinity Publishing, 2003) and Ray "Hap" Halloran, *Hap's War: The Incredible Survival Story of a P.O.W. Slated for Execution* (Menlo Park, CA: Hallmark Press, n.d.).

30   Richard Cartwright Austin, ed., *Letters from the Pacific: A Combat Chaplain in World War II* (Columbia, MO: University of Missouri Press, 2000), pp. 187 and 188.

31   Allan R. Millett, *Semper Fidelis: The History of the U.S. Marine Corps* (New York: Macmillan, 1980), p. 432.

32   Vandegrift, A. A. *Once A Marine: The Memoirs of General A. A. Vandegrift, USMC* (New York: Norton, 1964), p., 289.

33   Millett, *Semper Fidelis*, 434.

34   Ibid., pp. 432–33; see also Clifford M. Drury, *The History of the Chaplains Corps, United States Navy*, Vol. 2 (Washington, D.C.: U.S. Gov't Printing Office, n.d.), pp. 195–206; Roy J. Honeywell, *Chaplains of the U.S. Army* (Washington, D.C.: Government Printing Office, 1958), Chapter 17; and Gushwa, *The Best and Worst of Times: The U.S. Army Chaplaincy, 1920–1945*, Vol. IV (Washington, D.C: Chief of Chaplains Office, 1977), Chapter 4.

35   O'Callahan, *I Was Chaplain*, p. 31.

36   Ibid., p. 37.

37   Millett, *Semper Fidelis*, p. 434.

38   Drury, *History of the Chaplain Corps*, Vol. II , p. 202, and Vol. I, p. 167.

39 Drury, *History of the Chaplain Corps*, Vol. II, pp. 201 and 202.

40 Ibid., p. 202.

41 Author's interview with Henry Sledge, April 26, 2010, Birmingham, Alabama.

42 E. B. Sledge, *With the Old Breed at Peleliu and Okinawa* (New York: Oxford, 1990), p. 242.

43 Hebrews 11:1.

44 Sledge, *With the Old Breed*, pp. 242 and 243.

45 Drury, *History of the Chaplain Corps*, Vol. I, pp. 102 and 208.

46 For background material on this and subsequent paragraphs, see O'Callahan, *I Was Chaplain*, and Drury, *History of the Chaplain Corps*, Vol. II, pp. 199–201.

47 Drury, *History of the Chaplain Corps*, Vol. II, p. 200.

48 Ibid.

49 Ibid., p. 201.

50 Ibid., pp. 200, and 201, and O'Callahan, *I Was Chaplain*, pp. 62 and 63.

51 Crosby, *Battlefield Chaplains*, pp. 240 and 241.

52 See Harry S. Truman, *Memoirs of Harry S. Truman*, Vol. I, *Year of Decisions* (New York: Doubleday, 1955), pp. 10 and 421–23. See also D. M. Giangreco, *Hell to Pay: Operation DOWNFALL and the Invasion of Japan*, (Annapolis, MD: Naval Institute, 2009) and Max Gadney, "Did the Bomb Ultimately Save Lives?" *World War II* 25, No. 5 (January-February 2011): 66 and 67.

53 Author's interview with Dr. Raymond P. Biehl, September 8, 2001, Wheaton, Illinois. See also Robert and Amelia Kraus, eds., *The 509th Remembered* (privately published, 2005), p. 38.

54 Downey's records are in the William Downey file, RG 247, National Archives, and the material about his personality and style is derived from the author's interview with Theodore J. "Dutch" VanKirk, February 24, 2006, Louisville, Kentucky.

55 Quoted in Liam Nolan, *Small Man of Nanataki* (New York: Dutton, 1966), p. 142.

56 Paul W. Tibbets, *Return of the Enola Gay* (Columbus, OH: Mid Coast Marketing, 1998), Chapter 29.

57 Sledge, *With the Old Breed*, pp. 313 and 314.

58 Albert G. Hayes to Mary Hayes, letter dated August 11 and 16, 1945, in the Dorsett Collection.

59 George W. Wickersham, III, *Marine Chaplain, 1943–1946* (Bennington, VT: Merriam Press, 1998), pp. 108 and 109.

60 Keith, *Days of Anguish*, p. 209.

61 An original copy of this service is in the Dorsett Collection.

CHAPTER TEN

1 Morris N. Kertzer, *With an H on My Dog Tag* (New York: Behrman House, 1947), pp. 45 and 46.

2 Christopher Cross, *Soldiers of God* (New York: Dutton, 1945), pp. 181–182.

3 Chaplain Richard H. Chase, "It Makes Christians," *Life*, October 4, 1943, pp. 57–64.

4 Ibid.

5 Cross, *Soldiers of God*, p. 182.

6 Deborah Dash Moore, *GI Jews: How World War II Changed a Generation* (Cambridge, MA: Harvard, 2004), p. 264.

7 Ibid.

8 Sloan Wilson, *The Man In the Gray Flannel Suit* (New York: Avalon, 2002).

9 Bernard S. King file, RG 247, National Archives, and King's diary, papers, and photos in the Dorsett Collection.

10 Document dated October 15, 1973, in the B. L. Rose file, Chaplain School Archives, Fort Jackson, South Carolina.

11 *Navy Chaplain's Newsletter* 3, No. 3 (May-June 1945).

12 Louis Barish, ed., *Rabbis in Uniform: The Story of the American Jewish Chaplain* (New York: Jonathan David, 1962), pp. 305 and 306.

13 Kertzer, *With an H on My Dog Tag*, p. 12.

14 A copy of this address is in the archives, U.S. Naval Station, Norfolk, Virginia.

15 Richard M. Dalfiume, *Desegregation of the U.S. Armed Forces* (Columbia, Missouri: University of Missouri Press, 1969).

16 The Dorsett Collection contains three unpublished photographs taken from April through October 1942 at Fort Benjamin Harrison. And blacks were fully integrated at the chaplain school at Harvard (see RG 247, National Archives).

17 H. L. Bergsma, *The Pioneers: A Monograph of the First Two Black Chaplains in the Chaplain Corps of the United States Navy* (Washington: U.S. Government Printing Office, NavPers 15503, 1980), pp. 3–8.

18 Ibid., p. 5.

19 Ibid.

20 Ibid., pp. 3–8.

21 Benis M. Frank and Henry I. Shaw, Jr., *Victory and Occupation: History of U.S. Marine Corps Operations in World War II* (Nashville: Battery Press, 1994), Vol. V, p. 726.

22 Kertzer, *With an H on My Dog Tag*, pp. 45 and 46.

23 *Army and Navy Chaplain*, January–February, 1946, p. 4.

24 Thomas Childers, *Soldiers from the War Returning: The Greatest Generation's Troubled Homecoming from World War II* (Boston: Houghton Mifflin, 2004), p. 3.

25 Ibid., p. 229.

26 Details of Harold Fickett's chaplaincy record are in Drury, *Navy Chaplains*, p. 92. The material on his emotional scars was given by Harold L. Fickett III in an author interview, March 25, 2011, from Atlanta, Georgia.

27 See Wiliam J. Leonard, S.J., *The Letter Carrier: The Autobiography of William J. Leonard* (Kansas City, MO: Sheed and Ward, 1993), Chapter 9; Kertzer, *With an H on My Dog Tag*, pp. 168–197; and Carol Lemons, typescript of unpublished autobiography in the Dorsett Collection, pp. 275 and 276.

BIBLIOGRAPHY

Abzug, Robert H. *Inside the Vicious Heart: Americans and the Liberation of Nazi Concentration Camps.* 1985.

Alexander, Jack. "He's Our Guy," *Saturday Evening Post.* April 26, 1945.

Ambrose, Stephen. *Citizen Soldiers.* 1997.

Ambrose, Stephen E. *D-Day, June 6, 1944: The Climactic Battle of WWII.* 1994.

Amoury, Daisy. *Father Cyclone.* 1958.

Barish, Lewis, ed. *Rabbis in Uniform: A Century of Service to God and Country.* 1962.

Beardmore, H. *The Waters of Uncertainty.* 1944.

Bergen, Doris L., ed. *The Sword of the Lord: Military Chaplains from the First to the Twenty-first Century.* 2004.

Bergsma, H. L. *The Pioneers: A Monograph on the First Two Black Chaplains in the Chaplain Corps of the U.S. Navy.* 1980.

Bowman, B.L. *Transport Chaplain.* 1947.

Brink, Chaplain Eben Cobb. *And God Was There.* 1944.

Burchard, Waldo W. "Role Conflicts of Military Chaplains," *American Sociological Review* 19. October 1954.

By Their Side: A Memorial. National Lutheran Service Council: 1940–1948. 1948.

Cain, L.W. *Chaplain Cain: An Autobiography.* 1989.

Caldwell, Dan T., and B. L. Bowman. *They Answered the Call.* 1952.

Carlson, Alvin O. *He Is Able: Faith Overcomes Fear in a Foxhole.* 1945.

Carpenter, Alton E., and A. Anne Eiland. *Chappie: World War II Diary of a Combat Chaplain.* 2007.

Chaplaincy of the Methodist Church in World War II. 1948.

Chaplains of the Fifth Army. 1945.

Chase, Richard H. "It Makes Christians," *Life.* October 4, 1943.

Childers, Thomas. *Soldiers from the War Returning: The Greatest Generation's Troubled Homecoming from WW II.* 2004

Claypool, James V. *God in a Battlewagon.* 1944.

Connelly, Kenneth A., Jr. *Chaplain's Assistant.* 1945.

Cook, Ruth Beaumont. *Guests Behind Barbed Wire.* n.d.

Cooper, Watt M. *With the Seabees in the South Pacific.* 1981.

Cosby, N. Gordon. *By Grace Transformed.* 1999.

Crosby, Donald F., S.J. *Battlefield Chaplains: Catholic Priests in World War II.* 1994.

Cross, Christopher. *Soldiers of God.* 1945.

Dalfiume, Richard. *Desegregation of the U.S. Armed Forces.* 1969.

Daniel, Eugene L., Jr. *In the Presence of Mine Enemies: An American Chaplain in WWII German Prison Camps.* 1983.

Davis, Mac. *Jews Fight Too!* 1945.

Dennis, Clyde H., ed. *These Live On: The Best True Stories Unveiling the Power and Presence of God in World War II.* 1945.

Drury, Clifford Merrill. *The History of the Chaplain Corps, U.S. Navy, Vol. II, 1939–1949.* n.d.

Drury, Clifford Merrill. *United States Navy Chaplains 1778–1945.* 1948.

Du Bois, Lauriston J. *The Chaplains See World Missions.* 1946.

Fallis, George O. *A Padre's Pilgrimage.* 1953.

Foley, Albert S. *God's Men of Color.* 1969.

Forgy, Howell M. *". . . And Pass the Ammunition".* 1944.

Frese, Janell T., and G. R. Barber. *O Chaplain! My Chaplain! Man of Service.* 2005.

Fricke, T. P. *We Found Them Waiting.* 1946.

Gadney, Max. "Did the Bomb Ultimately Save Lives?" *World War II* 25, No. 5. January-February 2011.

Giangreco, D. M. *Hell to Pay: Operation DOWNFALL and the Invasion of Japan.* 2009.

Gilroy, William F. R. and T. J. Denny. *A Brief Chronology of the Chaplain Corps of the U.S. Navy.* 1983.

Glasser, Arthur. *And Some Believed: A Chaplain's Experience with the Marines in the South Pacific.* 1946.

Grant, Dorothy Fremont, ed., *War Is My Parish.* 1944.

Grobman, Alex. *Rekindling the Flame: American Jewish Chaplains and the Survivors of European Jewry, 1944–1948.* 1993.

Gushwa, Robert L. *The Best and Worst of Times: The U.S. Army Chaplaincy, 1920–1945,* Vol. IV, *The U.S. Army Chaplaincy.* 1977.

Hale, Wallace M. *Battle Rattle.* 2004.

Hayden, Mark. *German Military Chaplains in World War II.* 2005.

Honeywell, Ray J. *Chaplains of the U.S. Army.* 1958.

Hutcheson, Richard G., Jr. *The Churches and the Chaplaincy.* 1975.

Jorgensen, Daniel B. *The Service of Chaplains to Army Air Units, 1917–1946.* Air Force Chaplains Series, Vol. 1. n.d.

Keith, Billy. *Days of Anguish, Days of Hope.* 1977.

Kertzer, Morris N. *With An H on My Dog Tag.* 1947.

Kimball, Clyde E. *Diary of My Work Oversees.* 1947.

Kinkopf, Father Jack. *The Chalice and the Heavy Hat.* 2002.

Kirksey, Robert Hugh. *With Me: Growing Up in the Faith.* 1996.

Klein, Isaac. *The Anguish and Ecstasy of a Jewish Chaplain.* 1974.

Kroll, C. Douglas. *A History of the Navy Chaplains Serving with the U.S. Coast Guard.* 1993.

Kurzman, Dan. *No Greater Glory: The Four Immortal Chaplains and the Sinking of the Dorchester in World War II.* 2004.

Lamb, David S. *"Till We Meet Again".* 1944.

Lack, Ernest A. *Chapel Vespers.* 1945.

Leonard, William J., S.J. *The Letter Carrier: The Autobiography of William J. Leonard.* 1993.

Leonard, William J. *Where Thousands Fell.* 1995.

Leuschner, M. L., C. F. Zummach, and W. E. Kohrs. *Religion in the Ranks.* 1946.

Loveland, Anne C. *American Evangelicals and the U.S. Military, 1942–1993.* 1996.

Maahs, Arnold M. *Our Eyes Were Opened.* 1946.

MacDonald, Charles B. *A Time for Trumpets: The Untold Story of the Battle of the Bulge.* 1984.

Maguire, William A. *Rig for Church: The Thrilling Life Story of a Navy Chaplain.* 1942.

Maguire, William A. *The Captain Wears a Cross.* 1943.

Manchester, William. *American Caesar: Douglas MacAruther 1880–1964.* 1978.

Manchester, William. *Goodbye Darkness: A Memoir of the Pacific War.* 1980.

Marshall, Catherine. *Mr. Jones, Meet the Master.* 1949.

Marshall, Catherine. *A Man Called Peter.* 1951.

McCanon, Rupert L. *Sometimes We Laugh—Sometimes We Cry or Tell It to the Chaplain.* 1969.

Miller, C. Windsor. *A Tanker's View of World War II: The Military Experience of C. Windsor Miller.* 2004.

Millett, Allan R. *Semper Fidelis: The History of the United States Marine Corps.* 1980.

Monks, John, Jr. *A Ribbon and a Star: The Third Marines at Bougainville.* 1945.

Moody, Paul D., et al. *Religion of the Soldier and Sailor.* 1945.

Moore, Deborah Dash. *GI Jews: How World War II Changed a Generation.* 2004.

Morison, Samuel Eliot, *History of U.S. Naval Operations in World War II.* 15 volumes, 1947–1962.

Morrett, John J. *Soldier-Priest: An Adventure in Faith.* 2003.

Nance, Ellwood C. *Faith of Our Fighters.* 1944.

Nolan, Liam. *Small Man of Nanataki.* 1966.

O'Brien, Steven. *Blackrobe in Blue: The Naval Chaplaincy of John P. Foley, S.J., 1942–1946.* 2002.

O'Callahan, Joseph T. *I Was Chaplain on the Franklin.* 1956.

Olson, Arnold T. *Give Me This Mountain: An Autobiography.* 1987.

Orr, J. Edwin. *I Saw No Tears.* 1948.

Palmer, Greg, and Mark Zaid. *The GI's Rabbi: World War II Letters of David Max Eichhorn.* 2004.

Phillips, Sid. *You'll Be Sor-ree! A Guadalcanal Marine Remembers the Pacific War.* 2010.

Proehl, F. C., ed., *Marching Side By Side.* 1945.

Rabey, Steve. *Faith Under Fire.* 2002.

Read, Francis W. *G.I. Parsons.* 1945.

Rogers, Edward K. *Doughboy Chaplain.* 1946.

Rood, Wayne R., and Anne Rood. *You Okay, Chappy? Memories of Infantry Field Chaplain WWII, and His Wife on the Home Front.* 2002.

Rooney, Andy. *My War.* 1995.

Sacco, Jack. *Where the Birds Never Sing.* 2003.

Salter, F. T. *An Englishman's Faith.* 1941.

Sampson, Joseph L. *Look Out Below: A Story of the Airborne by a Paratrooper Padre.* 1989.

Searle, Robert W. *Tell It to the Padre.* 1943.

Shaw, Henry I., Jr., et al. *History of U.S. Marine Corps Operations in World War II.* 6 volumes, 1958–1971.

Silcox, S. G. *A Hillbilly Marine.* 1977.

Sitzer, Gerald. *A Cautious Patriotism: The American Churches and the Second World War.* 1997.

Sledge, E. B. *With the Old Breed at Peleliu and Okinawa.* 1990.

Slomowitz, Albert Isaac. *The Fighting Rabbis: Jewish Military Chaplains and American History.* 1999.

Smith, Joseph S. *Our Padre: The Inspiring Stories of Fr. Kilian Dreiling, World War II Army Chaplain.* 1942.

Society for the Propagation Faith. *The Priest Goes to War.* 1945.

Spellman, Archbishop Francis J. *V: The Road to Victory.* 1942.

Spellman, Francis J. *Action This Day: Letters from the Fighting Fronts.* 1943.

Spellman, Francis J. *No Greater Love: The Story of Our Soldiers.* 1945.

Sperry, Willard L., ed., *Religion in the Post-War World.* 1945.

Spooner, Rick. *The Spirit of Semper Fidelis: "Reflections from the Bottom of an Old Canteen Cup".* 2004.

Stroup, Russell Cartwright. *Letters from the Pacific: A Combat Chaplain in World War II.* 2000.

Taggart, William C. *My Fighting Congregation.* 1943.

Taylor, Allan. *Front Line.* n.d.

Temple, William. *Social Witness and Evangelism.* 1943.

Thorne, Ennis P. *This Day I'll Remember.* 1983.

Thorton, Francis B. *Sea of Glory: The Magnificent Story of Four Chaplains.* 1953.

Tibbets, Paul. *Return of the Enola Gay.* 1998.

Tregaskis, Richard. *Guadalcanal Diary.* 1943.

Truman, Harry S. *Memoirs.* 1955.

U.S. Navy Department, *U.S. Navy Chaplains.* 1948.

Vandegrift, A. A. *Once a Marine: The Memoirs of General A. A. Vandegrift, USMC.* 1964

Vanderbreggen, Cornelius. *A Leatherneck Looks at Life.* 1945.

Vanderbreggen, Cornelius. *Letters of a Leatherneck.* 1948.

Van Schouwen, Cornelius. *The Life and Work of a Chaplain: My Diary: 1943–1946.* 1985.

Venzke, Robert R. *Confidence in Battle, Inspiration in Peace: The U.S. Army Chaplaincy, 1945–1975.* 1977.

Wickersham, George W. II. *Maine Chaplain 1943–1946.* 1998.

Willard, W. Wyeth. *The Leathernecks Come Through.* 1944.

Williams, Robert. *Return to Normandy.* 2002.

Wilson, Charles E. *From Bastogne to Bavaria with the Fighting Fourth Armored Division, 1944–1945.* 1993.

Wilson, Robert R. "Status of Chaplains with Armed Forces," *American Journal of International Law.* July 1943.

Woodward, C. Salisbury. *Clergy in Wartime.* 1939.

Wuest, Padre Karl A. *They Told It to the Chaplain.* 1953.

Yost, Israel A. S. *Combat Chaplain.* 2006.

Zahavy, Zev, ed., *Chaplain on Wings: The Wartime Memoirs of Rabbi Harold H. Gordon.* 1981.

INDEX